PRAISE FOR *EMPLOYEE EXPE*

For many people work is a cause of stress and anxiety – this book is here to solve that. Using the latest research and evidence – while being fantastically readable – the book gives a positive, people-first approach to making work better!
Bruce Daisley, author of *The Joy of Work*

This is a must-read book for anyone working in the field of employee experience. It offers simple, practical tools and advice to help you make a positive difference to your employee experience. Bringing together the latest research and thinking from positive psychology and human-centred design, Emma Bridger and Belinda Gannaway demystify EX and provide everything you need to start making a difference today.
Mark Levy, EX adviser and former pioneer of employee experience at Airbnb

Employee experience is now rightly starting to be viewed as being as important as customer experience. This book is therefore a timely and vital read for leaders wanting to have high-performing businesses powered by great people. The insights and tools included are highly practical and you can start using them straight away to make a real difference in the life of your team and your business.
Pete Markey, CMO, Boots

As the global pandemic has accelerated our transformation to a fully digital economy and society, dubbed the fourth industrial revolution, too many focus on the technology tools. This is a mirage because tools need humans. What we are really entering is the human capital era where human talent is the most valuable resource. Our ability to adapt through leading our teams on learning tours will be the hallmark of the most successful and resilient organizations. Engaging talent in

continuous learning and adaptation requires designing the ultimate employee experience. Drawing on their deep expertise in leading transformational change, talent engagement, employee experience and the psychology underpinning human motivation, Emma Bridger and Belinda Gannaway have crafted an approachable handbook to do just that. My advice: read it with your teams so you can rethink your organization to unleash maximum human potential.
Heather E McGowan, future-of-work strategist and co-author of
The Adaptation Advantage

Successful companies understand that employee experience must be intentionally designed and delivered to both drive impactful business outcomes and meet the needs of their people. *Employee Experience by Design* takes you on a guided tour of employee experience from the foundational basics to the future of what's next. More importantly, packed within is a comprehensive reference of practical guidance and techniques for building an EX mindset and elevating your organization's EX practice today.
Damon Deaner, Director, Employee Experience & Design, IBM Talent & Transformation

This book provides an extensive insight into creating a successful employee experience. A step-by-step approach in how to implement a user-friendly job–worker experience is put forward. The book also provides the reader with methodological advice on how to measure the employee experience.
Dr Julian Edwards, Research Fellow, The Open University

A must-read for anyone with an interest in employee experience. *Employee Experience by Design* is a practical guide for both beginners and more practised EX professionals, providing a valuable methodology for approaching EX design at a strategic and solution level.
Ann-Marie Blake, Board Member, International Association of Business Communicators (IABC)

A great introduction to what employee experience is and how it can be developed using design thinking. Anyone taking an employee-centric approach to internal communication will find this useful in terms of connecting communications to experience.
Dr Kevin Ruck, co-founder, PR Academy, and editor of *Exploring Internal Communication: Towards informed employee voice*

Finally, a practical and accessible guide that is a must-read for designing better employee experiences. Filled with easy-to-execute activities to bring EX to life anywhere and real-life examples from organizations, this book will be your go-to resource. The blend of research, context and lived experiences comes together seamlessly to show the way.
Lindsay Bousman PhD, former Senior Director of Talent Programs, Expedia Group

It's brave to talk of employee experience in the current guise of work. Often one of those overly used phrases, it could be construed as the latest tactic in convincing people they have it good when in reality they don't. With *Employee Experience by Design* there's no longer a hiding place for falsehoods and platitudes regarding EX. If you're NOT following what's in this book, then you're not designing, developing and delivering a considered, optimized and fulfilling employee experience. This book is that useful: it should be the touchstone for all who aspire to really show they care about their people and their experience of work. Leaders, ignore this at your peril.
Perry Timms MCIPD and FRSA, founder and Chief Energy Officer at PTHR, TEDx speaker, and Adjunct Professor/Visiting Fellow at four UK business schools

Clearly written and very practical, *Employee Experience by Design* is a perfect companion guide for anyone in HR and EX who wants to take a user-centric approach to design employee experience. With a friendly tone and lots of examples, it is a thoroughly enjoyable read to learn about design thinking.
Dr Bonnie Cheuk, digital and business transformation leader

Employee Experience by Design acts as a clever coach to business leaders, giving them the tools to discover for themselves how EX is defined in their organizations. From EVP and employee journey mapping, to design thinking and onboarding, this book is a one-stop shop for anyone working or interested in employee experience. It is peppered throughout with up-to-date, real-life examples of EX in action – many taken from the authors' own extensive work in this field. Just like the times we're currently living through, the skill of Bridger and Gannaway in drawing together this comprehensive and complete guide is unprecedented. For any organization seeking to improve EX, this has to be the starting point.

Sarah Harrison, President, International Association of Business Communicators UK&I

Employee Experience by Design

*How to create an effective EX
for competitive advantage*

Emma Bridger

Belinda Gannaway

KoganPage

First published in Great Britain and the United States in 2021 by Kogan Page Limited

2nd Floor, 45 Gee Street	122 W 27th St, 10th Floor	4737/23 Ansari Road
London	New York, NY 10001	Daryaganj
EC1V 3RS	USA	New Delhi 110002
United Kingdom		India

www.koganpage.com

Kogan Page books are printed on paper from sustainable forests.

© Emma Bridger and Belinda Gannaway, 2021

Illustrations by Andy Willard.

The right of Emma Bridger and Belinda Gannaway to be identified as the authors of this work has been asserted by them in accordance with the Copyright, Designs and Patents Act 1988.

ISBNs

Hardback	978 1 78966 773 8
Paperback	978 1 78966 771 4
eBook	978 1 78966 772 1

British Library Cataloguing-in-Publication Data

A CIP record for this book is available from the British Library.

Library of Congress Cataloging-in-Publication Data

Library of Congress Cataloging-in-Publication Data is available. Control Number: 2020056238

Typeset by Integra Software Services, Pondicherry
Print production managed by Jellyfish
Printed and bound by CPI Group (UK) Ltd, Croydon CR0 4YY

CONTENTS

FOREWORD

When I was first hired by Brian Chesky, Airbnb CEO, we talked about what my role would involve. He told me straight: 'Don't f*ck up the culture.' And so began my employee experience journey. In a few short years, employee experience (EX) has made its way into the lexicon of HR. But if we are going to do this right, we need a shift: a shift in mindset that translates into ways of working. It's time to understand that our people are as important as our customers.

Employee experience is much broader than the traditional HR function. The focus has to be on the end-to-end journey for our people, and this is going to involve much more than the traditional people functions and teams. What we need is a wholesale shift in the HR approach. We must consider which parts of the organization to involve to deliver a fantastic EX. We need facilities, safety, operations, office managers and more, to bring the culture to life and deliver the experience our people want and need.

But this is not just about what we do. How we do it is vital too. To create the shift we need, we must change the way we approach EX. It's time to stop assuming we know what our people want from their experience at work. And it's time to talk in the language of opportunities rather than problems to fix. At its heart, EX needs humanity and this starts by giving our people a voice, and making sure we listen.

The call for a more human-centred approach to business has been amplified by the global COVID-19 pandemic. In many ways the pandemic served to validate what we started back at Airbnb. It showed us that we can work differently at a moment's notice, that flexibility doesn't mean a drop in productivity, and that tech can be a force for good. But more than that, the pandemic taught us that human connection is at the heart of EX.

The future of work has never been more uncertain. But my hope is that organizations are now more open minded about how they can function to benefit all: their people, their customers, and society. Getting your EX right has power; it can make a fundamental difference to your people and deliver a positive social impact. But to do this we can't go back to the way things were before. Getting your EX right needs a rethink and a different approach. EX can't be about a superficial rebrand of the HR function.

The pages of this book will enable you to re-imagine your EX. The thinking, insights and tools that Emma and Belinda share will give you what you need to make the shift. There has never been a better time to do this. We have an opportunity to genuinely put our people at the heart of what we do, and give our attention to the experience they want and need at work. I'm excited to see what happens next.

Mark Levy, EX adviser and
former pioneer of employee
experience at Airbnb

DEDICATIONS

Emma's dedication

I wrote my half of the book during the COVID-19 pandemic. During lockdown people got busy making sourdough, quizzing on Zoom, and baking banana bread. Some people took on lockdown puppies, started lockdown romances and others got busy making lockdown babies. My lockdown experience was all about writing this book.

Initially I thought I might be able to use the enforced house arrest to my advantage. Fewer distractions and the fact that everyone was in the same boat would mean no 'fear of missing out', no temptation to procrastinate and plenty of book writing time. How wrong I was. I, along with many others, travelled the lockdown rollercoaster of highs and lows – on top of which was a fast approaching deadline for the book.

It could have all gone horribly wrong, but it didn't thanks to some amazing people in my life – and I want to thank them. First, a big thank you to my co-author Belinda, for her patience at my procrastination and for challenging me (in a good way) to be better. Huge thanks also to my amazing circle of friends, for being there through thick and thin and feigning interest when I talk to them about employee experience. A huge thank you to the People Lab team, for keeping everything going when I was head down and stressed with the impending deadline.

And to my family, the biggest thanks of all for everything they do. Thank you to Harry for the cups of tea at exactly the right moment. To Teddy for the hugs just when I needed them. To Eadie for making sure we ate a gorgeous home-cooked meal every night. And to Ted in his unwavering belief that I could do this.

And finally, I want to dedicate this book to my Grandad Martin, who sadly passed away in the summer of 2020. He was a born storyteller and inspired a love of tales and books. I'm not sure this was the kind of book he would have ever read, but I do know that it wouldn't matter. He would've been proud I'm sure, and regaled me with stories of his experiences at work over a pint or two, as he did many times over the years.

To Grandad Martin, with love X

Belinda's dedication

I started work on the book on a flight back from Sydney to London in January 2020. It was a wonderful holiday with dear friends and the year stretched out optimistically in front of me. How a few weeks changed all of that thanks to COVID-19. Co-writing this book during this time has been a privilege. I've had the time, the space (mental and physical) and security to do it. I realize not everyone has had the same experience of this pandemic, and for mine I am incredibly grateful. I've also had the good fortune to be doing this with Emma, without whom we never would have started, let alone finished. I've learned so much from you and your positivity.

As the granddaughter of two librarians and the daughter of another two, who are also writers in their own right (yes mum, you too), I'm thrilled that life has given me the opportunity to do this. So my dedication is to my parents, Norman and Evelyn, for showing me it's possible. Dad, who will be 90 by the time this comes out, has written about 30 books on local sport history (so many we've lost count). I remember vividly the launch party of his first in 1982 at Lymington Cricket Club and how excited I was to see my name in the front. It's taken me nearly 40 years to repay this in kind. Thank you mum and dad for everything and for sharing your rich and varied memories of your experiences of and at work as well as those of my grandparents from the late 1930s onwards.

To my boys, Bill and Reuben, good effort for making lockdown such a positive and sunshine-filled time. You nailed it. Thank you for being my number-one cheerleaders. And to Martha for our walks on the beach. To my sister Clare and my friends, I am in awe and eternally grateful for your limitless love, hilarity, your constant check-ins, your energy and riotous good humour xx

ACKNOWLEDGEMENTS

Thank you to Andy Willard who drew the fantastic illustrations for this book, and to all the people and organizations who have supported and contributed to the creation of it by sharing your thoughts, ideas, experiences and positivity:

Esther Poza Campos

Carlos Erazo-Molina

Romain Quicq

Nebel Crowhurst

Sarah Corney

Lucia Abugattás

Perry Timms

Tim Fleming

Marie Kretlow

Dennis Field

Bonnie Cheuk

Sacha Connor

Niall Ryan

Pierre Delinois

Matt Matheson

Lindsay Bousman

Damon Deaner

Nicole Dessain

Christian Rytting

Sam Maxwell-Reed

Rose Tighe

Sarah Rachel Jones

Anna Penrose

Sam Knowles

Mark Levy

Kerrie Hughes

Engage For Success

Sander de Bruijn

Karen Notaro

Andrew McIlwaine

Sacha Harris

CIPD

Jane Roques-Shaw

Ted Hewett

Ruth Dance

Matt Manners

Katie Austin

Sarah Osborne

Sally Camm

James Hampton

Jennie Pitt

Nikki Williams

Charlotte Dewar

Lorne Armstrong

Katie Burke

Lizzy Barker

MANAGERS THAT COACH.

01

' Consumers of the Workplace '

Introducing employee experience design

Definitions and approaches

Setting the scene

The psychological contract at work is changing, and with it employees' expectations of work. It's no longer enough to receive pay for a job well done; we look for purpose and meaning at work. We want to move beyond satisfaction to be motivated and engaged, with a focus on our development. We look for managers who will coach us to be our best, rather than simply telling us what to do. We expect more than the annual performance review; we want ongoing conversations that focus on our strengths, as well as our development areas. In short, employees are fast becoming 'consumers of the workplace' (Gallup, 2019). Before the COVID-19 crisis, the business case for employee experience (EX) predominantly focused on competition for talent, with studies indicating that employees were actively looking for other openings. In Mercer's 2019 Global Talent Trends Study, 97 per cent of executives said that they believed there would be increased competition for talent, with just over half expressing concern about the time it could take to fill open positions.

There's no doubt that the COVID-19 crisis has forced a sudden shift in the way we work, and created new and different challenges for organizations. At the time of writing, the impact of COVID-19 is already being felt, and once the immediate physical health emergency has passed, there is a longer-term challenge that organizations will need to rise to. The COVID-19 crisis presented an opportunity to do things differently and 'reset' the EX approach within organizations. It's fair to say that the business driver for focusing on EX might have changed for a post-COVID world, but there's no doubt that the business case is still compelling.

Set against this backdrop, it's little surprise that we are observing a significant increase in interest in EX. Deloitte's Human Capital Trends survey (2017) reported that nearly 80 per cent of executives rated EX as important, but only 22 per cent said their companies are excellent at building a differentiated EX. LinkedIn (2020) reported that the number of members who have employee experience in their job title has increased by over 240 per cent. Organizations are investing in initiatives, activations, programmes and transformations for their people. However, the global picture on engagement, which is the outcome of a great experience, is still pretty depressing, with 43 per cent of companies reporting low or declining employee engagement (Mercer, 2020).

Clearly there is a gap here, which is why we decided to write this book. Designing and delivering a compelling EX isn't just good for business; it's good for our people, customers and society as well. If employees are consumers of the workplace, a significant shift in mindset needs to happen. Josh Bersin (2019), global industry analyst, describes EX in the following way:

> EX means we work for the employees and not the other way around. In other words, we've spent the last 30 years building new ways to understand, segment and listen to our customers – now we are doing the same for our employees.

We need to approach EX with the same rigour and dedication that we approach the customer experience, but just how do we start to value our employees in the same way we do our customers? If Spotify can remind us what music we were listening to as teenagers, why is it that companies often struggle with something as simple as making sure there is a working swipe card to access the office on day one? Surely with the advances in customer experience, employee experience

doesn't need to be this way? We believe that we need to move from an organization-led focus on transactions, processes and procedures to an explicit focus on designing an end-to-end experience that begins by truly understanding our people.

Kerrie Hughes has worked in the field of customer experience for nearly 20 years in a number of organizations, including financial services and energy. Here she shares some thoughts from the world of customer experience (CX) that are helpful to EX practitioners.

CX nuggets for EX

I've been working in the field of CX since 2001, when the company I was at had the vision to set up a customer experience team. As a new team we were passionate and ready to fight the fight on behalf of our customers. But being a very new discipline, this wasn't something you could buy a book about or google – in fact, Google was barely a thing! So we went with our gut and what felt right. Our early focus was on defining our brand and translating that across our touchpoints. We did journey mapping sessions and banned our SMEs from talking process and instead asked them to 'be the customer'. I loved it and have never looked back. So, as a veteran of CX, I've been asked: 'What can EX learn from CX?'

A good place to start is at the beginning. If you google 'design process', you will see that all good design starts with words such as research, analyse, understand and listen. In the design thinking process this step is known as 'empathize'. Essentially this step is about developing a deep understanding of the people you are designing for and the problem you are trying to solve. As a CX practitioner, this can be the trickiest and most difficult part to get an organization to commit to. There is an urgency and therefore a tendency to jump straight to solutions. It takes time and money to empathize. But spending time up front to get out there and find the people you are designing for is critical. Utilizing one or more of the many methodologies to truly understand and discover who they are, what their needs are, what frustrates them, what motivates them, what the real problem is that needs solving, is perhaps the most crucial step.

This is where my jealousy kicks in, because in the world of EX, this Holy Grail of insight – that is the difference between good design and, well, guess work – does not even require you to leave the (virtual) building! No expensive recruitment, just your employees' time. So, seize this opportunity with both hands. Build in this time to your work. I promise you that time spent here will make a significant and positive impact on your employee experience design. It also has the added benefit of providing research and insight to call on when dealing with HIPPOs (highest-paid person's opinion).

My next tip for EX by design is… don't be afraid of emotions. It's an often used quote because it's too perfect not to call on, but as Maya Angelou said: 'People will forget what you said, people will forget what you did, but people will never forget how you made them feel.' This emotional layer is something that should always be captured when creating the 'as-is' journey map. Personally, I always capture 'thinking' and 'feeling' separately and use these in the write-up to draw the emotional curve and identify the good, bad and neutral points. A great tool I use when designing new experiences is the Dramatic Arc, also referred to as 'Boom. Wow. Wow! WOW! BOOOM!' Taken from films, stories and plays, it makes you consider how you want to design the emotional experience and be deliberate and appropriate with where your Booms and your Wows are.

Finally, remember: it's a marathon, not a sprint; the work is never finished and things always change. So, identify the key experiences, the moments that matter, and prioritize to avoid being overwhelmed. Monitor and manage the experiences by building in mechanisms for employees to easily feed back and continue to iterate, refine and adapt.

It's no accident that we titled this book *Employee Experience by Design*. Ultimately our aim is to demystify EX and give you a simple, user-friendly framework with which to design great experiences for your people. We believe design thinking is a framework and approach that can provide us with the tools to design a truly compelling experience for our people. However, designing experiences is a very different proposition from specifying, building and delivering systems, transactions and processes to manage and optimize people as resources. Deloitte (2017) reported that just 10 per cent of executives said their companies are excellent at understanding and using design thinking as part of the EX, with 48 per cent saying they are weak in this area. Design thinking begins with developing a deep understanding of the people you are designing for – in our case, employees. You can only get to the heart of your EX if you practise deep empathy to understand and design around your people's emotions, attitudes, beliefs, perceptions and behaviour. Empathy is one of our core principles for creating a compelling EX and underpins our philosophy and approach. We believe it's critical to get curious about understanding people's emotions, their needs and behaviours.

It therefore makes sense to begin by understanding the nature of experience and what makes an experience good and/or positive. Over the course of the book, we'll draw insights from the world of positive psychology to help us to answer this question.

An experience, then, can be understood as practical contact with, and observation of, facts or events, which leaves an impression on us. Ultimately an experience makes us feel something and is subjective in nature. We define 'employee experience design' as the application of design principles and positive psychology, first to how we understand people and their needs and expectations, and then to how we develop, test and iterate solutions to intentionally curate the experience.

Our approach works at both a strategic solution and everyday level, helping you to:

- design an EX vision or approach to support your desired outcomes;
- identify the gaps where you fall short (or over deliver), to understand where there is an opportunity to optimize the experience;
- redefine the problem, or identify the opportunity, seeking a solution through the lens of your people;
- develop, test and iterate experience solutions;
- get hyper-focused on the 'everyday' experiences your employees have and empower them to improve them.

As you will discover, EX design can be applied at multiple levels and in different ways. Designing and implementing a compelling EX can feel overwhelming and ambiguous. Our EX design framework set out in the following chapters is clear and simple and will enable you to navigate the world of EX and make a tangible difference. The tools we'll share will help to overcome potential biases that can get in the way of great design. Unlike previous HR transformations, there is no blue-print that dictates what a move from a traditional HR service delivery model to an EX design approach should look like. The opportunity is to make sense of, and work with, EX design in ways that are right for your organization and people. Ultimately EX design is all about a mindset that can be put to work as a strategy, tool or a framework.

Focusing on delivering a brilliant employee experience is a no-brainer – it will create a competitive advantage, help you differentiate, attract and keep the best people, and ultimately make a positive contribution to your organization. The potential a brilliant EX has to positively impact your business is big. For example, research shows that companies who are leading the way in EX have four times the average profitability and twice the average revenue of companies that lag behind (Dery and Sebastian, 2017). We'll explore the business case more in Chapter 2, but the research is clear that your EX matters.

To create a compelling EX, though, we need to start at the begin-ning; you need to be clear that when you are talking about EX in your organization, there is shared understanding of what this really means. To help get you there, we will look at different definitions and approaches, emerging concepts and ideas, as well as some examples from companies who are leading the way.

A brief history

EX is nothing new – employees have always had experiences at work, good, bad and sometimes downright ugly. The difference is we are now purposefully thinking about how employees experience organi-zations and designing ways to make these experiences better. Jacob Morgan (2017) talks about the evolution of EX in the following way:

- Initially the focus was on utility, providing employees with the tools they need to do the job and seeing them as nothing more than a cog in a machine.

- Next came productivity, focusing on what employees needed to work better and faster.

- Then came engagement, a radical new concept which for the first time took a more employee-centric approach, asking what employees need to be their best at work.
- And finally we are now in the era of EX, which involves purposefully designing experiences from the view point of our employees.

Increasingly we are seeing practitioners getting bogged down in the semantics of engagement versus experience, which isn't helpful. We think it's quite simple: a great employee experience will contribute towards engagement. But if the employee experience is poor, it's doubtful employees will be engaged.

Should EX replace employee engagement?

It's been well documented that Airbnb made a deliberate decision to replace their HR department, instead choosing to focus on employee experience, with a team headed up by a chief employee experience officer rather than the traditional HR director. When the company made this move it sparked a great deal of interest from the HR community and beyond. Airbnb's mission is to create a world where you can belong anywhere, and they believe that central to achieving this mission is creating memorable workplace experiences across the entire employee lifecycle. This is why they made the move to set up an employee experience function. They argue that this is different from the more traditional HR set-up because the focus is much broader. This wider scope includes the office environment, facilities, food and CSR. In addition, it includes a group of employees that they call 'ground control', who are tasked to help bring their culture to life via a range of activities such as internal communications, events, celebrations and recognition.

While this sounds like a fantastic approach to creating a great place to work, the more cynical might argue that this is simply a name change. In Emma's first engagement roles back in the late 1990s, she worked as part of an organizational development team and the various departments that were part of the team included all of the above. There was even an equivalent to the 'ground control' concept, which was called the 'smile' team. The point is, employees have always had experiences. And there have always been those more forward-thinking companies that focused on purposefully designing and creating positive experiences for their people.

As EX gains interest and attention, it's inevitable that some commentators are asking if it should replace employee engagement. Unsurprisingly, our answer to this question is no! Quite simply, if we get the experience right, employees are more likely to be engaged. And if the experience is poor, then guess what, there is less likelihood of engagement. Companies leading the way when it comes to EX know that great experiences lead to higher engagement and all of the business benefits this brings.

Many commentators argue the case for a move away from employee engagement to employee experience by citing the lack of improvements seen in employee engagement despite the continued focus – we call this the 'employee engagement gap'. However, our own research has shown that it is precisely because companies are not purposefully designing great experiences for their people that we are seeing continued low levels of engagement globally (People Lab, 2018). For example:

- Many companies do not have a definition, engagement strategy or a plan to address EX and engagement.
- The focus is more often than not on running a survey rather than what they actually do in response to the data.
- There is little investment in practitioners' development or in improving line managers' skills.
- And there is little requirement to demonstrate any ROI on the actions they are undertaking.

Is it any wonder we are not seeing the improvements in engagement despite the continued focus?

In his book *The Employee Experience Advantage* (2017), Jacob Morgan argues that we need to purposefully design a work experience to create a truly engaged workforce, which will unlock business performance. Some commentators argue that engagement is organization-centric, whereas a shift to focus on employee experience is employee-centric. We would argue that those organizations excelling in this space know that we need to understand how employees experience the organization. We need to involve them in designing solutions to create great places to work. We're really clear that we absolutely cannot make assumptions about what engages our people and teams, nor can we assume what constitutes a great experience for employees. This is why we advocate a design thinking approach to developing a compelling EX.

In summary, we need to consider both employee experience *and* engagement if we are to develop workplaces that people want to join and contribute their best to. If we design and improve EX, we'll contribute towards developing an engaged workforce, which ultimately benefits not only our employees but our customers and partners too.

EX as a concept is much more user-friendly and accessible than employee engagement. We believe part of the reason that we observed overuse and abuse of the annual engagement survey was precisely because employee engagement is an abstract term. Practitioners, through no fault of their own, were unsure where to begin so reached for the survey, which gave the illusion of doing something. If you think this feels harsh, just consider the budget allocation for the annual engagement survey versus what happens afterwards. The emphasis, and the money, were often on measuring engagement, rather than on designing interventions, experiences or changing cultures to actually deliver engagement. EX, however, feels much more tangible and concrete, which we believe is contributing to the increased focus we're observing. As employees, we all have experiences and therefore can easily grasp what improving an experience might involve.

THE ROLE OF TECHNOLOGY IN EX

There's no doubt that technological advances have also contributed to the rising interest in EX. As companies begin to move away from the annual employee survey, there are an increasing number of opportunities to gather data and insight on, and from, employees. Swedish start-up

Epicenter even offers implants to employees via microchips that are basically like a swipe card: enabling access to offices, operating printers, or buying their lattes at the coffee bar, all with a swipe of a hand. It is easy to see how these technologies and other wearables are enabling companies to gather a range of data to help them understand employee experience and behaviours in real time. It is still early days for these technologies and our subsequent understanding of how they might be used to help improve EX and positively impact engagement. As practitioners, we need to understand how we can use these new technologies and approaches internally. Spending some time with our colleagues in marketing, IT, digital and customer experience is a great place to start. We need to make the business case to stakeholders to show that focusing on employee experience is every bit as critical as focusing on customer experience. We need to embrace big data, AI and machine learning inside organizations to help create a brilliant employee experience. However, we know that for many companies, these types of technology are still a long way off. Indeed, for many companies we work with, technology as a critical component of their EX doesn't feature at all. Employees have experiences at work regardless of the technological maturity of the organization, and lack of technology should not be a barrier for focusing on developing and improving your EX.

Defining EX

How do we define an experience? We can think of an experience as something that happens to you that has an impact on how you feel:

Working for that company is an experience I'll never forget!

It also refers to the way that something happens to you and how that then makes you feel:

My employer goes out of their way to make sure I have a great experience at work.

Unsurprisingly, as a result of this, there are numerous ways that individuals and organizations define EX:

Employee experience is about creating a great work environment for people. It involves understanding the role that trust plays in the employment relationship and making sure people are listened to and have a voice in issues that impact (CIPD, 2020).

The intersection of employee needs and wants, and the organizational design of those expectations needs and wants (Morgan, 2017).

It's the sum total of all the touchpoints an employee has with his or her employer, from the time of being a candidate (active or passive) to becoming an alumnus or alumna (Bersin, 2019).

Employee experience is the 'user experience' of your company – it's the intersection of employees' expectations, their environment and the events that shape their journey within an organization (Mercer, 2019).

The employee experience is the journey an employee takes with your organization. It includes all the interactions an employee has with your organization before, during and after their tenure (Gallup, 2019).

EX is the intentional design, and engineering of a high-value, integrated, end-to-end experience. From pre-hire to rehire, using the holistic employee experience as a lens, we can maximize all the interactions an individual has with an employer over the long term, to create a deep sense of belonging and co-create high performance and stronger business outcomes (Whitter, 2019).

What these all have in common, though, is the recognition that experiences make you feel something. It must be an inclusive practice, however you chose to define it, or whatever you want it to mean within your own organization. It can be tempting to overthink definitions, though, which is why we really love this definition from a company we work with:

EX is all about enabling our people to have more good days at work.

This definition is simple and clear and positions EX as a concept everyone can understand. Kennedy Fitch conducted a survey in 2018 of 250+ companies that revealed that only 15 per cent of respondents had an EX definition and no two definitions were exactly alike.

There were, however, some themes that were consistent across the different definitions they found. For example, most definitions involved 'scaling design of the organization around the employee to ensure the best possible experience'. Interestingly, there was a strength-based theme that emerged focusing on enabling the 'best work possible'.

The purpose of considering your definition of EX within your organization is to ensure alignment – that you, and others responsible for the intended EX, are on the same page. Engaging in a discussion about your organization's definition and approach to EX is a great place to start your journey with EX.

However we choose to define EX, though, we cannot simply take the HR functions and services of old and just rename them EX. We have observed a number of organizations who have done just this and simply taken the current HR offer, services and tactics and transposed them onto an employee lifecycle model. This approach is fundamentally flawed, given it is still top–down and 'done to' your people rather than designing experiences that start by understanding their needs. Adopting our EX design approach ensures you can avoid this. We would argue that delivering a compelling EX requires much more than what HR can do alone. EX involves a big shift within the HR function, covering areas including engagement, productivity, L&D, wellbeing, safety, security, technology, facilities, employee trust and more.

WHAT DO WE MEAN BY EX IN OUR ORGANIZATION?

Having a conversation about the nature of EX and what it means for your organization is a great place to start your EX design and journey. The following activity will help you to do this. We recommend using these questions in a workshop setting with a diverse range of stakeholders to gather views that are representative across the entire organization:

- Ask people to take a few minutes to individually capture some examples of their own experiences at work – the good and the not so good.
- Then ask everyone to share the examples they have come up with.
- Ask the group to cluster the different words into themes.

- Consider the different examples that emerge. Do the themes represent everyday experience, eg 'the people are really friendly here', or the 'conceptualized experience', ie that which the organization deliberately designs and intends, eg the onboarding experience?

- Consider and talk through the themes emerging: are they from the perspective of the employee or the organization?

- Use these outputs to generate a discussion on what EX could mean to your organization and what you mean when you talk about EX.

A good question to ask is what EX is and what it isn't. This discussion could form the basis of a definition for your organization.

Approaches to EX design

There are a range of different models and frameworks that exist to help you navigate the world of EX. Some are more prescriptive, detailing the areas you need to focus on to improve EX. For example, Ben Whitter (2019), a leading expert within EX, has developed a holistic employee experience (HEX) model, which outlines the key components of EX. Derived from evidence gathered over a number a years, it is positioned as a lens to help companies focus on the things that really matter at work. The model has six elements, which Whitter argues contribute to the overall quality of EX: human, leadership, structure, technology, workplace and community. These elements surround what Whitter terms 'the truth', which involves the purpose, mission and values of the organization.

Other approaches offer more of a framework to guide EX. For example, in his book *The Employee Experience Advantage* (2017), Jacob Morgan shares his 'employee experience equation', which states that culture plus technology plus physical space equals a good EX. LinkedIn (2020) Talent Solutions talks about the 4Ps as a framework for EX, involving people, place, product and process, whereas Mercer (2019) focuses on the quality of an EX that people crave, which involves being enriching, empathetic, efficient and embracing.

We do not believe in a 'one size fits all' approach to EX design; indeed, this is counter to using design thinking to develop a compelling EX.

It is impossible to assume that we know what will work for your organization, and this would fly in the face of our 'empathy principle'. Our aim is to share with you different frameworks, approaches, models and tools that you can make work for you and your organization. Our intention is not to be overly prescriptive, with a list of rules to follow, but – by sharing different models and approaches – to try to make it simple and easy to design a compelling EX, one that is right for your organization and, crucially, your people.

The starting point for EX design is intention: that is, intentionally designing an experience that is right for your people, and the work they do, at the same time as being right for your organization, your culture, your purpose and your values. Our three EX design lenses model (Figure 1.1) illustrates this point; a compelling EX needs to work for the individual, for the work they do and for the organization. It is often the case that HR practices are simply repackaged as EX, exposed by the fact they only take into account organizational needs. Our EX design approach will always involve understanding individuals' needs as well.

Considering how to develop and improve EX can be overwhelming – experiences exist at different levels, are diverse in nature and can be both planned and unplanned. As we've already said, a compelling EX requires more than what HR can do alone, and there are often many different teams involved in developing a great EX. It can be confusing trying to make sense of the specific role you do and how

FIGURE 1.1 Three EX design lenses

this fits into the EX landscape. When running our EX by design workshops, we typically have a wide range of practitioners attend, all trying to make sense of the piece of EX they have responsibility for. For example, you could be an HR practitioner responsible for re-designing the EX of a specific process, such as your performance development. Or maybe you're an HR director looking at your employee value proposition and how to use this as a blueprint for the overall experience your employees have. Perhaps you're a head of internal communications looking at how the experience of your people supports your company values (or not, in many cases!). Or you might be an L&D professional who has recognized that leaders make a big difference to your EX and you want to understand how your development programmes can support them to facilitate a great experience with their teams. You could be an employee engagement professional who needs to understand which experiences have the biggest impact on engagement to enable you to focus on the right things. And so the list goes on. The principles and frameworks we share throughout the pages of this book work at all of these levels, for all of these experiences, for whichever element of the EX you are focusing on. To help make sense of the EX landscape, we have developed the model shown in Figure 1.2.

The purpose of this model is to help practitioners understand the different types of EX and where they have the opportunity to contribute. At one end of the landscape are those experiences that are intentional and designed. This is the obvious home of EX design and most often what we think of when talking about EX. This could involve hygiene experiences, such as ensuring employees get paid on time and that they have the right tools for the job. Hygiene experiences may or may not be organization-specific – for example, every employer takes steps to ensure paying employees and having the tools for the job happens. Typically these types of experience are owned by a team somewhere in the business.

We then have what we call lifecycle experiences, which are intentional, designed experiences such as induction, performance management, exit and more. These experiences are more likely to be organization-specific and align with company culture and values. Again, these experiences will be designed and managed by different teams within the organization depending on the specific experience.

FIGURE 1.2 The EX landscape

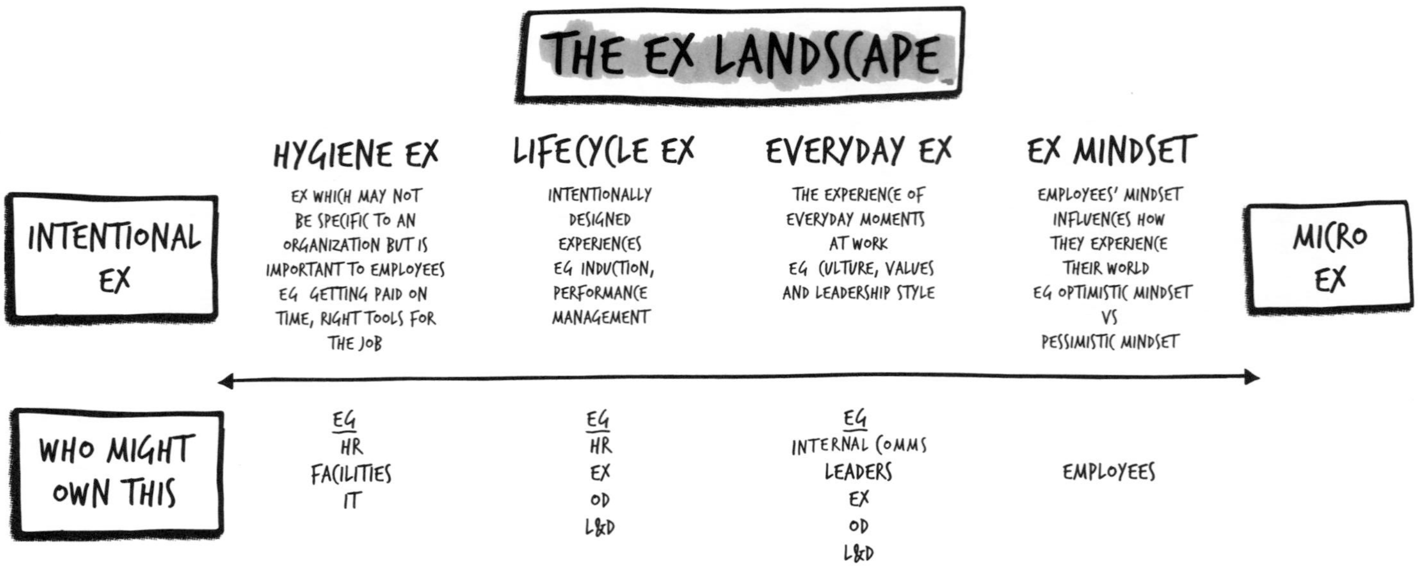

THE EX LANDSCAPE

HYGIENE EX
EX WHICH MAY NOT
BE SPECIFIC TO AN
ORGANIZATION BUT IS
IMPORTANT TO EMPLOYEES
EG GETTING PAID ON
TIME, RIGHT TOOLS FOR
THE JOB

LIFECYCLE EX
INTENTIONALLY
DESIGNED
EXPERIENCES
EG INDUCTION,
PERFORMANCE
MANAGEMENT

EVERYDAY EX
THE EXPERIENCE OF
EVERYDAY MOMENTS
AT WORK
EG CULTURE, VALUES
AND LEADERSHIP STYLE

EX MINDSET
EMPLOYEES' MINDSET
INFLUENCES HOW
THEY EXPERIENCE
THEIR WORLD
EG OPTIMISTIC MINDSET
VS
PESSIMISTIC MINDSET

INTENTIONAL
EX

MICRO
EX

WHO MIGHT
OWN THIS

EG
HR
FACILITIES
IT

EG
HR
EX
OD
L&D

EG
INTERNAL COMMS
LEADERS
EX
OD
L&D

EMPLOYEES

Then there is the everyday EX, which is where we find practitioners designing experiences that bring to life the company culture, brand and values. For example, the way we are led and managed each day will have an impact on how we experience the organization. While there are specific teams who will take ownership of the design and implementation of everyday experiences, these experiences are much more than this – for example, the way a colleague replies to an email, the greeting we receive from the receptionist each morning, being able to find information we need for our job. These small micro-experiences add up to form our overall EX and some of the responsibility for everyday EX lies with employees themselves.

And finally, we often forget to look at the role of our mindset in how we experience our world. We can choose how we wish to experience the organization, and this can have a profound effect on our overall experience. For example, the impact of a negative experience on an optimist may be different to a pessimist. This is something we will explore further in Chapter 3; it is often overlooked within the EX landscape.

It is also helpful to consider the difference between what we call the 'umbrella experience' and 'nested journeys'. Our levels of experience model (Figure 1.3) helps to illustrate this. The umbrella experience refers to the overall, end-to-end EX employees have with the organization, which begins before they even join on day one and extends after they exit the company. As a practitioner you might be focusing your work on this umbrella experience. Underneath the umbrella experience are what we call nested journeys, which might include experiences that last months or years, such as the employee journey on a graduate scheme or in their first business unit. And there are shorter nested journeys, such as the experience someone has in their first role. And along the way there will be moments that matter to the employee, such as their first promotion or taking maternity or paternity leave. The purpose of this model is to enable practitioners to consider the different types and levels of experience employees have and how they might impact each other.

The way we experience the world, including the world of work, is deeply personal. This is why one of our fundamental principles of EX

FIGURE 1.3 Levels of experience

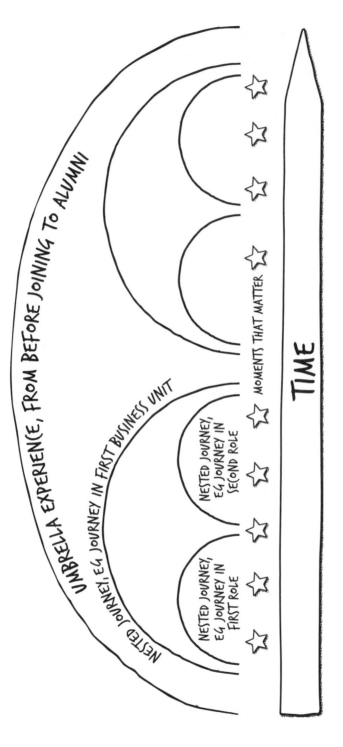

UMBRELLA EXPERIENCE, FROM BEFORE JOINING TO ALUMNI

NESTED JOURNEY, EG JOURNEY IN FIRST BUSINESS UNIT

NESTED JOURNEY, EG JOURNEY IN FIRST ROLE

NESTED JOURNEY, EG JOURNEY IN SECOND ROLE

MOMENTS THAT MATTER

TIME

design is empathy. Whichever model or framework you choose to discover, define and deliver your intended EX, empathy must feature. This is why our three EX design lenses model very deliberately places the employee at the centre, or the heart, of EX.

We must seek to view the experience, whatever that might be, through the eyes of our people. This is why we are cautious with using off-the-shelf, 'EX by numbers' models or frameworks. While there will be elements of these models that are relevant to your EX, ultimately, they are prescriptive and have made assumptions about what constitutes a great experience for your people. For example, many EX models include technology as a key element of a great experience. While this may be true for a great many people, there are numerous examples of individuals working jobs where technology is not (yet) on the radar, including a client of ours that makes metal products in a foundry. When working with the team there to understand their experience and how it could be improved, technology did not feature.

Another example is highlighted via the COVID-19 experience. During the lockdown conditions that were implemented in many parts of the world, millions of employees found themselves working from home for the foreseeable future. Suddenly the role of the physical office space to EX was of little importance. This is why we advocate using positive psychology and design thinking to provide you with your EX design framework. Our approach ensures you don't fall into the 'we know what's best for our people' trap, or blindly follow a model of EX that may not be relevant to your organizational context. EX design also ensures you work on the parts of the experience that will make the biggest difference to your people and organization. EX design gives you everything you need to design and implement a compelling EX while avoiding a prescribed list of what you should focus on.

Using positive psychology also enables us to really understand and empathize with our people. Positive psychology is the study of what makes life most worth living. It involves an approach to practice that seeks to understand strengths, not just weaknesses, looking to learn from and build the best things in life, as well as repairing the worst. The tools we recommend using throughout this book provide a strength-based, solution-focused approach that means we will invest time and energy in the right things. Positive psychology also helps us to understand the nature of experiences, involving emotions, attitudes, beliefs, norms and more. Design thinking then adds to this foundation, enabling us to understand what really matters to our people, and design solutions to respond to this. Using tools from the world of design thinking helps to define the problem we're trying to solve, or indeed to identify the opportunity to improve EX, avoiding the pitfalls of going straight to a solution.

Everyday EX

Let's provide a true story to illustrate why this approach works. Your survey findings tell you your people don't feel recognized for a job well done. A team is tasked with addressing this finding. Over the course of months they spend a great deal of time, effort and money putting in place an employee recognition approach, involving an app, monthly awards, internal communications and a big, glittering year-end event. A year later, though, the results haven't improved and employees still don't feel recognized for a job well done. Why? Because the team, although well meaning, made assumptions about the problem they were trying to solve. The tools we share throughout the book will help you to either validate your problem, or identify what the opportunity is, then ideate and prototype to deliver a successful outcome.

Now let's imagine you approached this scenario with an EX design mindset. First of all, no assumptions would be made about the problem you're trying to solve, and you would be open-minded and curious about the potential opportunity. Time would be spent understanding the situation from the perspective of employees, using a strength-based approach: asking when you are recognized for a job well done, what does this look like, or mean, to you? Using empathy at this point enables us to really understand what the problem definition or opportunity is. In our real-life example, taking this approach gathered insight from employees that revealed this was actually about being thanked for a job well done and not about the need to be recognized in a company-wide scheme. The opportunity was to develop a culture of feedback, between peers and leaders, not about awarding trophies at an event.

In fact, as we mentioned before, it is most often the everyday EX, sometimes called micro-experiences, that makes the biggest difference to our overall experience at work. We cannot overemphasize the impact of the everyday EX. However, it can feel like an overwhelming task to begin to first understand these everyday experiences and then positively impact them. A great place to begin your EX design journey is to start with a strength-based conversation by asking what good looks like for your people. This can be at the strategic level, for example, by asking:

Tell me about your best experience(s) at work.

Or it could be more focused to address a specific area, such as:

Tell me about a time when you felt recognized at work and how it felt.

We've collected hundreds of these stories from employees over the years, and the insight they reveal is invaluable for developing and improving EX. These types of conversations uncover very quickly and easily the 'everyday' EX that can make a big difference. Starting your EX journey with a 'best experience conversation' sets you off on the right path for EX design in the following ways:

- It's strength-based, gathering insight to alert you to what works rather than focusing on what is broken.
- The conversations very quickly uncover the everyday EX that makes a big difference.
- Having these conversations enables you to empathize, putting the end user – the employee – at the heart of the process.
- The insight uncovers the personal nature of EX, helping to avoid the 'one size fits all' approach.
- The insight also helps to identify opportunities, ensuring you are solving what needs to be solved.

BEST EXPERIENCE

The following activity is a great way to uncover what a great experience means to your people. It provides a quick and easy way to get started with your EX design journey and can be used for any type of EX you are working on. At a big picture level, you can use this activity to understand what constitutes a great experience for your people. It can also be effective as a tool to explore specific employee experiences, such as the onboarding journey, to understand what good looks like. You can then use insights as part of the design thinking process in a variety of ways:

- to develop a definition or approach;

- to uncover the 'everyday EX' insights;

- to define the problem;

- to ensure you avoid assumptions and resist going straight to solution;

- at a strategic level, to understand what a great EX means to your people;

- for a specific area of the EX you are seeking to improve, eg induction.

We have used this activity for over 15 years as a way of designing experiences, which begin by developing a deep understanding of employees. If you have Emma's previous book, *Employee Engagement* (Bridger, 2018), you'll recognize the activity, which is also shared there. The reason for this is that we always advocate you begin by seeking to understand what good looks like for your people and avoiding making assumptions about what this entails.

Ask your team, or the group you are working with, to think about their best experience within their work life: a time when they were really engaged at work, when they loved what they were doing. Ask them to get into pairs and spend 10 minutes interviewing each other (5 minutes each), using the questions below:

- Tell me about your most valued or engaging experience you have had in your work life – a time when you really loved coming to work.

- What were the conditions that made it possible?

- How did this experience make you feel?

Ask pairs to capture an overview of their partner's story, thinking about what made it possible, and how it felt, and to also capture any key themes they observe emerging. Each pair will then feed back their partner's story to the rest of the group. When they do this, capture the key themes on a flip chart.

Outputs

As pairs are sharing their partner's stories, capture the key words that they feed back. Typically, this will include intrinsic motivators associated with a great EX (whatever that EX is) such as:

- feeling valued;
- being proud;
- building confidence;
- having autonomy;
- developing and getting better at something;
- being trusted;
- working with great people;
- having fun;
- working for an inspiring manager;
- having challenging work;
- delivering and succeeding;
- achieving.

This activity allows people to reconnect with the emotional side of work: by telling their stories, people remember what it feels like to have positive experiences at work. This is also a great exercise to get a group into a positive state of mind to talk about their experience.

Discuss and explain

When everyone has shared their stories, take a look at the words you have noted:

- What are the group's observations of the words you have recorded?
- Using the words, ask the group to develop a definition or description of what a positive and compelling experience means in your organization.

As mentioned, you can also adapt this activity to explore a specific experience you are looking to redesign. For example:

- returning to work;

- induction;

- performance management conversations;

- career progression.

You can adapt the questions to work for your specific scenario – for example, by asking people to share stories about brilliant return-to-work experiences or great induction experiences. The basic premise is to gather insights that help you understand what a positive experience involves for your people, whatever the experience you are focusing on.

When looking at organizations who are doing great things within the world of EX, attention often turns to the obvious suspects: the Silicon Valley superstars, tech companies and the digital cool kids on the block. This can make EX feel inaccessible, something that only certain types of organization are embracing – which is why we wanted to share stories from the less obvious organizations, who are nonetheless leading the way in EX. Throughout the following chapters, we'll share examples of companies that are leading the way with EX design to help bring to life the concepts and ideas we will share.

EX DESIGN – THE ASTER STORY

Aster is one the UK's largest and most innovative housing associations. Their corporate vision is that everyone has a home, which, despite being a bold statement, is one that everyone across their business is passionate about. Their purpose is to improve people's lives via reliable landlord services and a wide range of housing options in response to the housing crisis. And, critically, they recognize their core strengths are their people and their ethical approach, which in EX is a key area of focus for the business.

Back in 2017 Aster made a conscious decision to change the way they approached HR in order to drive forward their transformation agenda. They took the decision to align the people, communications and IT teams under one directorate. The driver for these changes was to move away from a process-focused people approach, operating in silos, to develop and build a people-first culture. The HR team was disbanded and new workstreams were established that included an EX team with the recruitment of a head of EX, and EX partners, working across the organization.

The approach Aster has taken to establish this new team, and way of working, is a great example of EX design in practice. The team's primary focus was to make Aster a great place to work and create an environment where their people could deliver their best work, whichever part of the organization they worked in. Early on they began by mapping the employee journey and evaluating the touchpoints to understand which moments mattered most to their people and which areas would contribute to the delivery of the corporate strategy the most, to enable prioritization. Their initial focus was their trade teams, as they knew how they experienced life at Aster was very different from others who work less remotely. Right from the off they gathered feedback and evidence to guide their work. Employee voice is at the heart of what they do, not only for the EX team, but to ensure it influences key business decisions. They talk about supporting big and little conversations, and this is to ensure employees have their say. Sacha Harris, head of EX at Aster, explains that their approach is still evolving:

> We are learning as we go, testing and piloting new approaches all with the aim of creating experiences that mean employees feel valued, motivated, and therefore want to deliver a great service to our customers. We have worked on areas such as how we onboard new employees, to building an award-winning wellbeing strategy, to really ensuring employee voice makes an impact at all levels of the organization. We have worked with our trade teams on what's important to them as well as creating opportunities to keep colleagues connected to the strategy and each other. It's been interesting, as we realized there were moments that mattered to our people that weren't under our direct influence to change. For example, we quickly realized the role of leaders is critical to EX, so we have been working with the organizational development team on the role of the leader to enhance the EX. We continue to build our leadership development programme with the employee experience at the heart.

As Aster continues to review their offer, they want to make sure it's as attractive and personalized as possible. They recognize what employees want will vary depending on who they are and their circumstances. They are working hard to ensure employees understand the whole offer and don't just see it as a series of initiatives, so communication is key.

Sacha is refreshingly open about the learning the team has gone through over the past few years, as they experiment with different solutions to improve the EX. She is comfortable talking about their approach to EX as an ongoing journey, with both successes and some failures they have learned from quickly.

Both she and the team embody an EX design mindset, being curious and empathic in the way they approach EX, as well as comfortable with experimentation and continuous improvement. The team knows it's important that the EX supports Aster's vision and continues to evolve in a world post-COVID as requirements and expectations of employees change. Sacha also recognizes that proving ROI is not always straightforward, and the team is now measuring EX via Culture Amp (pulse) surveys to achieve this. They hope to start using data to better shape experiences and also begin to explore predictive analytics. The EX approach at Aster also embodies the principles of positive psychology that we advocate as part of our EX design framework. Sacha explains that one of the biggest differences in the way the team now approaches EX is the switch from a deficit-based approach, ie focusing on what needs fixing, to a strength-based approach, learning from what works.

The Aster story is a great example of an organization using an EX design approach to make a difference to the business. The EX at Aster is helping the organization with their business transformation by creating a positive experience where people are engaged, valued and motivated. And it is a fantastic example of EX design in action.

In this chapter we have introduced the concept of our EX design approach, which we will expand on in the following chapters. Combining positive psychology and design thinking will really help to develop and improve EX in your organization, in a simple and practical way.

Takeaways

- EX requires much more than what HR can do alone.

- It is not the same as engagement – a great EX will facilitate engagement – and a great EX is crucial for engagement.

- It must be employee/human-centric – you need to know your people.

- It's subjective – it involves our emotions, attitudes, beliefs, perceptions and behaviours.

- There is no single definition or a one-size-fits-all approach.

- Use the 'Best experience' activity in this chapter to begin your EX by design journey.

References

Bersin, J (2019) [accessed 10 August 2020] Employee experience: it's trickier and more important that you thought [Online] https://joshbersin.com/2019/03/the-employee-experience-its-trickier-and-more-important-than-you-thought/ (archived at https://perma.cc/GAJ8-MEZ3)

Bridger, E (2018) *Employee Engagement*, Kogan Page, London

CIPD (2020) [accessed 10 August 2020] Employee experience [Online] https://peopleprofession.cipd.org/profession-map/specialist-knowledge/employee-experience (archived at https://perma.cc/7LVW-BECM)

Deloitte (2017) [accessed 10 August 2020] Human capital trends [Online] https://www2.deloitte.com/content/dam/Deloitte/global/Documents/About-Deloitte/central-europe/ce-global-human-capital-trends.pdf (archived at https://perma.cc/LN3K-5ZWE)

Dery, K and Sebastian, I (2017) Building business value with employee experience, MIT CISR, *Research Briefing*, 17 (6). https://cisr.mit.edu/publication/2017_0601_EmployeeExperience_DerySebastian (archived at https://perma.cc/V6WN-54M9)

Gallup (2019) [accessed 10 August 2020] State of the global workplace [Online] https://www.gallup.com/workplace/238079/state-global-workplace-2017.aspx (archived at https://perma.cc/DYV5-R64M)

Kennedy Fitch (2018) [accessed 10 August 2020] Employee experience: how to build an EX-centric organization [Online] http://www.kennedyfitch.com/KFwebsite-new/wp-content/uploads/Employee-Experience-How-to-Build-an-EX-Centric-Organization.pdf archived at https://perma.cc/7H9Q-6P93)

LinkedIn (2020) [accessed 10 August 2020] Global talent trends 2020 [Online] https://business.linkedin.com/talent-solutions/recruiting-tips/global-talent-trends-2020 (archived at https://perma.cc/BYH6-PFY4)

Mercer (2019) [accessed 10 August 2020] Global talent trends [Online] https://www.uk.mercer.com/gbm-risk-department/global-talent-trend.html (archived at https://perma.cc/T57N-UUSK)

Mercer (2020) [accessed 10 August 2020] Global talent trends [Online] https://www.mercer.com/our-thinking/career/global-talent-hr-trends.html (archived at https://perma.cc/3GQZ-5FD8)

Morgan, J (2017) *The Employee Experience Advantage: How to win the war for talent by giving employees the workspaces they want, the tools they need, and a culture they can celebrate*, Wiley, Hoboken, NJ

People Lab (2018) [accessed 10 August 2020] *Spotlight on employee engagement* [Online] https://peoplelab.co.uk/spotlight-on-the-employee-engagement-profession-launches/ (archived at https://perma.cc/6FJ8-GLBJ)

Whitter, B (2019) *Employee Experience: Develop a happy, productive and supported workforce for exceptional individual and business performance*, Kogan Page, London

02

Making the case for EX

In this chapter we'll cover:

- building the business case for EX;
- the evidence of the positive impact of a compelling EX;
- how to convince your stakeholders that focusing on EX is good for the business;
- where to focus;
- getting clear on what you want to achieve.

Building the business case for EX – the evidence

There is a growing body of evidence that demonstrates that the experience our people have at work matters. While this is a given for those of us working in the field of EX, we often encounter stakeholders who need convincing. It seems obvious that the experience our people have at work will ultimately impact organizational performance, but there are many who challenge this assumption. To overcome these objections we have included some of the latest research to help make the business case for a focus on EX. EX by design often begins with getting buy-in from leaders and stakeholders, so we've included insights and tools to help you achieve this.

The Sears 'employee–customer–profit chain' was one of the first pieces of empirical research to make the link between employee attitudes and organizational performance. The research, published in the *Harvard Business Review* in 1998 (Rucci *et al*, 1998), found a positive correlation between employee attitudes, customer behaviour, and subsequent impact on the bottom line. In summary, the focus was on creating a compelling place to work, in order to facilitate a compelling place to shop, which in turn led to a compelling place to invest. While the company used a 70-item survey to understand employee experience and engagement, analysis revealed that a subset of 10 items, specifically relating to attitudes to the job and the company, made the biggest difference. Although the research was not explicitly asking about the employee experience, it seems reasonable to suggest that positive experiences facilitate positive attitudes; it's difficult to have a positive attitude towards the job you do, or the company you work for, if the experience of either is poor.

In 2017, MIT conducted a global survey of 281 senior executives exploring the role of EX in building business value (Dery and Sebastian, 2017). In the study they defined employee experience as 'the work complexity and behavioural norms that influence employees' ability to create value'. They found that companies focusing on these two factors outperformed their competitors. Those companies that were placed in the top quartile for EX, using the MIT definition, had twice the innovation, double the customer satisfaction, and 25 per cent greater profitability when compared with those companies placed in the bottom quartile for EX.

Further evidence demonstrating the impact of a great EX on subsequent business performance is provided via research from Jacob Morgan (2017). He found that those companies that invested most heavily in EX were:

- included 11.5 times as often in Glassdoor's Best Places to Work;
- listed 4.4 times as often in LinkedIn's list of North America's Most In-Demand Employers;
- 28 times more often listed among Fast Company's Most Innovative Companies;

- listed 2.1 times as often on the Forbes list of the World's Most Innovative Companies;

- twice as often found in the American Customer Satisfaction Index.

And perhaps most compelling is the finding that those companies Morgan classes as 'experiential' have more than four times the average profit and more than two times the average revenue.

Further evidence comes from Willis Towers Watson (2020), who survey over 500 companies annually covering almost 10 million employees. Their research has shown that those companies with more effective EX outperform their peers on top-line growth, bottom-line profitability and return to shareholders. And research from IBM (2017) found that discretionary effort was almost twice as likely to be reported when employee experience is positive. In addition, they found that a good EX, as measured by their EX index, was linked to employees' intention to stay. In fact, employees with positive experiences are 52 per cent less likely to say that they intend to leave their organizations. Research from Gartner in 2019 tells a similar story. They found that employees who are satisfied with their experience are 60 per cent more likely to say they want to stay with their employer, 52 per cent more likely to report high discretionary effort, and 69 per cent more likely to be a high performer. They also discovered that employees who report they have a good EX are 48 per cent more likely to meet organizational customer satisfaction goals, 89 per cent more likely to meet organizational innovation goals, and 56 per cent more likely to meet organizational reputation goals.

In Chapter 1 we discussed the relationship between EX and employee engagement; in summary, engagement is what we get when employees have great experiences. The business case for employee engagement is well documented. Companies with top-quartile engagement enjoy twice the net annual profit compared with those with bottom-quartile engagement. They also have 12 per cent higher customer satisfaction, 40 per cent lower employee turnover, are 35 per cent more efficient, and have 62 per cent fewer accidents than companies with bottom-quartile engagement (Engage for Success website). While there's no doubt that engagement positively impacts a range of desired business outcomes, it has come under increasing criticism from commentators over the past few years. The criticism levied at the field of employee engagement often involves commenters citing the failure of companies to improve it. Although there are a diverse range of engagement scores shared via published research and white papers, it's fair to say that global engagement is still fairly poor. However, we believe the problem is not with the concept of engagement per se, but with the lack of understanding of how to go about developing engagement. For too long companies have taken a transactional approach to engagement, running a survey and seeking to fix problem areas identified via short-term initiatives. At the opposite end of the spectrum are those companies that take a transformational approach to engagement. They understand that they need to build a culture and workplace that facilitates great experiences. It is these companies – that understand that engagement is born from positive experiences at work – that are reaping the rewards.

The evidence for working on your EX outlined so far has focused on the big picture, explaining why, at the strategic level, EX is good for business. You may be looking to make the case for a more specific focus on EX; perhaps to improve the experience of onboarding, or internal communications, or performance management. In their *Global Talent Trends 2020* report, LinkedIn share some research that demonstrates the impact of specific EX components, providing evidence again that a great experience yields great rewards. They researched over 1,000 companies looking at key EX elements, such as training and flexibility, and then cross-referenced them with employee behavioural data. The results found that companies that rated highly on employee training enjoyed 53 per cent lower attrition, and those that had a purposeful mission had 49 per cent lower attrition. The study found that those with flexible work arrangements had 137 per cent higher headcount growth. However, in the same survey they found that just 52 per cent of employees said their company provides a positive employee experience, meaning almost half aren't enjoying a positive experience at work. There is clearly a huge, untapped potential for companies to focus on improving their EX and all of the benefits this brings.

Building your business case – finding your why

The evidence for focusing on EX, and the subsequent benefits this brings, is useful to help convince sceptical stakeholders. However, organizations are unique, and getting clear on your scope is a great place to begin building your case. The business case you build will very much depend on your business context and the needs you have identified, whether solving a problem or identifying an opportunity. Our EX by design approach will enable you to effectively scope your approach and help you to identify where to focus your efforts.

Being clear from the outset about either the problem you are trying to solve, or the opportunity you wish to seize with EX, enables you to both make the business case and then demonstrate impact. In this section, we will explore a range of reasons that companies are investing in EX to provide some context as you 'find the why' for your organization.

So why do companies choose to invest in EX? In 2018, Kennedy Fitch conducted a survey of 250+ companies and researched what they call 'EX Pioneers' to better understand the business case for EX. Their findings ranked the most important reasons for building EX as follows:

1 business growth;

2 engagement;

3 creating competitive advantage;

4 productivity;

5 profitability;

6 successful business transformation;

7 building a customer-centric HR.

They then repeated their survey and found a similar list of reasons underpinning the business case for EX:

1 engagement and retention;

2 business growth and strategic requirements;

3 increasing customer satisfaction;

4 foster an employee-centric culture;

5 competitive advantage;

6 building a more customer-centric HR;

7 increase performance.

These are all relevant strategic drivers for focusing on EX within your organization, and there is some compelling data that helps to make the case for investing in EX for each of these. To take engagement and retention as an example, in their 2020 Global Culture study of some 20,000 employees, O.C. Tanner found that 59 per cent of respondents would accept a role in a different company today if it offered the same work, pay and benefits: less than half of respondents have loyalty to their organization. Research from Gallup in 2018 had already indicated a similar trend, with 63 per cent of employees believing they could find a job as good as the one they have. In addition, research from Deloitte (2017) found that nearly one in five employees, especially Millennials, left their jobs in 2017 due to a poor employee experience. Though in a post-COVID-19 workplace you could argue that EX and the impact on areas such as retention are not as relevant, we would argue the opposite is true. When the labour market is buoyant, it is easier for unhappy employees to make the move to a new place of work. But when we are in a recession, unhappy employees are more likely to stay with you, which is far from ideal.

So while data in the public domain might not be specific to your organization, it can help you to make the business case for a specific focus on EX as well as for broader strategic goals. For example, research by Gallup (2018) found that just 12 per cent of employees strongly agree that their organization does a great job of onboarding, which could be useful data if this is an area you wish to focus on. Gallup also found that 23 per cent of employees said that they experience burnout very often or always, and 44 per cent feel burnt out sometimes. A high level of burnout within organizations then impacts absenteeism, performance and more, so using EX to reduce burnout may also be another approach to explore.

Whatever element of the EX you are looking to make the case for, there will no doubt be some evidence in the public domain which you can use to help you make your case. The key is to be clear about what it is you are trying to impact – to find your why – and then source some data to help make your case.

The reputation driver is also useful to help you make the case for investment in EX, a further 'why' to add to your business case. Internet sites such as Glassdoor enable employees, past or current, to share their experiences of your organization in the public domain. Sites such as these are increasingly used by potential employees when choosing which jobs to apply for and where they would like to work. In addition, a study conducted by Norwich Business School in 2018 (Symitsi *et al*, 2020) uncovered a link between Glassdoor ratings and performance:

> First, we find that UK firms rated highly by their current employees in terms of satisfaction achieve superior profitability (ROA) compared to those rated poorly. Second, the significant positive relationship between employee satisfaction rating and profitability indicates that similarly to the case of US firms, online employee reviews can be used to forecast the financial results of UK firms.

More and more companies, such as Unilever and Nandos, now actively use their Glassdoor ratings and profiles as part of their marketing, not only for potential employees but for investors too. Organizations are also increasingly coming under fire for the way they treat, or mistreat, employees. During the COVID-19 lockdown, there were a number of high-profile brands that attracted the wrong kind of column inches because of the appalling experience of their employees. Time will tell if this treatment of their employees impacts consumer behaviour, but corporate reputation can be a compelling way to make the case for EX.

EXERCISE

Finding your why – aligning your EX objectives to your business strategy and goals

What this is: This activity is designed to enable you to understand how a compelling EX could help to contribute to achieving your company's strategy, goals, ambitions and objectives. This will help you to make the business case for EX investment.

Why use it: Your EX approach should contribute to what your company is trying to achieve; using this activity will help you to make sure that this is the case.

How to use it: To run this activity you'll just need the activity instructions and any relevant company information such as mission, goals, etc. You'll also need a flip chart and pens if you're running the activity in person, or an online collaboration tool such as Miro if you're running this online.

Who to use it with: This activity is helpful to use with those people who have some responsibility for designing your EX approach, for example your senior team, HR team and EX team.

Background

In our 'three EX design lenses model' (see Figure 1.1) we talk about the organizational context and need for EX. When making the case for EX investment, this is a useful place to start. A compelling EX is of course good for our employees, but should contribute to the strategy, goals, priorities, issues, challenges or opportunities the business is working on.

A compelling EX should contribute to the overall purpose and strategy of your organization, and yet often EX initiatives are disconnected from corporate goals.

Instructions

- Set the scene for the activity by explaining that it is important to ensure EX contributes to your business strategy, and the starting point for this is to check in that everyone is clear about what your company is trying to achieve.

- Share any relevant company background and information at this point, eg company strategy, mission, vision, goals, ambitions, strategic priorities.

- Discuss: facilitate a discussion on your company data and insight to answer the following questions:

1 What are the key themes and broad areas your company is currently focusing on?

   o This could include themes such as:

      – growth;

      – innovation;

      – improved customer experience;

      – improved reputation;

      – health and safety focus;

      – operational effectiveness;

      – cost-cutting;

      – productivity;

      – sales;

      – compliance.

2 Once you have discussed and identified the broad themes, agree the three to five areas you are going to focus on and prioritize.

3 To help you do this, analyse each theme by looking at the potential impact your employees have on each theme and its subsequent success.

4 You can use the template in Table 2.1 to help you; the worked examples are there to illustrate how this might work.

The outcome of this activity is to agree which business priorities can be most impacted by your people. Focus on these areas first and start to consider how a

TABLE 2.1 Worked examples

Company focus: 3–5 themes	Priority	Examples of the impact your employees could have on each area
Innovation	1	Employees producing great ideas for new products
Growth	3	Employees increasing sales to help grow revenue
Customer experience	2	Employees care about customer needs
Sales	4	Employees increasing sales to help grow revenue
Health and safety	5	Employees having fewer accidents

compelling EX could create a competitive advantage, where your employees have the potential for the biggest impact on your high-priority business areas. This information can be included in any business case you need to make. Depending on your focus, you can search for relevant evidence in the public domain to back up your conclusions. You can then use this information to help you develop your EX focus: goals and outcomes.

Think about your EX team

EX roles are on the increase, but the idea of an EX team can be misleading. In many ways EX is everyone's responsibility and should not fall at the feet of one person or team. But having a dedicated EX professional, or team, helps to ensure the right things will happen. Interestingly, research from Kennedy Fitch (2018) found that while 96 per cent say EX is important, it's currently understaffed and under-resourced.

In their EX leaders research, the HX Leaders Network (2020) identified different stages of maturity for EX, which indicated where companies are on their journey:

- 'no plans' – 14 per cent;
- researching EX – 32 per cent;
- starting EX – 25 per cent;
- building capability – 18 per cent;
- 'new ways of working – 6 per cent;
- merging CX and EX – 6 per cent.

Famously, in 2014, Mark Levy at Airbnb brought together a diverse range of teams under its 'EX' function, including culture, recruiting, events, facilities, real estate, design, etc. This was specifically to create an end-to-end journey for employees, and he is widely regarded as the person to coin the term 'employee experience'.

We're still feeling our way when it comes to EX team and resource structure and, in our experience, organizations are approaching this in a number of different ways. It's important to be mindful, however, that this is not about simply renaming a current team, as such an approach will not deliver the potential benefits a focus on EX can deliver.

Building the case for EX by design

We've shared the evidence for EX, but what about the 'design' element? We advocate using principles from the world of design thinking as a key component of our EX by design approach, and this is not accidental. There is compelling evidence that using design thinking principles, and establishing a culture where these behaviours are the norm, yields impressive results. McKinsey (2018) tracked the design practices of 300 publicly listed companies over a five-year period across multiple industries to study the design actions that are taken to unlock business value. Their findings found a correlation between those companies scoring high on the 'McKinsey Design Index', and higher revenue growth and higher returns to shareholders.

In their research they uncovered four 'clusters' of design actions that were most strongly correlated with subsequent financial performance, namely:

1 measuring and driving design performance with the same rigour as revenues and costs;

2 breaking down internal walls between physical, digital and service design;

3 making user-centric design everyone's responsibility;

4 de-risking development by continually listening, testing and iterating with end users.

In response to these findings, McKinsey make the following recommendations:

• Develop analytical leadership to measure and drive design performance with the same rigour as financials.

• Develop cross-functional teams to break down silos and ensure a design thinking approach is everybody's responsibility.

- Help de-risk the development of solutions with continuous iteration.
- Focus on user EX to help break down silos.

Our EX design framework incorporates all of these principles, and by using our framework you will be following some best practice thinking within your EX approach.

In a further study in 2018, InVision surveyed 2,200 organizations around the world to understand how companies can create better business outcomes with design practices. Although not focused solely on design thinking, what the study did find was that a design-led approach makes a positive difference to organization performance. They found that those companies with high design maturity enjoy cost savings, revenue gains and brand and market position improvements as a result of their design efforts. And in these companies employees are involved in the design process.

Further research from the HX Leaders Network (2020) found that one of the themes of those organizations leading in EX was their EX leaders' design thinking capabilities, which they use to discover and define EX. In particular, the research found that by using these capabilities they were very disciplined in the way they gained insights: 'EX leaders observed, interviewed, surveyed, combined data sets in their analytics, they experimented with different ways of working, using a variety of workspace arrangements and tools.' There does appear to be a growing body of evidence to back up the benefits of using a design thinking approach to develop your EX.

EXERCISE
Developing your EX vision

What this is: This activity is designed to enable you to develop your future vision for EX, whether that be at the big-picture, cultural level, or a vision for a specific element of EX such as onboarding.

Why use it: A clearly articulated vision for EX is important to ensure everyone is on the same page and heading in the same direction.

How to use it: You can run this activity in a number of ways. If you're online, use an online whiteboard, such as those found in Miro or similar. Or if you are in person, you can use a whiteboard or create mood boards using art materials.

Who to use it with: This activity is helpful to use with those people who have some responsibility for designing your EX, for example your senior team, HR team and EX team.

Overview

- Begin your session by asking the group if they have ever experienced any weird coincidences, such as deciding to buy a new car and then seeing that car everywhere. Or for the parents in the room, or online, maybe finding out that they, or some they know well, was pregnant, and then suddenly seeing pregnant women everywhere.

- Ask the group for any examples of this phenomenon they might be able to recall and share.

Then share the following information to explain why this phenomenon occurs:

- These situations aren't a coincidence at all but actually the result of our own in-built spam filter. We are bombarded with sensory images, sounds and data all day long. There is a part of our brain called the reticular activating system (RAS) that helps filter out unnecessary stimulus that we're bombarded with.

- The RAS consists of a bundle of densely packed nerve cells located in the central core of the brainstem. You can think of it as your own personal assistant for your conscious mind. It acts as a gatekeeper to screen or filter the type of information that will be allowed to get through.

- What is amazing is that you can deliberately program the reticular activating system by intentionally focusing on messages to send from your conscious mind to your subconscious. Therefore, if we focus on a blue Volvo, we start seeing blue Volvos everywhere.

- This is why it's so important to set goals and visualize our future. What we need to do is to create a very specific picture of our future vision in our conscious mind.

- The RAS will then pass this on to our subconscious, which will then help us move towards this future vision we have created.

- It does this by bringing to our attention all the relevant information that otherwise might have remained as 'background noise'.

- This is why we need to develop a clear vision for our EX.

Ask the group to brainstorm on a whiteboard, or create a mood board, to communicate the future vision for EX, whichever element you are working on. Ask the following questions:

- Imagine anything is possible – what *could* EX be like in the future?
- Describe what would be happening: what will it look like and feel like?
- How does it feel for our employees or the specific audience group?
- What will a typical day/journey be like?
- Why will people talk about this EX in the future?

Ask the groups to then present back their whiteboard capture or mood boards. After all the presentations, ask the group to reflect on:

- the common themes;
- the differences between the mood boards.

Finally, conclude the session by asking the group to come to a consensus on a possible future vision for EX.

___

Overcoming objections and barriers

It is stating the obvious, but gaining executive-level buy-in and support to your work in EX is critical, and not always straightforward. Here are some strategies that have helped us over the years we've been working in this space to convince sometimes sceptical senior leaders that a focus on EX is the right thing to do.

- Practise empathy to get into the mindset of the leaders you are seeking buy-in from. What do they care about? What keeps them awake at night? Use the principles we share in Chapter 7 to build a persona of those people you wish to convince and use this insight to build rapport and make the case.

- Speak in the language of the business and your stakeholders. You might not even need to explicitly mention the term 'employee experience'. If talent attraction is an opportunity area, talk about this and how you can help. If growth is a key area of focus, again talk about how you and your colleagues can contribute with your capabilities and expertise.

- Build your business case using clear objectives that are aligned with the business strategy and outline potential ROI, or ROX, which we'll take a deeper look at in Chapter 10, where we look at measuring EX.

- Use evidence wherever possible to back up your case. This could be via analytics – for example, demonstrating that the biggest flight risk with employees is up to the three months mark, and exit surveys revealed that the experience of employees from onboarding to that point is substandard. You can put a cost against the reality today and the projected future savings, if you get the green light for your proposal.

- If you have a strong focus on customer experience, you can use this as your way in. Share research that makes the link between employees and customers and ask to spend time with your customer experience (CX) colleagues to understand how this expertise could be applied to employees.

- Conduct small-scale pilots to test and learn, then share the findings with stakeholders to evidence a focus on EX and potential business benefits.

- Build your team of supporters. There will no doubt be influential stakeholders across the business you can use as allies to help you to make your case or sponsor the work you are proposing. Find these people and build good relationships with them.

- Undertake some scenario planning and include the scenario of 'do nothing' to bring your proposal to life for stakeholders.

- Run a best experience activity with stakeholders, as outlined in Chapter 1, getting them to share stories about times when they were at their best. Encourage a conversation about what the organization could be like if there were more opportunities for people to have more best experiences.

EXERCISE

Defining the goals and outcomes of your EX activity

What this is: This activity will help you to design and agree the goals and outcomes of your EX activity, whether at a big picture, strategic level, or at a specific, process, or everyday level.

Why use it: Good EX objectives should be aligned to what your company is trying to achieve; using this activity will enable you to do this.

How to use it: To run this activity you'll just need the activity notes, any relevant company information, such as mission, goals, etc, and a flip chart and pens.

Who to use it with: This activity is helpful to use with those people who have some responsibility for designing your engagement strategy and approach, for example your senior team, HR team and EX team.

Background

The process of defining the goals and outcomes of your EX strategy and/or focus will enable you to ensure that it is aligned to your business strategy. Understanding the purpose of EX within your company, and why and how it will help you achieve your overall business strategy, is the cornerstone of achieving alignment. In addition, an EX strategy and approach that can be clearly linked to the overall business strategy enables practitioners to demonstrate value to the business and get buy-in from key stakeholders.

There are a whole host of reasons why you may be focusing on EX. It is sometimes the case that the call for action for investment in EX can be quite abstract. For example, in their Global EX survey, Kennedy Fitch (2018) found the following reasons for focusing on EX:

- To create a working environment that allows people to realize their potential.

- To attract, engage and inspire employees to be their best in a safe, transparent and engaging environment.

- Defining and developing the optimal EX is crucial to our business success and, in particular, our High-Performance Culture.

- To build a better place to work.

These are all valid and desirable reasons for focusing on EX. In some cases the link to business outcomes is explicit, eg to attract employees, whereas in other cases it is less obvious. It is helpful when making your business case to include both goals and outcomes for EX investment and focus. For example, you may wish to build a better place to work, which is a goal, to contribute to an outcome of attracting and retaining talent.

Table 2.2 sets out some example EX goals and business outcomes.

Overview

- You can either work up your EX goals with a small group or as an individual.

- You can use the outputs from the previous two activities in this chapter on 'finding your why' and 'defining your vision' as inputs for this activity.

- After reflecting on these outputs, consider what your EX goals and subsequent business outcomes could be.

Top tips

We're all familiar with the acronym SMART when it comes to setting objectives or goals. As a quick reminder:

- Specific – goals must be clear and unambiguous in what they need to achieve.

TABLE 2.2 Example EX goals and business outcomes

Example EX goals	Example business outcomes
Strategy level:	• Reduce employee turnover
• Become a great place to work where people can realize their potential	• Reduce absenteeism
	• Increase productivity
• Become an employer of choice	• Increase sales
• Increase employee engagement	• Improve customer experience
Process level:	• Improve company reputation
• Improve our onboarding	
• Develop the EX of our performance management approach	
• Improve the EX of our internal communication	

- Measurable – goals must include concrete criteria to allow progress and delivery to be tracked.

- Achievable – goals must be within the organization's power to reach.

- Realistic – goals must be attainable given the resources available within your organization.

- Timely – goals should have a timeframe allocated for delivery.

It's important to ensure our goals and objectives are tangible and concrete, so that we can track performance and ultimately measure our success in achieving them. A good way to assess how concrete your goals and outcomes are is to ask yourself, 'How will I measure that?' and 'How will I prove that we have been successful in achieving this goal?' We will cover measurement in Chapter 10; however, we highly recommend that when you set your goals and objectives for your EX strategy or focus, you also define your measures and metrics at the same time. If you are struggling to articulate how you will measure the success in achieving one of your goals, it probably isn't concrete enough.

A few questions you might wish to consider include:

- What do you need EX to deliver for your organization and employees?

- What does success look like?

- Where do you want to be in five years?

- Why do you want a compelling EX?

- What are the outcomes you are hoping to achieve?

- How are they tethered to organization or business outcomes?

- For what purpose?

Using your employee value proposition (EVP) to design a compelling EX

An EVP is an expression of what an organization uniquely offers its employees that answers the question, 'What's in it for me?', and acts as a key differentiator within the workplace. It should be consistent with the corporate brand and is most often partially descriptive of the current state and partially aspirational. By identifying and adopting an EVP, you can identify what makes your organization a great place to work and focus activity on those experiences that will bring this to life. An EVP can help to motivate and inspire those already within the business and attract high-calibre potential employees, no matter the role. An EVP will give you a blueprint for EX across the entire employee lifecycle.

We view the employee value proposition (EVP) as the employee deal: what is expected of employees within your organization, and also what can they expect in return? Clearly the EX is central to this. Many companies simply view this as the balance of rewards and benefits that are received by employees in return for their performance in the workplace. However, we believe this approach is too transactional and that an EVP should be much broader than this and encompass the entire EX.

A strong EVP will:

- align with the culture of the organization, stating clearly what behaviours are expected of employees and then rewarded;
- outline how it should feel to work within the organization and what the EX should be;
- be informed by existing employees and culture;
- be unique, relevant, and compelling if it is to act as a key driver of talent attraction, engagement and retention.

We use the model in Figure 2.1 to help develop and use your EVP.

We recommend starting the process of creating your EVP with a research phase. It won't come as a surprise to hear that we advise involving your people to develop your EVP, rather than inventing it in isolation. Gathering insight from employees enables a true understanding of your organization's unique strengths, as well as the current reality of the EX. Typically we recommend running short workshops with a range of employees using appreciative inquiry to facilitate rich conversations about the current and future culture and EX. We'll go into more detail about what appreciative inquiry is and how you can use it in Chapter 3. It is also helpful to run one-to-one

FIGURE 2.1 Developing your EVP

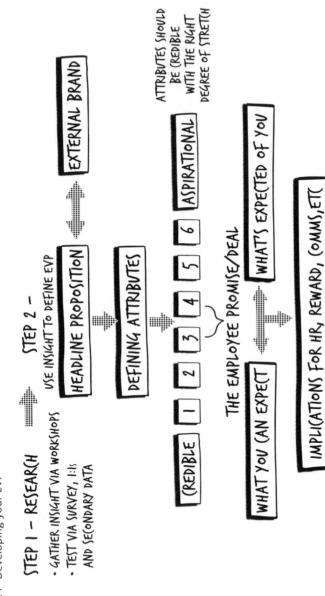

STEP 1 – RESEARCH

- GATHER INSIGHT VIA WORKSHOPS
- TEST VIA SURVEY, 1:1s AND SECONDARY DATA

STEP 2 –

USE INSIGHT TO DEFINE EVP

HEADLINE PROPOSITION ⟷ EXTERNAL BRAND

DEFINING ATTRIBUTES

CREDIBLE [1] [2] [3] [4] [5] [6] ASPIRATIONAL

ATTRIBUTES SHOULD BE CREDIBLE WITH THE RIGHT DEGREE OF STRETCH

THE EMPLOYEE PROMISE/DEAL

WHAT YOU CAN EXPECT ⟷ WHAT'S EXPECTED OF YOU

IMPLICATIONS FOR HR, REWARD, COMMS, ETC

interviews with stakeholders, which can include customers and other external partners if relevant.

Gathering insight enables the creation of a draft EVP, populating the framework set out in the model we share here. This can then be tested with employees and further refined. Once the headline proposition and defining attributes are agreed, we can look at what this means for the EX. For example, for each attribute we can outline what the deal is, that is, what employees can expect working for our organization, but equally what is expected of them.

In summary, your EVP can be used as the blueprint for your EX, informing touchpoints within the employee lifecycle. It helps to direct the design, build and communication of your EX.

Takeaways

In this chapter we have shared some of the key pieces of evidence that demonstrate the positive impact of EX and that will help you to make the business case. Demonstrating how your EX activity will positively impact the business is key, and the tools included in this chapter will help you to do that. In summary:

- There is a growing body of evidence that demonstrates that EX positively impacts a range of business outcomes.
- Getting buy-in from your executive teams will help you to deliver your goals.
- Creating a vision for your EX is a helpful starting point and will help to align those involved with EX and ensure you are all on the same page.
- Spend time mapping your goals and outcomes to your business needs, and consider how you will measure success.
- Developing your EVP is a great way to create a blueprint for subsequent EX efforts.
- Time spent on a well-argued business case will make life easier in the long run and ensure you spend time on the right things.

References

Deloitte (2017) [accessed 10 August 2020] Human capital trends [Online] https://www2.deloitte.com/content/dam/Deloitte/global/Documents/About-Deloitte/central-europe/ce-global-human-capital-trends.pdf (archived at https://perma.cc/LN3K-5ZWE)

Dery, K and Sebastian, I (2017) Building business value with employee experience, MIT CISR, *Research Briefing*, **17** (6). https://cisr.mit.edu/publication/2017_0601_EmployeeExperience_DerySebastian (archived at https://perma.cc/V6WN-54M9)

Engage for Success [website] [accessed 10 August 2020] www.engageforsuccess.org (archived at https://perma.cc/XCU9-X6FQ)

Gallup (2018) [accessed 10 August 2020] Designing your organization's employee experience [Online] https://www.gallup.com/workplace/242240/employee-experience-perspective-paper.aspx (archived at https://perma.cc/BH3J-SH9F)

Gartner (2020) [accessed 10 August 2020] The modern employee experience: Increasing the returns on employee experience investments (published 13 January) [Online] https://www.gartner.com/en/documents/2020/1/3979529-the-modern-employee-experience-increasing-the-returns-on (archived at https://perma.cc/CHN4-3GU9)

HX Leaders Network (2020) [accessed 10 August 2020] *Employee experience 2020* [Online] https://hxleadersnetwork.com/2020-ex-report/ (archived at https://perma.cc/C6XV-9WGJ)

IBM (2017) [accessed 10 August 2020] The Employee Experience Index: A new global measure of a human workplace and its impact [Online] https://www.ibm.com/downloads/cas/JDMXPMBM (archived at https://perma.cc/HE3V-5TLU)

InVision (2018) [accessed 10 August 2020] The new design frontier [Online] https://www.invisionapp.com/design-better/design-maturity-model/ (archived at https://perma.cc/ZU9Y-ZFKV)

Kennedy Fitch (2018) [accessed 10 August 2020] Employee experience: how to build an EX-centric organization [Online] http://www.kennedyfitch.com/KFwebsite-new/wp-content/uploads/Employee-Experience-How-to-Build-an-EX-Centric-Organization.pdf (archived at https://perma.cc/7H9Q-6P93)

LinkedIn (2020) [accessed 10 August 2020] Global talent trends 2020 [Online] https://business.linkedin.com/talent-solutions/recruiting-tips/global-talent-trends-2020 (archived at https://perma.cc/BYH6-PFY4)

McKinsey (2018) [accessed 10 August 2020] The business value of design [Online] https://www.mckinsey.com/business-functions/mckinsey-design/our-insights/the-business-value-of-design (archived at https://perma.cc/3CXF-QKSA)

Morgan, J (2017) *The Employee Experience Advantage: How to win the war for talent by giving employees the workspaces they want, the tools they need, and a culture they can celebrate*, Wiley, Hoboken, NJ

O.C. Tanner (2020) [accessed 10 August 2020] Global culture report [Online] https://www.octanner.com/uk/global-culture-report.html (archived at https://perma.cc/ET3F-8YUN)

Rucci, AJ, Kirn, SP and Quinn, RT (1998) The employee-customer-profit chain at Sears, *Harvard Business Review*, 76 (1), pp 82–97

Symitsi, E, Stamolampros, P, Daskalakis, G and Korfiatis, N (2020) The informational value of employee online reviews, *European Journal of Operational Research*. http://dx.doi.org/10.2139/ssrn.3140512 (archived at https://perma.cc/C4MW-GKU7)

Willis Towers Watson (2020) [accessed 10 August 2020] Identifying the factors that make a high-performance employee experience [Online] https://www.willistowerswatson.com/en-us/insights/campaigns/breakthrough-research-on-employee-experience-download (archived at https://perma.cc/6UUQ-C45A)

03

Busting myths

What's really driving your EX?

In this chapter we'll cover:

- an introduction to the psychology and neuroscience of what makes a great experience and why they're good for business;
- how to use this knowledge to underpin your EX approach and activity (spoiler alert: it's way more than perks and benefits);
- the role of the individual's mindset in the world of EX;
- simple tools to help apply the theory in practice.

Introduction

Research from Gartner (2019) found that the return on investment (ROI) on EX is disappointing: despite an average spend of $2,420 for each employee, only 13 per cent of those participating in the study said that they were satisfied with their experience at work. But we know that when you get the EX right, it pays off. Caroline Walsh, VP at Gartner's HR practice, says:

> Simply investing in these programs is not enough – companies taking that approach only drive up expectations, creating a vicious cycle in which employee desires and organizational spending fuel each other.

We believe that part of the foundation for getting your EX right is developing some understanding of the psychology of experiences. An understanding of the science adds value to your EX design approach. Throughout this chapter we'll share with you the theories and models from psychology and neuroscience that we believe are most relevant to EX design. And more importantly, you'll understand how to use this knowledge to ensure you generate ROI from your EX focus. We'll explain how to apply the science in a practical way, and you'll see that our EX design framework has the science baked in.

We talk about 'employee experience design' as the application of design principles and positive psychology. At the heart of our approach is the empathy principle; we need to invest time to understand the people we're designing for. We need to understand their needs and expectations. Once we genuinely comprehend our employees' needs and expectations, we can develop, test, and iterate solutions to design a compelling experience.

There is no substitute for taking time to understand the people you are designing for, or with. Being intentional about understanding your employees ensures you avoid making assumptions about what a good experience means to them. As humans we all have implicit biases, and this means we have assumptions about what constitutes a great experience. Our natural biases can be the downfall of good intentions when it comes to EX design. Developing an understanding of the psychology and neuroscience of experiences is beneficial to anyone involved in EX design. The field of psychology and neuroscience is vast, and we could dedicate an entire book to this topic alone. Therefore in this chapter we'll share with you those theories and models we have found most helpful to EX by design.

Positive experiences – why bother?

It seems obvious to say that positive experiences are a good thing, for both employees and businesses. You might be interested to learn that there is some pretty compelling evidence from the world of positive psychology to back this up. And the science helps to explain why a positive EX is a good thing. Positive psychology is a branch of psychology originally born out of Martin Seligman's research (eg Seligman and Maier, 1967) on learned helplessness. While positive psychology does not claim to have discovered the value of a positive approach and thinking, it does enable us to understand how to help people flourish and thrive. Positive psychology takes a strength-based approach, seeking to learn from what works, rather than always focusing on what doesn't work and how problems can be fixed. This is a subtle, but significant, shift in the way we approach and think about human behaviour.

In Chapter 2 we outlined the business case for focusing on EX. There is some robust science that explains why this is the case. Shawn Achor, an educator, speaker and consultant, spent 12 years at Harvard researching what makes people happy. In his book, *The Happiness Advantage* (2011), he describes how positive experiences at work lead to improved performance. In his research he found that being in a happy or positive state is actually a precursor to success, rather than the result of such success. These findings help to explain why positive experiences have an impact on subsequent performance in organizations.

The science shows that there is a fairly simple, scientific explanation as to why this is the case. When we have a positive experience, we experience positive emotions and we observe a rise in levels of serotonin and dopamine, which are neurotransmitters: chemicals released by nerve cells to send signals to other nerve cells. These particular chemicals not only make us feel good, but they also enhance the learning centres within our brains. These learning centres help us to organize new information more effectively, retain information for longer, and retrieve information more quickly. They also enable us to make and sustain more neural connections, which then allow us to think quicker, more creatively, see things in a different way, improve our problem-solving capability, and analyse complex information more skilfully. To summarize, when we experience positive emotions, the release of associated chemicals enables us to perform at a higher level, which then leads to improved performance.

There are numerous studies that provide evidence to back up these claims. For example, in one study doctors who were primed to be in a positive state before making a diagnosis showed three times more intelligence and creativity than doctors in a neutral, stressed or negative state. They also made accurate diagnoses 19 per cent faster. A team of positive psychologists conducted a meta-analysis to further test this hypothesis, looking at over 200 studies on 275,000 people worldwide. What they found was that in nearly every domain the findings were the same: positive emotions lead to success.

Obviously priming employees to be in a positive state before they perform critical tasks each and every time they perform them would be fairly intensive. However, creating a workplace that develops, supports and enhances the employee experience means that there is much higher likelihood of employees experiencing positive states and emotions.

What really makes a brilliant EX?

When it comes to designing employee experiences, there is often a gap between what science knows and what businesses do. The approach to designing a compelling employee experience regularly focuses on what are known as the 'hygiene factors'. Hygiene factors are those elements at work which we need to get right to ensure employee satisfaction, such as pay, benefits and environment. But while hygiene factors facilitate satisfaction, they don't always result in positive emotions. We worked with a client some years ago who was going through the process of moving some 2,000 employees from a rather outdated office into a lovely, shiny new office. They came up with what they thought was a brilliant idea – to give all employees a free breakfast. They believed a free breakfast would be a great experience for their people and contribute towards their overall engagement. And despite our best efforts we couldn't convince them otherwise. So what happened? Initially the free breakfast went down a treat, lots of smiley faces in the morning queuing up for free toast or cereals. But pretty soon there were rumblings: some people didn't like cereals or toast and wanted porridge or a piece of fruit. But these items weren't on the free breakfast list. Other people started to abuse the company's generosity, taking three or four boxes of the free cereal to see them through lunchtime and beyond. The rumblings grew into discontent. The company actually had to publish and enforce a 'free breakfast policy' detailing the rules for the free breakfast. And it wasn't long before they were wishing they had not gone down the free breakfast route to start with, given the discontent it had caused. The free breakfast very soon became yet another hygiene factor – it was simply expected as part of the employee deal. Despite the initial positive experience, employees very quickly came to perceive the free breakfast as simply part of the package, such as receiving their pay each month.

On the face of it perks such as a free breakfast might sound pretty cool, and something that you'd focus on when designing your EX. However, the problem is that these are all examples of hygiene factors, rather than experiences that result in positive emotions, at least in a sustainable way. It's easy to imagine that if you worked for an organization where these things are present, initially you'd think they were great, but pretty soon you may well take them for granted. Let's refer back to the 'best experience' activity in Chapter 1. We have collected hundreds of stories and insights over the years about what constitutes a 'best experience' for people. Never once has anyone said it was the free coffee, the ping pong table, beer on Fridays, the gym membership, the cool office, the free breakfast, or indeed any of the usual perks. These types of perks, although well-meaning, very quickly morph into hygiene factors – stuff that's just expected from our employer and workplace. Hygiene factors such as free food, pay and benefits and the office environment are important to help ensure we avoid dissatisfaction at work, which results in a negative experience. But they aren't that useful when it comes to facilitating a positive experience. The initial high from such perks quickly becomes the norm.

The limitation of perks to facilitate an ongoing positive EX can be explained by Herzberg's hygiene–motivation model. This is a useful framework to consider when designing compelling employee experiences. Sometimes referred to as the 'two-factor' model, Herzberg first developed his model in 1959, and in summary it makes the distinction between hygiene factors and motivators as seen in Figure 3.1.

FIGURE 3.1 Hygiene–motivation model

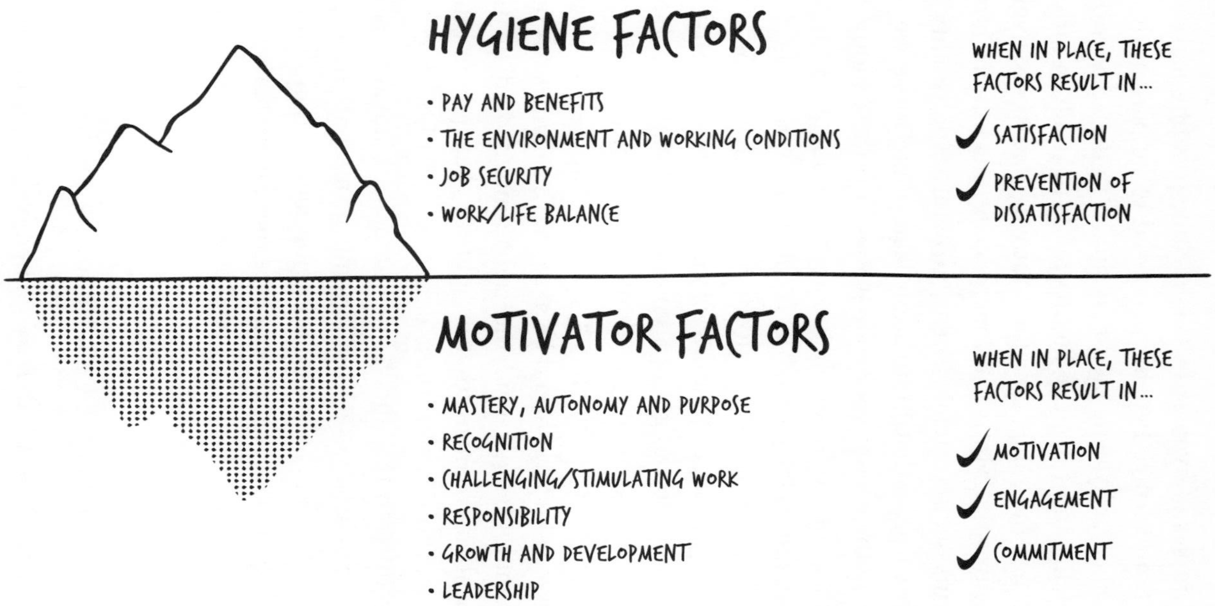

HYGIENE FACTORS

- PAY AND BENEFITS
- THE ENVIRONMENT AND WORKING CONDITIONS
- JOB SECURITY
- WORK/LIFE BALANCE

WHEN IN PLACE, THESE FACTORS RESULT IN...

✓ SATISFACTION
✓ PREVENTION OF DISSATISFACTION

MOTIVATOR FACTORS

- MASTERY, AUTONOMY AND PURPOSE
- RECOGNITION
- CHALLENGING/STIMULATING WORK
- RESPONSIBILITY
- GROWTH AND DEVELOPMENT
- LEADERSHIP

WHEN IN PLACE, THESE FACTORS RESULT IN...

✓ MOTIVATION
✓ ENGAGEMENT
✓ COMMITMENT

Herzberg differentiates between what he calls hygiene factors and motivation factors. Hygiene factors are those elements of a job, or indeed your experience at work, that are necessary foundations for satisfaction. Examples of hygiene factors include pay, physical working environment, and fringe benefits perceived to be part of the job you do. The absence of hygiene factors is linked to dissatisfaction at work, but the inclusion of hygiene factors tends to result in satisfaction. But this is not the same as being motivated at work; hygiene factors do not motivate. Motivation factors are much more innate, including elements such as achievement, growth, responsibility and meaning. It's no surprise that motivation factors are those we hear when people share their best experience stories. It is these motivation factors that illicit a positive emotion and are the foundation for positive experiences and engagement. It is of course possible to be motivated at work but dissatisfied, although probably not for long!

What's interesting is that companies very often focus on the hygiene factors when it comes to designing a compelling EX. Of course we aren't saying that the hygiene factors don't matter – get these experiences wrong at your peril. Having a positive experience when it comes to the hygiene factors should be a given. Companies of course should ensure employees get paid the right amount and on time, work in a physical environment that is right for their job and much more. We'd argue, though, that these experiences, although critical, are less likely to differentiate and create competitive advantage. The opportunity for your EX to set your organization apart from your competitors lies in first uncovering motivation factors that matter to your people, and then designing experiences that facilitate them. And using the best EX activity from Chapter 1 is a great way to do this.

What really makes a brilliant EX – introducing the best EX model

Over the past decade, People Lab have gained insight into the workings and experiences of many hundreds of employees across diverse, global organizations. They have collated data from hundreds of 'Best Experience' workshops to provide data to develop evidence-based practices to help design great experiences. These workshops enabled individual perspectives on what truly matters at work to be unearthed and understood. The insights gathered have highlighted and reinforced universal themes for an exceptional employee experience.

The workshops sought to gather stories of employees' most valued or engaged experiences of work, where the job has been loved and individuals felt at their best. Unique to these workshops was the strength-based, open, constructive path they took, focusing on what works and what good looks like.

Qualitative data from these workshops was then analysed to assess common themes. Categories of similar meanings were distilled from the data, and used to inform what exceptional employee experience is.

Introducing the MAGIC-CA model of EX

The model (Figure 3.2) involves the 'universal themes' of a positive EX, which are common across the hundreds of best EX stories collected and analysed by People Lab. When employees have a best experience it gives them:

FIGURE 3.2 MAGIC-CA model

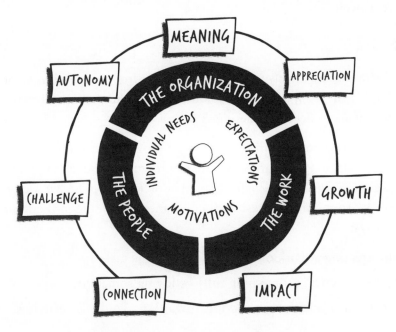

Meaning

Appreciation

Growth

Impact

Connection

Challenge

Autonomy

However, at the same time the model also emphasizes the need to understand individual differences, and deliberately places the requirement for empathy at its centre. While the universal themes will take you so far, it is critical to take time to understand what a 'best EX' means to your people. This approach supports the 'empathy principle' and overcomes issues with using an 'off the shelf' model of EX. It helps avoid making assumptions about what good looks like for your people. With this approach you get the best of both worlds to truly understand what a best EX means to your people.

The universal themes proposed by the MAGIC-CA model of EX are all backed up by the science and discussed further throughout the rest of this chapter and book. We'll take a quick look at the themes here as well:

MEANING

> We're not sure exactly where meaning comes from, if it is inherent, or if it is 'real' at all; what we do know is that humans flourish when they have it and suffer when they don't (Irvine, 2013).

Meaning is certainly present when employees share their best EX stories. Meaning is subjective to our own individual experience; however, Viktor Frankl, in his seminal book *Man's Search for Meaning* (1962), proposed that we can discover meaning in life in the following ways:

- by creating a work or accomplishing some task;
- by experiencing something fully or loving somebody;
- by the attitude that one adopts toward unavoidable suffering.

We're hard-wired to search for meaning in our lives. Finding meaning in life seems to provide a biological advantage. Research from Dr Patricia Boyle and colleagues in 2012 studied over 900 older people who were at risk for dementia. In short, those who had a sense of meaning in life, outside of themselves, were only half as likely to develop Alzheimer's. Having meaning in our lives positively impacts the biological strength and resilience of our brain cells to injury and degradation. It also lowers our risk of a stroke and cardiovascular disease. It therefore seems reasonable that our best experiences will feature an element of meaning.

APPRECIATION

Experiences where we have some level of appreciation and gratitude from others also featured as a key element of a best EX. When we experience appreciation, this results in a release of positive emotions and all the benefits that this brings. Being appreciated results in positive feelings, great memories, higher self-esteem, feeling more relaxed and more optimistic.

What is interesting, though, is that the person showing us appreciation, or sometimes called gratitude within psychological studies, also gets a boost. Showing others gratitude is linked to a range of positive outcomes, including increased wellbeing, better sleep habits, increased metabolism, and lower stress. Appreciation is good for everyone.

GROWTH

As humans we have an innate need for personal growth, and this was a key feature of best EX stories; they nearly always involved some element of growth. This may involve a more traditional idea of intentional learning and development at work. Or something less tangible, such as a feeling that we have grown as a person as a result of an experience. Growth is linked to challenge; we often find ourselves experiencing personal growth when we have a challenge to overcome. In addition, growth is also somewhat predicated via our mindset, highlighting the role of employee mindset in EX.

The concept of a growth mindset was initially developed by Carol Dweck and popularized in her book *Mindset: The new psychology of success* (2006). In summary, a mindset is a perception, or theory, that people have about themselves. For example, you might tell yourself you are bad at maths, or good at art, you are not creative or you are a great writer, a bad parent or a great teacher. Dweck's work focused on two different types of mindset: fixed or growth. As the name suggests, those with a fixed mindset believe their qualities and traits are fixed and can't be improved or developed with effort. However, those with a growth mindset believe the opposite to be true – that basic abilities can be developed through dedication and hard work. People with a growth mindset tend to learn more, learn it more quickly, and view challenges and failures as opportunities to improve.

Having a fixed mindset is often a result of the praise and feedback we have received throughout our lives, but the good news is that we can change our mindset. Developing a growth mindset would seem to be a good foundation for great experiences.

IMPACT

Having a positive impact is also a key feature of our best experiences. The majority of best experience stories involve the idea of 'making a difference' somehow. This of course links to the concept of meaning, but it is different: it is more visible and external to the individual. It is possible to find meaning from an experience without it having a positive impact.

When we have a positive impact and make a difference, it stimulates a rush of positive emotions, we feel good about that experience. When we experience positive emotions, our serotonin and dopamine levels rise. These are neurotransmitters (chemicals released by nerve cells to send signals to other nerve cells). These chemicals make us feel good and enhance our ability to learn and absorb information. Having an impact also teaches our brains that our actions matter.

CONNECTION

Experiences involving positive social connections feature strongly in best EX stories. This could be with an employee's manager, leaders, team-mates, colleagues or people from outside the organization. The nature of these connections is personal to individuals and their own context and stories. For example, some people might talk about being supported by a colleague; for others it might be a social connection resulting in a fun experience; sometimes people talk about feeling appreciated and valued by those they are working with. As social creatures, feeling connected is rudimentary to our wellbeing.

The biological foundations of this are tied to oxytocin (Zak, 2017) and its impact on serotonin. When oxytocin is released through any type of social connectivity, it triggers the release of serotonin. Serotonin then activates the 'reward circuitry' in our brain, resulting in a happy feeling. It's no surprise that our best experiences feature connection.

AUTONOMY

Direction and control of our own lives is important and a key feature of intrinsic motivation. In work, autonomy brings with it flexibility, another often cited element of best experiences. Autonomy also promotes a feeling of respect – respect for individual abilities within the organization that would otherwise be missed.

Autonomy sets employees free from limiting micromanagement and demands good communication within the organization. This instils freedom for employees and communicates a level of trust, both of which are associated with great experiences.

CHALLENGE

Overcoming a challenge elicits positive emotions, but developing purposefully hard experiences is not the answer. Challenges require problem-solving, bring novelty, and demand personal growth. Challenges provide us with intrinsic motivation, via 'our spontaneous tendency seek out novelty and challenges, extend capacity, to learn and explore' (Deci *et al*, 2001). Building experiences with an element of challenge into workplace practice engages the essence of employee wellbeing in organizational culture. An EX with the right amount of stretch provides opportunity for personal development, and freedom to tackle challenges creatively features in creating best experiences.

Understanding the psychology of our best experiences is a great foundation for designing EX. When we take this model and add it to the insight we gather from employees in our organizations, we have the foundations to create genuinely brilliant experiences that will create a competitive advantage. Ultimately, you need to seek to understand the human in your employee.

A positive experience is not all about positive emotions

We've established that a compelling experience elicits positive emotions, but that doesn't mean the experience is necessarily without challenge or pain. Thinking back to our best experience stories, we never hear anyone say an experience was their best because it was easy and required no effort. Most often our best experiences involve overcoming challenges, solving a problem, some kind of personal growth or similar. What we never hear is, 'It was a brilliant experience because it was really easy.' There are a few ways we can look at both understanding this finding and applying the learning to the way we design EX.

The idea of 'pain is good' within customer experience has been around for a while. Have you ever heard about the IKEA effect? It's a cognitive bias that occurs when consumers place a disproportionately high value on products they have partially created. Researchers from Harvard, Yale and Duke University (Norton *et al*, 2012) discovered that self-assembly impacts the evaluation of a product by its consumers. Their findings suggest that when people use their own efforts to make something, they value it more than if they didn't put any effort into its creation, even if it is done poorly. While there are probably few people who would describe assembling flat-pack furniture as a positive experience, the outcome of such an experience can elicit positive emotions. It's not just about the experience itself, but how it ultimately makes you feel and the lasting impact on you.

Just think about those people who describe running a marathon as a compelling experience. Once again let's use the lens of the 'best experiences' stories to understand this phenomenon. First, involvement and autonomy often feature in these stories. Our research has shown that involvement and autonomy are significant elements of a great EX. If an EX facilitates autonomy and features employee involvement, employees are more likely to value it. Second, as we've already mentioned, best experience stories very often involve an element of challenge, problem-solving or difficulty. We're not advocating you design painful experiences necessarily, but these ideas are useful to keep in mind as you develop EX. It is easy to fall into the trap of assuming that good, or positive, equals easy, and this is not often the case. What is interesting is that, broadly speaking, experiences that relate to hygiene factors tend to be more positive if they are easy and straightforward. Whereas those experiences that link to motivator factors are more likely to require an element of challenge or mastery. And of course it's likely that, as practitioners, we are involved in the design of experiences that cover both hygiene and motivator factors. Let's take the example of onboarding. Having the right kit and access on day one of employment is hygiene. These experiences should be simple, straightforward and easy. But those elements of onboarding that relate to motivator factors, such as being given some autonomy, involvement in work, and more, should have some challenge. No one wants to sit there bored and twiddling their thumbs for the first few weeks of a new job.

The science of motivation

A quick history lesson on management practice can be useful to understand why so many EX practices fall short, no matter how well intentioned. In the early 1900s Taylor (1911) argued that work involved mostly simple, uninteresting tasks. He wrote that incentivizing employees, together with careful monitoring, was the most effective way to get people to fulfil their roles. This approach is still prevalent in many organizations today: reward the behaviours you want to see and punish those you don't. A whole billion-dollar industry of rewards and benefits is the result of this approach, and there are numerous EX products, services and approaches that are based on the 'carrot and stick' approach. It seems intuitive that an EX based on rewards is a good thing, but in fact this approach is flawed and out of date. We now know that using the reward–punishment approach doesn't often produce the outcomes we would expect. And we would argue that the reward–punishment approach doesn't make for a compelling EX. Research from Dan Pink (2009) shows that with the onset of more complex and creative jobs, traditional rewards can actually lead to less of what is wanted and more of what is not wanted. Pink's research gives evidence to demonstrate that the reward–punishment approach can result in:

- lower intrinsic motivation;
- lower performance;
- less creativity;
- unethical behaviour;
- short-term thinking.

The explanation for this phenomenon is that 'rewards, by their very nature, narrow our focus'. We need to move beyond a model of reward–punishment to consider the role of intrinsic motivation. Intrinsic motivation can be defined as being motivated to do something because it is driven by internal rewards, that is, it is naturally satisfying to you. On the flipside is extrinsic motivation, which is all about external rewards. For example, at work you might decide to mentor a more junior colleague because it feels like the right thing to do: you want to help them out and you find it rewarding. This is an example of intrinsic motivation. A colleague might also mentor a more junior colleague, but they are doing it to earn recognition from their manager and to be seen by others as doing the right thing. This is extrinsic motivation.

Harry F. Harlow (1950) first talked about the concept of intrinsic motivation in the 1940s. He originally developed this theory while studying primates solving puzzles. What he found was that primates appeared to enjoy solving the puzzles, even in the absence or expectation of a reward. This idea of intrinsic motivation was built on the work of Deci and Ryan in the 1960s and 1970s (Deci *et al*, 2001). They replicated Harlow's studies with humans and developed their theory of self-determination (SDT). SDT proposes that we have an innate drive to be autonomous, competent and connected to each other. When these conditions are present, research demonstrates links to a whole range of positive outcomes, including higher levels of positive emotion, wellbeing and employee engagement. Deci *et al* (2001) concluded that human beings have an 'inherent tendency to seek out novelty and challenges, to extend and exercise their capabilities, to explore, and to learn'.

We have already established that great experiences often involve intrinsic motivation; therefore understanding more about the science of motivation is helpful for those of us designing EX. In his book *Drive*, Dan Pink (2001) builds on SDT, arguing that motivating employees involves three essential elements:

1 *autonomy* – the desire to direct our own lives;

2 *mastery* – the urge to get better and better at something that matters;

3 *purpose* – the yearning to do what we do in the service of something larger than ourselves.

It is not a coincidence that best experience stories we have gathered nearly always feature these three themes, as well as the concept of connectedness from SDT. When designing experiences we should focus on our innate need to be self-directed (autonomy), to learn, grow, be challenged and create new things (mastery), to do better by ourselves and our world (purpose) and to be connected to others.

Applying the science of motivation

The insights gathered from your best EX conversations will uncover those intrinsic motivator factors that matter to your people. While it's important not to make assumptions about what a great EX looks like for your people, it is highly likely that at least some of the intrinsic motivator factors outlined in this chapter will come up. But how can you use this insight within your EX design? The ideas below are a useful starting point and will hopefully spark some ideas for ways in which you can build motivator factors into different parts of the EX.

Autonomy

This involves experiences that provide employees with autonomy over some (or all) key elements of their work. There is an opportunity to consider how to build autonomy into the design of the EX of the work they do:

- When they do it (time) – examples include:
  - focusing the roles on outputs rather than time;
  - flexibility over when employees complete tasks;
  - flexibility over working patterns and hours.
- How they do it (technique) – examples include:
  - freedom to figure out the best way to do their jobs;
  - involvement in defining how they do their jobs.
- Who they do it with (team) – examples include:
  - facilitate opportunities for collaboration;
  - opportunities to join cross-company projects.
- What they do (task) – examples include:
  - using design thinking tools to enable creativity over the role they do;
  - hackathons and open-source projects to enable people to work on different projects.

Mastery

Mastery involves experiences that enable employees to grow and develop:

- Provide 'Goldilocks tasks' – Pink (2001) talks about 'Goldilocks tasks' to describe those tasks that are neither too difficult nor too easy. The right amount of stretch results in a good experience for people. If tasks are too easy, people become bored, but if they are too difficult, this can result in stress.

- Focus on creating a culture that encourages risk-taking and doesn't punish failure – central to design thinking is the notion of failing fast and learning from experimentation. The design thinking tools set out in later chapters will help to facilitate this, by giving permission to get things wrong and learn from the experience.

Purpose

Purpose involves experiences that provide a sense of purpose. This might be purpose linked to your brand or it could be purpose linked to an individual's own values:

- Communicate your brand purpose – ensure your people understand the organization's purpose goals, not just its profit goals. Understanding the purpose and vision of your organization and how employees contribute to this purpose is often a key theme of best experience stories.

- Place equal emphasis on purpose maximization as you do on profit maximization – research shows that the attainment of profit goals has no impact on a person's wellbeing. Organizational and individual goals should focus on purpose as well as profit. Many successful companies are now using profit as the catalyst to pursuing purpose, rather than the objective.

- Take time to understand individuals' own values – at a team level this is possible and experiences can be designed to support this – for example, redesigning an employee volunteering programme that is meaningful to your people.

The role of positive emotions in EX

A compelling EX will involve positive emotions, even if the EX itself is challenging or difficult. Think back to the 'running a marathon' example – definitely challenging, probably painful at times, but often cited as a best experience. Within the work context we often hear stories of difficult projects, highs and lows, moments of self-doubt, working with challenging people, but the overall EX is described as positive for many reasons: autonomy, mastery and purpose are just three. It is helpful to understand the psychology of positive emotions and how we can apply this thinking to EX design.

Barbara Frederickson (2000) developed her broaden-and-build theory, which helps to explain the mechanisms of positive emotions. First let's start by looking at the consequences of negative emotions. In summary, when we have an experience that elicits negative emotions, it narrows our focus. We go into 'fight–flight' mode and our resources are focused on this response. From an evolutionary perspective this was a helpful, adaptive response; we want to overcome threats to our survival. The problem is that this response doesn't differentiate between, for example, the threat of a bear attack versus working for a bad boss that results in negative emotions. Clearly a poor EX is not helpful in the workplace; it stimulates negative emotions that are unhelpful for a host of reasons, not least stimulating our flight–fight response and narrowing our focus. So what is the role of positive emotions and how are they helpful at work?

Fredrickson (2000) argued that positive emotions have the opposite effect to negative emotions. Rather than narrowing our focus, they have a 'broadening effect'. This enables us to look for creative, flexible and unpredictable new ways of thinking and acting. This then contributes to building lasting physical, intellectual, psychological and social resources. This theory contributes to our understanding of the positive outcomes we observe when a compelling EX is present. For example, if we prime people to feel either amusement or contentment, they can think of a larger and wider array of thoughts and ideas than individuals who have been primed to feel either anxiety or anger.

There are a vast array of studies that make the case for facilitating positive emotions at work. For example, they have been linked to greater job satisfaction and improved mental health (Schutte and Loi, 2014). They have also been linked to a reduction in turnover intentions and stress levels (Siu *et al*, 2014). In summary, if we design an EX that facilitates positive emotion, we're more likely to see higher productivity, more innovation, increases in employee wellbeing and resilience and higher levels of engagement.

There are a number of ways the broaden-and-build theory can be used in EX design. First of all, it's important to be mindful of creating a culture of psychological safety. Creating a place where employees aren't fearful of failure provides opportunities to work on new and challenging projects, which Frederickson argues promotes the positive emotion of 'interest'. In addition, she talks about 'positive leadership' as an enabler of positive emotion at work. While there are a number of different definitions of positive leadership, essentially it involves role-modelling and being intentional about enhancing positive emotions.

Not all experiences are created equal

We receive 11 million bits of information every second and we can only consciously process 40 bits – which means 99.9999996 per cent is unconscious. Our brains have evolved to help us make sense of the world and process information quickly via the development of some 150-plus cognitive biases. Our cognitive biases have evolved for a reason: they help us navigate our world more quickly and ultimately have helped us to survive. However, they can trip us up and lead us to the wrong conclusions. Understanding a little more about how these biases work can enable us to design more compelling experiences for our people in a number of ways. First, a basic understanding of the science of cognitive biases helps those involved in EX to be more aware of them, and therefore more likely to avoid them. And second, we can use the science of biases to design more compelling experiences for our people.

Daniel Kahneman, in his seminal book *Thinking, Fast and Slow* (2011), explains the role of these cognitive biases in a really simple way. He differentiates between system 1 and system 2 thinking. System 1 thinking is fast and impulsive; it happens automatically, with little or no effort, often at an unconscious level. It's at this level that our cognitive biases come into play. This type of thinking is useful and has helped us survive. These biases are essentially short-cuts to enable us to quickly make sense of our world. System 2 is slow(er) and is intentional and deliberate; we're conscious of our thinking at this level. We need both types of thinking, but system 1 thinking has the potential to catch us out and lead us to the wrong answer.

Our EX design framework in itself will help you to overcome some of the cognitive biases that have the potential to trip us up. For exam-ple, our confirmation bias means we tend to seek out data to back up our prior beliefs and assumptions. Using the principles of design thinking, which we detail in later chapters, can help to avoid this bias. Our emphasis on empathy within our framework also helps to overcome our stereotyping bias. In addition, we can use our knowl-edge of cognitive biases in EX design to our advantage. The halo effect is the idea that our overall impression of someone, or some-thing, will directly impact how we perceive almost everything they do. So if we have a great experience with an organization or indeed another person, we're more likely to perceive everything they do more positively.

The peak–end rule is another cognitive bias that is useful to consider in EX design. This bias relates to the way in we which remember and evaluate an experience after the event. What sticks in our mind are any intense moments, both positives and negatives (the 'peaks'), as well as the last moments of an experience (the 'end'). This helps to explain why sometimes experiences involving pain can be looked back upon fondly – again, we can think about marathon runners as an example of this. Within the workplace the peak–end rule could apply to our overall experience of working at an organization, as well as other, specific experiences along the way. And this is why the experience our people have when leaving an organization, or a team, is so critical. Our leaving experience is heavily weighted to stay with us and inform our lasting impression – and is often overlooked.

Taking control of our EX

Experiences don't just happen to us. Our mindset plays a critical role in how an experience impacts us. To date EX, as a practice, has felt very 'done to' employees. But we believe that an individual's mindset, and personal responsibility, has a role to play that is under-represented in EX design. We're not in any way abdicating the role of the organization here; it's a given that companies should focus on designing experiences that help people to thrive. But, if all else is equal, and the company does all the right things, employees' mindset will play a critical role in how they experience work.

Let's consider for a moment the nature of experiences. It is fair to say that many experiences are subjective. For example, pain is a subjective experience. Take the example of being stung by a wasp – the way we all experience this pain is subjective. No one else can measure or feel our pain in this respect. A subjective experience involves both emotional and cognitive components. An objective experience, however, is the actual event itself, eg the wasp sting. Let's consider a work-based example. For your onboarding experience you bring together a group of new starters for a day-long, face-to-face event. The introverts in the group may be apprehensive about the event, given it involves meeting lots of new people. At the end of the event there may be some introverts who, on balance, report that it was a positive experience. Despite the fact they might have found some parts of the day uncomfortable, they appreciated the chance to meet new colleagues, they learned more about the organization, they had some fun, and they were grateful to the company for running the event. Alternatively other introverts might report that the experience was negative for them, focusing more on how they felt having to meet new people and being out of their comfort zone. The objective experience was the event itself, but different people will have different subjective experiences dependent on their individual mindset. In summary, our subjective experience is unique to us, given it is produced in our mind. This is why our personal mindset, and psychology, has a critical role to play in the overall EX.

What is fascinating is that our mindset doesn't only influence how we feel about and interpret an experience, but it can actually change the outcomes of an experience as well. A study from Kirsch and Lynn (1999) illustrates this. It involved a group of blindfolded students who were told their arm was being rubbed with poison ivy. All of the students' arms reacted with symptoms of poison ivy; however, the plant used wasn't poison ivy at all, but a completely harmless plant. Then, on the students' other arm, the researchers rubbed real poison ivy, but told them it was a harmless plant. Even though all of the students were allergic, only a few of them came out in a rash. While this study is no longer considered ethical, it does demonstrate that the expectation of a positive outcome, or indeed a positive experience, makes it more likely to arise. This is referred to as 'predictive encoding'. If we prime ourselves to expect a positive outcome, what we are doing is encoding our brain to recognize the outcome when it does in fact arise. This adds weight to the argument that our company reputation and our attraction and recruitment experiences are so critical. Great experiences at this stage raise the likelihood of employee expectations of a positive EX when they join us.

But just how do you define the right mindset to support a better experience? While we can't answer exactly this question (yet), a recent study by Leadership IQ (Murphy, 2020) has revealed those traits required for 'self-engagement', which we believe will contribute to the right mindset for an enhanced EX. In their study of over 11,000 employees, they gathered insight on what they termed 'self-engagement', ie their optimism, resilience, proactivity, assertiveness and ambition. Their model of self-engagement involves what they call 18 outlooks, and in summary reflects the extent to which employees have personal control. The questions were designed to understand the role that employees themselves play and included items such as:

- I expect that more good things will happen to me than bad things.
- The tough times I've had in my career have helped me to grow and improve.
- I find something interesting in every task/project I do.

It's no surprise that their findings demonstrated that our mindset at work plays a significant role in the way we experience work and subsequent levels of engagement. What was interesting, though, was that the research found that often self-engagement is more critical than other engagement enablers, such as the role of the line manager.

The research found the following elements all played a significant role in explaining engagement at work:

1 Optimism – the study found that having an optimistic outlook explains 30 per cent of an employee's inspiration at work. This finding makes sense when viewed through the lens of positive psychology. We know that an optimistic mindset can protect against a downward spiral, as well as reduce levels of anxiety.

2 Having an internal locus of control – this is when an employee believes that they control their successes and failures, and it is not down to luck but hard work. The study found an internal locus of control explained 26 per cent of an employee's inspiration at work. Again, this result is not actually that surprising: studies have demonstrated time and again that people with a high internal locus of control experience more career success, better health, less anxiety and lower stress.

3 Resilience – being resilient, eg coping well when things get tough, explained 25 per cent of an employee's inspiration at work. We know that resilience is a key skill for overall wellbeing, so it makes sense that it would play a role here. Being resilient means being able to bounce back from setbacks and cope when things don't go the way you had hoped.

4 Assertiveness – high assertiveness was found to explain 23 per cent of a worker's engagement. Being high in assertiveness means being able to communicate effectively and clearly express needs, views and boundaries. Research has found that assertiveness is often correlated with higher levels of self-esteem, and healthy assertiveness skills can even reduce conflicts and aggressiveness in the workplace.

5 Meaning in your job – finding something interesting in the work you do explains 24 per cent of an employee's inspiration at work. People who find meaning in their work are more inspired and more likely to stay with their employer, more likely to give their best effort at work, and more likely to recommend their employer to others.

The elements outlined here can all be developed and taught; they are not fixed. We believe that developing this type of mindset will positively influence the experience you have at work. In summary, we can support employees to develop the right mindset and own self-engagement, which will positively impact the experience they have.

The everyday EX and where to begin

In Chapter 1 we talked about the everyday employee experience, sometimes referred to as micro-experiences. Once again, the insight gathered from best EX conversations helps us to understand this. What this insight tells us is that our people often see the EX quite differently from the way the organization and practitioners see it. Best EX stories will rarely, if ever, mention specific employee lifecycle components, or specific employee journeys, nor will they mention perks and benefits. Best EX stories are very personal and the range of experiences they involve are broad. For example, a story involving delivering a big project could involve relationships with leaders and colleagues, personal growth, appreciation of the company for taking a chance on them, brilliant communication, access to decision-makers and resources to get the job done. We need to consider the everyday EX in our EX design, given it is the sum of these micro-experiences that contribute to the overall EX. Research from O.C. Tanner (2020) indicates that 92 per cent of employees describe their employee experience as their 'everyday' experience. And in the same research just 42 per cent of employees rate their employee experience as positive or extremely positive. But just where do you begin to design the everyday EX?

In their book *The Power of Moments* (2017), Chip and Dan Heath share insights on why certain experiences stay with us, and we can use this insight to help us create an everyday EX that makes a positive difference to how our people feel. We already know about the 'peak–end' rule, that is, when reflecting on how an experience made us feel, we evaluate based on the best or worst moment, the peak and the ending. So we need to understand how we can create peak moments, or more peak moments, at work, rather than trying to ensure every moment of every day is peak. In their book they explain that we need to 'fill the pits and build the peaks' – that is, sort out those experiences that aren't good and focus on building more peaks to design a compelling everyday EX. In their book, Chip and Dan recommend the following five steps to design peak experiences:

1 Look for small peaks.
2 Celebrate and honour relationships.
3 Find and acknowledge strengths.
4 Identify new possibilities.
5 Look for spiritual insight.

And we have the ideal approach to help you to do just this: appreciative inquiry (AI). AI was originally developed by Dr David Cooperrider, Dr Suresh Srivasta, and Dr Frank Barrett at Case Western Reserve University (Cooperrider and Whitney, 2009). In summary, AI is a simple, strength-based tool that enables you to learn from, and use insights about, what works. For our purposes, it helps uncover and learn from peak moments. The approach provides a simple framework to follow that enables groups, teams and the organization to have different conversations about their experiences at work. The methodology is based around what is known as the 5-D cycle (see Figure 3.3).

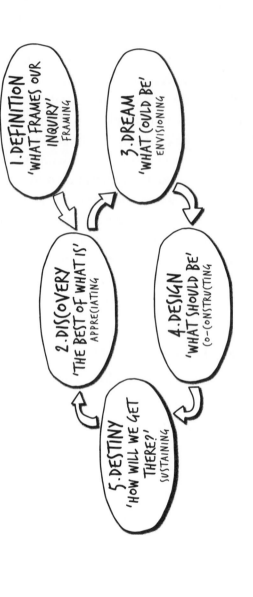

FIGURE 3.3 Taking a strength-based approach to EX using AI

The 5-D cycle offers a simple process to follow when planning any AI intervention. The inquiry takes place by following the cycle through its entirety in the following way:

1. Definition

This stage sets up the topic for the AI intervention, essentially framing the inquiry. There are a number of ways in which this can be done. You could use AI to address 'the pits', that is, those experiences you know aren't working. The trick is to ensure you reframe this definition in a positive light. For example, rather than saying we want to address the problematic onboarding EX, you'd reframe this to say we want to create a brilliant onboarding EX. We can also use AI to help design and deliver more peak moments and experiences as part of the everyday EX. For example, you may define the topic as creating a great place to work.

Once the topic for AI is defined, we then move on to the process itself. Essentially participants are taken around the cycle, and given the opportunity to talk in depth about the topic using a different lens. Questions are often drafted before the session to prompt stories and discussion at each stage, but flexibility is helpful. What is great about this process is that it can be run in small groups, with teams, or in large-scale summits with hundreds or even thousands of employees.

2. Discovery

Once the topic for the inquiry has been established, the process begins with the discovery phase. This part of the process is all about reflecting on 'best of' or positive experiences, by collecting stories from participants. This is where we use the best EX activity or similar, to uncover examples of peak experiences from our people.

3. Dream

Once we have spent time thinking about current or previous experiences within the theme of the AI intervention, we then move on to the dream phase. These conversations focus on what could be, and ask employees to envision a future that is different from today. This phase is all about the art of possibility, really emphasizing participants to focus on what *could* be. Here participants are challenged to stretch their thinking and allow themselves to get excited about a different future and possibilities. Questions or activities are designed to inspire participants to create a clear and tangible view of where they want to be, asking them to describe this future in detail.

The dream phase builds on the learning and discussion from the discovery phase, encouraging participants to create something new. So, for example, if the theme for the AI intervention is to create a great place to work, the dream phase would encourage participants to imagine anything is possible and create a future vision of a great place to work for their organization: asking questions such as, 'What will it look like? What will it feel like? How will it be?'

Using creativity and expressive forms in the dream phase works really well and takes people out of their usual patterns of thinking. For example, in the past we have asked groups to create a mood board, or visual, for a future great place to work. In the dream phase you can use a 'future vision' activity like the one we shared in Chapter 2.

4. Design

Next comes the design phase, which moves thinking on from what *could* be to what *should* be. This stage of the process enables the participants to build on their learning and conversations from the previous stages to begin planning and prioritizing what would work well. Questions are asked about what needs to change in order to bring to life their thoughts, ideas and vision from the previous stages. Changes are identified and the seeds of plans and projects are put into place.

In our experience, by following the cycle of AI, by the time you reach this stage participants are far more open about what is possible, and what is within their own gift to change, than they might be if the more usual deficit approach is followed. The mind the gap activity is an example of a conversation you can have to help you design the EX you wish to see.

EXERCISE
Mind the gap

Once the peak moments are uncovered via a best EX conversation and the desired future is identified via a future vision conversation, a gap analysis can be done to determine what action is needed. This activity helps you to identify the gaps that need to be filled.

This session will help you conduct a gap analysis for your EX as defined via the definition stage of AI.

Filling the gap

Remind the group about themes emerging from the previous sessions:

- where we are today – from best EX activity;
- where we want to be – from future vision activity.

Divide the group into smaller workgroups and ask them to discuss and document:

1 how near we are to where we would like to be;
2 how far away we are from where we would like to be, listing all of those areas we need to develop in.

Then look at what the gap is. Talk about what the gap tells us and therefore what our thoughts are on areas for possible actions.

Time to talk

Undertaking a gap analysis is a great exercise to begin to analyse and understand what we do, how we do it, and what we can do to make things better. Discuss and identify the gaps as a group.

What to do

Capture any actions in a simple 'stop, start, continue' template.

---

5. *Destiny*

The final stage of the AI cycle is destiny. This stage really focuses on what needs to happen in order to deliver or act upon the design discussed in the previous stages. This stage looks at how employees can be accountable for their own EX and what they are going to personally take forward, be responsible for, or even experiment with. This stage really emphasizes the potential and value of small changes participants can make today in order to move the organization closer to where they want to be. You can use the team reflection activity to help you to do this.

EXERCISE
Team reflection

It's helpful to make time to think about actions and behaviours that can positively impact upon EX – in particular, what individuals and teams can do differently to improve their everyday EX.

This session will give your team the space to reflect on previous discussions and consider how they can impact everyday EX.

Activity

Ask the group to consider the outputs and actions from all of the previous sessions you have run. Ask them to discuss and consider the following questions:

- How does our future vision make you feel?
- Identify the three commitments you can make to achieving the changes we want to bring about.
- List the top three things that need to change and ideas for how you would change them.
- List any actions you need to take.

Talk about it

Ask the group to feed back and capture the outputs in a central place. Ask for feedback and discussion from the rest of the team as each group feeds back.

Write it down

Capture any actions in a stop, start, continue template and agree next steps.

AI as a tool for EX design

AI is a powerful tool to use within EX design. And although it is not taken from the world of design thinking, there are many common principles in the framework and approach – for example, ensuring the definition statement is solution-focused and positive. The discovery phase helps to facilitate empathy and insight-gathering, and the dream phase is all about divergent thinking. Its power is in the fact that it encourages participants to talk about, and share, real-life experiences and stories: looking at what has already worked in the past or is working today. These real-life stories and experiences are a great foundation to then imagine future possibilities, which then don't seem so far-fetched or overwhelming.

From a psychological perspective, given AI is strength-based, the process itself generates positive emotions and experiences: it is a positive experience in itself, which people usually enjoy. The process also sets out a clear purpose at the outset and facilitates autonomy amongst participants: they contribute their own stories and ideas and develop their own solutions.

Finally, having a group work together to imagine future possibilities is an excellent way of both involving employees and giving them a voice. In summary, the AI process incorporates the principles advocated by Chip and Dan Heath to help uncover and design experiences that will stay with us, including the everyday EX:

1 Look for small peaks – use best EX activity to do this.

2 Celebrate and honour relationships – the AI process in its entirety will support this by focusing on what we have in common, rather than looking at differences, and by sense-making with colleagues.

3 Find and acknowledge strengths – the AI approach is a strength-based approach.

4 Identify new possibilities – use future vision activity to do this.

5 Look for spiritual insight – use best EX and future vision activities to do this.

Takeaways

In this chapter we have outlined the key psychological models and approaches that can help us to understand what makes a great EX and outlined how we can use this knowledge to design great experiences. In summary:

- Positive experiences release a cocktail of neurotransmitters to give us a psychological advantage.
- We need to differentiate between hygiene and motivator factors when designing experiences and ensure we focus on what really matters to our people.
- A great EX is not all about positive emotions.
- While EX is subjective and personal, there are some universal themes of a great EX.
- EX design can help overcome cognitive biases.
- The peak–end rule can help us focus on what really matters when designing EX.
- Our individual mindset plays a critical role in how we experience our world.
- We can use AI to help understand and design better everyday experiences.

References

Achor, S (2011) *The Happiness Advantage: The seven principles of positive psychology that fuel success and performance at work*, Random House Group Publishing, London

Boyle, PA, Buchman, AS, Wilson, RS, Yu, L, Schneider, JA and Bennett, DA (2012) Effect of purpose in life on the relation between Alzheimer disease pathologic changes on cognitive function in advanced age, *Archives of General Psychiatry*, **69** (5), pp 499–504. doi:10.1001/archgenpsychiatry.2011.1487

Cooperrider, DL and Whitney, D (2009) *Appreciative Inquiry: A positive revolution in change*, Berrett-Koehler, San Francisco, CA

Deci, EL, Koestner, R and Ryan, RM (2001) Extrinsic rewards and intrinsic motivation in education: Reconsidered once again, *Review of Educational Research*, **71** (1), p 14

Dweck, CS (2006) *Mindset: The new psychology of success*, Random House, London

Frankl, VE (1962) *Man's Search for Meaning: An introduction to logotherapy*, Beacon Press, Boston

Fredrickson, BL (2000) Why positive emotions matter in organizations: Lessons from the broaden-and-build model, *The Psychologist-Manager Journal*, **4** (2), pp 131–42

Gartner (2019) [accessed 10 August 2020] The modern employee experience: Increasing returns on employee experience investment [Online] https://www. gartner.com/en/human-resources/insights/employee-experience (archived at https://perma.cc/JGT7-UCTT)

Harlow, HF (1950) Learning and satiation of response in intrinsically motivated complex puzzle performance by monkeys, *Journal of Comparative and Physiological Psychology*, **43** (4), pp 289–94

Heath, C and Heath, D (2017) *The Power of Moments: Why certain experiences have extraordinary impact*, Bantam Books, New York

Herzberg, F, Mausner, B and Bloch-Snyderman, B (1993) *Motivation To Work*, Routledge, New York

Irvine, M (2013) [accessed 10 August 2020] Approaches to po-mo, *Georgetown University Communication, Culture, & Technology Program* [Online] http://faculty.georgetown.edu/irvinem/theory/pomo.html (archived at https:// perma.cc/NQ4L-3Q8Y)

Kahneman, D (2011) *Thinking, Fast and Slow*, Penguin, London

Kirsch, I and Lynn, SJ (1999) Automaticity in clinical psychology, *American Psychologist*, **54** (7), pp 504–15

Murphy, M (2020) [accessed 10 August 2020] These 18 outlooks explain why some employees are happy at work (and others are miserable) [blog] [Online] https://www.leadershipiq.com/blogs/leadershipiq/these-18-outlooks-explain-why-some-employees-are-happy-at-work-and-others-are-miserable (archived at https://perma.cc/XQA7-3XN4)

Norton, MI, Mochon, D and Ariely, D (2012) The IKEA effect: when labor leads to love, *Journal of Consumer Psychology*, **22** (3), pp 453–60

O.C. Tanner (2020) [accessed 10 August 2020] Global culture report [Online] https://www.octanner.com/uk/global-culture-report.html (archived at https://perma.cc/S4J2-8SBU)

Pink, D (2009) *Drive: The surprising truth about what motivates us*, Canongate, Edinburgh

Schutte, NS and Loi, NM (2014) Connections between emotional intelligence and workplace flourishing, *Personality and Individual Differences*, **66**, pp 134–39

Seligman, MEP and Maier, SF (1967) Failure to escape traumatic shock, *Journal of Experimental Psychology*, **74**, pp 1–9

Siu, O, Cheung, F and Lui, S (2014) Linking positive emotions to work well-being and turnover intention among Hong Kong police officers: The role of psychological capital, *Journal of Happiness Studies*, **16**. https://doi.org/10.1007/s10902-014-9513-8 (archived at https://perma.cc/7ZEC-7SZD)

Taylor, FW (1911) *The Principles of Scientific Management*, Harper & Brothers, New York and London

Zak, PJ (2017) The neuroscience of trust, *Harvard Business Review*, January–February. https://www.emcleaders.com/wp-content/uploads/2017/03/hbr-neuroscience-of-trust.pdf (archived at https://perma.cc/HW7A-WUSN)

04

Culture, leadership and EX

In this chapter we'll cover:

- the significant relationship between culture and employee experience;
- the different definitions of culture and what they tell us;
- how culture impacts at a big picture and micro level and what to do about it;
- why values matter (even when they're more aspirational than lived) and how to make them more meaningful;
- the impact of culture on design and design on culture;
- the role of leaders in creating a compelling EX;
- setting leaders up for success;
- evaluating managers' competencies.

The relationship between culture and employee experience

Culture is one of, if not the, most significant influences on employee experience. EX only happens within the context of your organizational culture. Or, to put it another way: 'Culture is the soup within which employee experience swims' (Wright-Wasson, 2019). While a great culture does not guarantee a great EX, it makes it a lot more likely. According to O.C. Tanner research in 2020, where organizations have a thriving culture, employees rate their satisfaction with employee experience 102 per cent higher. Culture is both a draw for potential employees and a significant factor in how they experience the organization when they get there. More than three-quarters of adults across four countries (US, UK, France and Germany) say they consider a company's culture before applying for a job (Glassdoor, 2019). And 71 per cent would start looking for another job if their company's culture deteriorates.

These facts, of course, have not gone unremarked. There is now a well-established 'cultural reform' movement among management thinkers, disciplines and schools. According to Richard Buchanan (2015), Professor of Design, Management and Innovation, Weatherhead School of Management, Case Western Reserve University, the movement is concerned with reforming the culture of organizations and developing a better understanding of cultural values and the purpose of the organization. What is interesting in the context of EX design is the fact, as noted by Buchanan, that some of the most important figures of this movement – such as Peter Drucker, Tom Peters and Peter Senge – have all recognized the importance of design as an element of cultural change.

What is culture – a definition

It clearly matters, but what is culture? If we're to understand how culture impacts EX and what to do about it, we first need a clear sense of what we mean when we talk about culture. Like EX and engagement, there are multiple definitions. More than 50 distinct definitions have been identified in academic literature. Definitions often cover the stories employees tell to interpret events, organizational rituals and corporate symbols.

Siobhan McHale (2020), in her book *The Insider's Guide to Culture Change,* describes culture as: 'The patterns or agreements that determine how the business operates.' Or, more simply: 'How things work around here.'

Daniel Coyle (2018) in *The Culture Code* alludes to a more organic picture: 'Culture is a set of living relationships working toward a shared goal.'

If you were to look at all the definitions of culture, what you'd sense is that culture operates at different levels – that means you can see culture, but you can also feel it. For example, it is partly what we do and is therefore observable – we can see culture all around us, from how work gets done, to the posters on the walls, the office environment, even organization charts and process maps. These are all visible artefacts of culture. But we can also feel culture – we know if we belong, if it feels easy or tense, if the organization is hierarchical or flat, fun or political. This is the stuff we can't always see but we sense. And this often emanates from a deeper level of culture. A lot of what we experience within a culture comes from the values, beliefs and assumptions that have been learned and reinforced, sometimes over the entire history of the organization – whether that's a few years or a few centuries. They have a significant impact, even though we can't actually see them. A quick watch-out: the values on the wall may not be the deeper values, beliefs and assumptions that actually operate at that deeper level of culture. Put it another way, just because organizations say things work like this around here, doesn't mean that they actually do.

For this reason, our preferred definition of culture comes from Edgar Schein, one of the most prolific thinkers on organizational culture. He defines the culture of a group in relation to how, over time, these deep values and assumptions come into being as a way for the organization to make sense of its internal workings, while also adapting to the changing conditions of the outside world:

> The culture of a group can now be defined as a pattern of shared basic assumptions that was learned by a group as it solved its problems of external adaptation and internal integration, that has worked well enough to be considered valid and, therefore, to be taught to new members as the correct way to perceive, think, and feel in relation to those problems (Schein, 2004).

This definition feels particularly apt at the time of writing. As organizations adapt to the ongoing impact of the COVID-19 crisis, they are rapidly having to find new ways to connect and collaborate as they seek to respond to the changing external context.

How culture impacts EX

As mentioned earlier, culture impacts people's experience of an organization before they even join because it informs people's expectations of what the organization is and what it stands for – this is big picture stuff. But it also dictates every micro-experience an employee has with and within the organization, the highs and lows that make up a memory long after someone leaves. Let's look at both in turn.

Micro-experiences

Reflecting on micro-experiences and culture in its 2020 report, O.C. Tanner puts it like this:

> Workplace culture and employee micro-experiences are deeply interconnected. They work synergistically. Culture affects how employees interact, think, and work. It causes people to have specific micro-experiences, including peak and valley experiences. These experiences then, in turn, reinforce your corporate culture.

So culture frames the everyday experience, including how people relate to one another. Writing in a now famous letter to the whole Airbnb business in 2013, co-founder and CEO Brian Chesky put it like this:

> Culture is a thousand things, a thousand times. It's living the core values when you hire; when you write an email; when you are working on a project; when you are walking in the hall. We have the power, by living the values, to build the culture. We also have the power, by breaking the values, to **** up the culture (Chesky, 2014).

Big picture

Culture impacts people's expectations because companies talk about it – all the time. According to research published in the *MIT Sloan Management Review* (*MIT SMR*) (Sull *et al*, 2020), more than 80 per cent of large American corporations publish their official corporate values on their website. And when they do, they invariably talk about the importance of their culture in guiding the actions and decisions of employees throughout the organization. And it's not just websites. Over the past three decades, more than three-quarters of CEOs interviewed in *Harvard Business Review* discussed their company's culture or core values – even when not specifically asked about it.

So values are a core part of culture. That is the case even when companies fall short of those aspirations or when the actual values in play are clearly something other than what's on the wall or the website. And that gap between what organizations say they value and what actually happens is the case more often than not. According to the *MIT SMR*-published research (Sull *et al*, 2020), there is *no correlation* between the cultural values a company emphasizes in its published statements and how well the company lives those values in the eyes of employees. No correlation. Check out the link to this research for more on the detail – it's a good read.

Despite this contradiction, value statements – sometimes called espoused values, ie the ones companies say are in play – are a part of culture because they cast light on what leaders consider critical for the success of the organization. They also spell out the cultural elements leaders believe set the organization apart in the eyes of employees, customers and other stakeholders. Here's the rub: when expectations do not translate into reality, it creates a cognitive dissonance that impacts people's experience. How often have you heard a friend say of a company they joined a few months previously: 'It's not what I thought it would be like'?

What to do about it

Edgar Schein is often quoted as having said when it comes to culture, we get what we settle for. And that's true. Culture will always emerge in some form because groups of human beings don't work together in a vacuum. If they don't already exist within a group, we quickly start to create our own rituals and processes for finding and acknowledging leaders and recognizing and rewarding success. Like your ideal EX, culture should be intentional, a deliberate construction of leaders brought to life in collaboration with all those who are led. When it isn't, cultures turn toxic, according to McGowan and Shipley, authors of *The Adaptation Advantage* (2020). So a thriving culture is intentional.

A thriving culture also requires a joined-up approach. When culture and EX initiatives are siloed you start to see disparities in the employee experience. Many organizations fail to approach culture in this way and miss out on the impact of a cohesive approach. Organizations need to connect culture efforts with employee experience initiatives. So where you have a clearly articulated view of the culture of your organization, your intentional EX needs to be in harmony and vice versa.

The authors of the *MIT SMR*-published research report (Sull *et al*, 2020) suggest a first step in improving culture is for leaders to take a 'hard evidence-based look at how well the organization is living up to its espoused values'. Which elements of the culture are working well and which are falling short? Where are the pockets of cultural excellence? Which teams are undermining the culture?

Leaders also need to make sure the values mean something. The authors suggest:

- Make values actionable, distinctive and linked to results.

- Ensure leaders communicate values effectively by providing concrete guidance on desired behaviour.

- Articulate what makes your organization distinctive – when employees identify with a distinctive culture, they are more likely to incorporate core values into their everyday activities and pursue the organization's goals.

- Explain *why* values matter and how they help the organization achieve something.

EXERCISE
See, feel, believe – cultural integrity activity

What this is: This activity enables you to consider the role your organizational symbols and systems play in supporting, or sabotaging, employee experience.

Why use it: Culture works on different levels, from what is observable – including the systems and symbols we can see – to the values and assumptions that are less visible but still impact experience. Be aware that the values on the

FIGURE 4.1 Employee life spiral

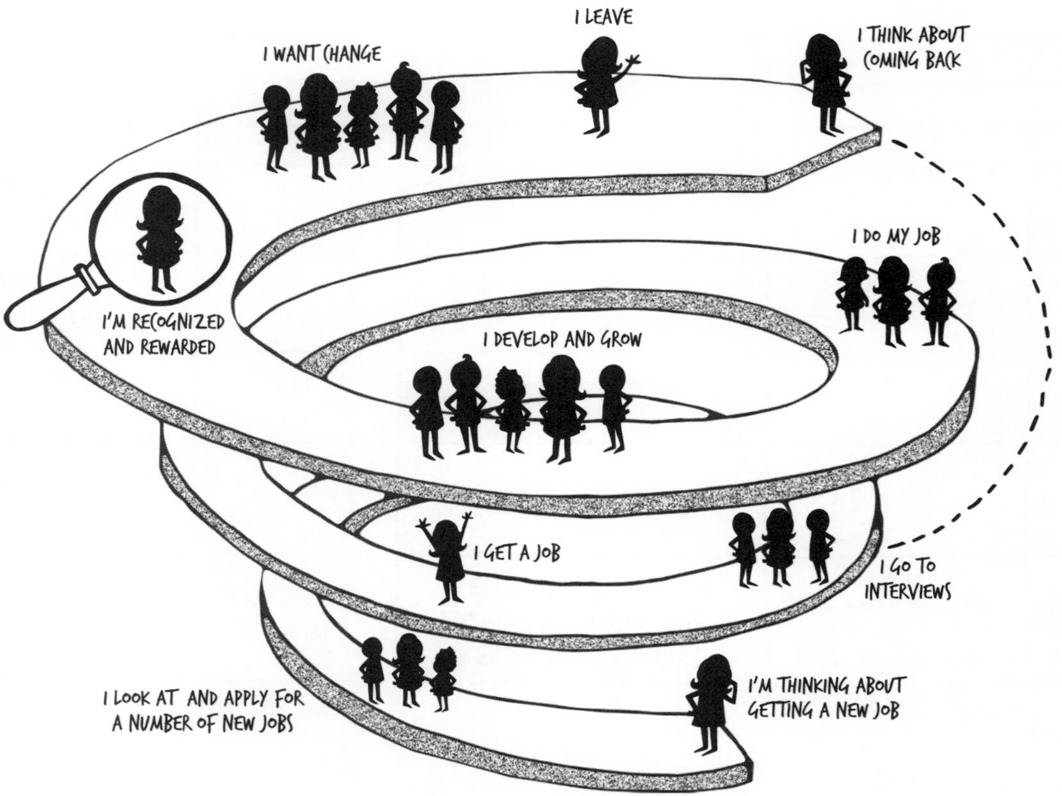

I THINK ABOUT COMING BACK

I DO MY JOB

I GO TO INTERVIEWS

I'M THINKING ABOUT GETTING A NEW JOB

I LEAVE

I DEVELOP AND GROW

I WANT CHANGE

I GET A JOB

I'M RECOGNIZED AND REWARDED

I LOOK AT AND APPLY FOR A NUMBER OF NEW JOBS

FIGURE 4.2 Cultural integrity action plan

CULTURAL SYSTEMS OR SYMBOLS	INTENDED EXPERIENCE	WHERE DOES THE LIVED EXPERIENCE ALIGN AND WHERE DOES IT FAIL TO?	WHERE DO OUR VALUES AND BELIEFS SHOW UP AND WHERE ARE THEY MISSING?	WHAT DO WE NEED TO DO?
EG PERFORMANCE MANAGEMENT SYSTEM				
EG OFFICE ENVIRONMENT				
EG EMPLOYEE COMMUNICATION				
EG ONBOARDING PROCESS				

wall might not be what is actively valued across the organization. This activity is a way to explore the coherence or integrity of your culture across these different levels to allow you to take an intentional approach to your culture.

How to use it: Use this activity to understand the gap between your intended and lived culture and what needs to happen to make it real. Here we demonstrate how to use it across the entire employee experience, but feel free to add and remove elements. Or use it to focus on just one element of employee experience, eg onboarding.

Who to use it with: Use this activity with a mixed group of employees. Or, if you are focusing on a specific element of the employee experience, for example onboarding, invite relevant employees, eg new joiners.

Facilitator instructions

1   Reorient the group around the intended culture of your organization.

2   As a group – or in smaller groups – work your way around the employee life spiral (see Figure 4.1), exploring the intended experience at each stage – what should people see and feel to meet this intention.

3   Now think about the reality of their lived experience. What do people actually see and feel at each stage – to what extent does it align with the intended culture?

4   Now explore where there is the biggest gap between what people see and feel and what the organization says it values. What needs to happen to close the gap? The cultural integrity action plan (see Figure 4.2) is a useful way to structure and capture the conversation. Remember, changing the most visible elements of your culture will not change the experience if the underlying values and assumptions are misaligned. Often you will need to work at this deeper level to change the lived experience.

Design thinking and culture

We borrow many tools and principles from design thinking and often see an interesting dynamic between culture and the design process. As the Design Council and Warwick Business School reported in 2014, design is most powerful when culturally embedded and with strong support, especially from senior management. When it comes to the reverse direction, researchers from the University of California and Imperial College London looked at 33 empirical studies and concluded that using design thinking tools may have a significant influence on culture (Elsbach and Stigliani, 2018). This, they suggest, is due to the experiential nature of the tools – ie people actively engage in hands-on work – affecting the norms, values and underlying assumptions about the right way to work.

Cultural impact shows up in three areas:

User-centricity

The use of empathy-based need-finding tools (discovery activities such as interviews and observing end users, see Chapter 7) encourages a culture of putting users' needs at the centre of activities. Jeanne Liedtka – professor of business administration at the University of Virginia Darden School of Business and well known for her work on design thinking – goes further, suggesting that such activities teach empathy and make us more curious: 'While we're out there getting data, we're immersing ourselves in someone else's lived experience. That's creating an emotional connection, it's shifting our perspective, it's showing us new ways' (Liedtka, 2020).

Openness to ambiguity, risk-taking and collaboration

Tools and activities associated with idea-generation – ie brainstorming and co-creation – encourage a culture where people are more willing to work without an initial clear direction and take on projects without a guarantee of success. People also become more open and able to work with others outside of their usual team or function and become less protective of their ideas.

Openness to experimentation and openness to failure

Design culture does not encourage failure. But it does recognize that the first attempt at something is about learning. Design is often an iterative process and not all eggs will hatch. Real-world experiments are an essential way to assess new ideas and identify the changes needed to make them workable. But such tests offer another, less obvious kind of value: they help reduce employees' normal fear of change.

To be clear, we're not suggesting design thinking, or the introduction of a design approach to employee experience, is a panacea. In some cultures, it will never establish itself beyond the odd quick and dirty workshop – not enough to shift a culture. However, design thinking can and does positively impact the team involved – and that impact spreads.

EXERCISE
Culture dimensions card sort – a conversation-led diagnostic

What this is: This activity is a diagnostic tool to create insights about the nature of the culture and where it may be most positively or negatively impacting employee experience.

Why use it: The objective is to identify cultural strengths and weaknesses that need further attention – not to find solutions. This would happen later in a different setting, for instance finding a problem area may kick off an EX design process (see Chapter 5).

How to use it: This activity can be run in small groups, or even in multiple groups simultaneously at a large event such as a town hall. It can be run multiple times to build a picture across the organization. And because it is quick and easy to do, it can be repeated frequently to keep a live perspective on what is happening that needs attention.

Who to use it with: This activity can be run with anyone. To get a broad insight into the culture, it would be run with multiple groups in different parts of the organization.

Background
• There are many tools and platforms that offer to analyse your organizational culture. We often find that simply starting a conversation is the best way to learn about the culture.

- There are numerous dimensions to your culture. It can sometimes feel overwhelming knowing where to begin, so we recommend starting with the attributes of what makes a great EX as defined by our MAGIC-CA model of EX. You can then add further culture dimensions you feel are relevant to your organization.

Facilitator instructions

1 Write the seven MAGIC-CA themes on Post-It notes, one per note, using the phrase 'I have...'. As a reminder they are:
   - meaning;
   - appreciation;
   - growth;
   - impact;
   - connection;
   - challenge;
   - autonomy.

2 Feel free to add any further culture dimensions that you believe are missing.

3 On a wall, draw a horizontal line. Above the line add a label that says 'strongly agree'; on the line, label it 'neither agree nor disagree'; below the line, add a label saying 'strongly disagree'.

4 Ask each participant to plot their dimension Post-Its in relation to the line – ideally do this in silence to avoid people influencing each other.

5 Discuss what is there and explore why people have chosen to put the dimensions where they have on the axis.

6 Ask people to give specific examples of where that dimension has been strong or absent for them, listen carefully to the words they use, and keep asking why to understand more about the experience.

7 At the end of the share, invite people to move their Post-Its if they have a better understanding of that dimension and have a new perspective on their experience of it.

8 At the end, invite people to vote on the top two dimensions they believe require attention to improve their experience at work. You might do this by giving people two stickers each to add to a Post-It.

Adaptation: You can run multiple sessions focusing on one dimension at a time and spending longer exploring that dimension. It is also possible to run this activity using a virtual whiteboard platform.

What next: The weakest areas of your culture that are a priority for your people could inform the beginning of an EX design process (see details in Chapter 5). However, if you want to respond to the insights in a more pragmatic way, a good extension activity is to look at the strengths in your culture (as evidenced on the wall) and ask what exists in the strongest dimensions of your culture that can be used to strengthen the weakest areas.

The role of leaders in creating a compelling EX

Before we delve into the topic more deeply, we wanted to let you know that, for ease, we will use the terms manager and leader interchangeably. There are numerous opinions, studies, books and more that offer up thoughts on the difference between leaders and managers. One view is that leaders are more focused on the future, have a strategic role, and should inspire others. Whereas managers are more focused on the here and now and getting the job done. The truth is that in reality it is more complex: managers need to lead and leaders need to manage. A diagnosis of the difference between the two is outside our remit here; therefore, when we refer to either leaders or managers, we are talking about people who have some kind of responsibility for other people at work.

Edgar Schein (2004) famously says that leaders' most important role is looking after culture – in particular, recognizing and changing culture where it no longer serves the organization. In fact, he suggests leadership and culture are two sides of the same coin. Cultural norms dictate how an organization defines leadership and chooses leaders.

Intuitively it seems that leaders will have a critical role to play in EX, but it's useful to take a look at some evidence to back these assumptions up. IBM (2017) conducted an in-depth research programme to understand the ideal EX, what drives it, and expected outcomes. They discovered that EX begins with the direction and support of leaders, who in turn facilitate the EX via what they term 'human workplace practices'. These practices include elements such as trust, relationships, meaning, empowerment, recognition, voice, growth and more.

The IBM research concluded that 'leaders and managers play a powerful role in setting the overall tone and direction of an organization, effectively setting the stage for a more positive employee experience' (2017). Further analysis revealed how leaders contribute towards a compelling EX, indicating that this begins with the provision of clarity around future direction and why employees matter, helping them to move the organization forward. However, at the same time they discovered that just 56 per cent of employees say their senior leaders are providing clear direction about where the organization is headed. Clearly there is work to be done. They also found that when leaders serve and support the team, this positively impacts the EX.

Research from Gallup (2019) adds further weight to the idea that leaders matter when it comes to EX. When reviewing different stages of the employee lifecycle, they found that an employee's interaction with their manager made the biggest different to EX. For example:

- Attract: Millennials say that 'quality of manager' is a top factor they consider when looking for a new job.

- Onboard: When managers play an active role in onboarding, employees are 2.5 times more likely to strongly agree their onboarding was exceptional.

- Engage: Managers account for an astounding 70 per cent of the variance in their team's engagement.

- Perform: Only two in ten employees strongly agree that their performance is managed in a way that motivates them to do outstanding work.

- Depart: Fifty-two per cent of exiting employees say that their manager could have done something to prevent them from leaving their job. Nevertheless, only 51 per cent of employees who left their job had a conversation about their engagement, development or future during the three months leading up to their departure (Gallup, 2019).

Further evidence is provided via a study to explore the influence of cultural environment factors in EX and subsequent impact employee engagement (Shuck *et al*, 2011). The findings revealed leadership as a critical component for employee experience, which then builds employee engagement. And in a further study leadership was found to have the highest importance for a positive EX (IBM, 2017).

We have established that a compelling EX is required for employees to be engaged, and there are a number of studies that make the link between leadership style and engagement. For example, one such study (Tims *et al*, 2011) looked at the effects of a transformational leadership style on employee engagement. The research from Tims *et al* explored the ways in which line managers' leadership style influences engagement. Their findings indicated that daily transformational leadership related positively to employees' daily engagement, and further investigation highlighted that it was in fact the optimism of leaders that mediated this relationship. So an optimistic leadership style, in this case, had an impact on the engagement of employees.

Authentic leadership has also been found to impact employee engagement. Authentic leadership can be defined as:

> a pattern of leader behavior that draws upon and promotes both positive psychological capacities and a positive ethical climate, to foster greater self-awareness, an internalized moral perspective, balanced processing of information, and relational transparency on the part of leaders working with followers, fostering positive self-development (Walumbwa *et al*, 2010).

Authentic leadership behaviours have been found to positively relate to employee engagement. For example, in a study by Xu and Cooper Thomas (2011), the following leadership behaviours were found to predict engagement:

- supports team;
- performs effectively;
- displays integrity.

Further analysis revealed that 'supports team' was the strongest predictor of subsequent engagement. It seems sensible to suggest that supporting your team would contribute to a positive EX.

In addition, a style of leadership known as intellectual stimulator leadership was found to increase job satisfaction, effort and effectiveness when positive emotions like enthusiasm, hope, pride, happiness and inspiration complement the leadership (Zineldin, 2017).

What these studies show is that the way in which leaders lead can have an impact on a range of outcomes that are associated with how employees experience work. And interestingly, both transformational leadership and authentic leadership are sometimes looked at via the lens of positive leadership. Positive leadership is an umbrella term for a number of different leadership models that have some key elements in common:

- It involves being purposeful about experiencing, modelling and positive emotions.
- It involves being interested in your team's development as well.
- And it involves attributes of high self-awareness, optimism and personal integrity.

Given our discussion of the role of positive emotions in EX in Chapter 3, it makes sense that positive leadership will help to facilitate a compelling EX. To understand more about positive leadership, we can look to the work of Kim Cameron (2013). In his book, *Practicing Positive Leadership*, he outlines not only a substantial body of empirical evidence for the impact of positive leadership, but also practical tools and techniques. In summary, Cameron argues that positive leadership practices enable employees and organizations to flourish, achieve their highest potential, experience elevating energy and become more effective.

Setting leaders up for success

Often organizations overlook the fact that their leaders are employees first, leaders and managers second. We have to focus on getting their experience right to help them ensure their teams have a great EX. Quite simply, your leaders can make or break the employee experience within the workplace, so investing in them makes sense: first, by intentionally designing compelling experiences for them, and second, by ensuring they are set up for success to support a compelling EX with their teams. Don't assume your leaders will naturally know how to facilitate a compelling EX with their teams; support may be required.

We know what great leadership and management looks like. There are huge bodies of research and numerous books on the subject. Gallup (2019) are leading experts in the subject and share some useful guidance on how we can support our leaders on creating a compelling EX with their teams:

- Choose your leaders and managers carefully, obvious but critical. So many people find themselves promoted to the role of manager or leader because they are technical experts rather than because of the requisite skills to lead and manage others.

- Give your leaders and managers the right support. In their research, Gallup (2019) find that leadership development programmes are not translating into managers feeling fully prepared for and inspired about their future.

- Practise empathy by taking time to understand how it feels for leaders and managers in your organization. Gallup's paper, 'The manager experience: Top challenges and perks of managers' (2019), is a great resource, sharing evidence from a study of more than 50,000 managers. However, there is no substitute for taking the time to listen to managers and leaders within your own organization. Gallup (2019) suggest designing learning programmes that are continual, multimode and experiential.

- Take steps to ensure your brand, purpose and culture are experienced at every stage of your employee lifecycle. This advice is relevant for all employees, not just leaders and managers. But we can't expect them to bring the organization purpose brand and culture to life for their teams if they are not experiencing it themselves.

In Chapter 3 we talked about the psychology of experience and made the case for focusing on positive psychology. The work of Shawn

Achor (2011) helps us to understand why focusing on the positive will contribute towards a positive EX. It stands to reason, then, that positive leadership is helpful for EX practice. Kim Cameron's (2013) work on positive leadership can also provide practical guidance to set our leaders up for success when creating a positive EX. Cameron outlines a number of positive leadership practices that are based on his four positive leadership strategies:

- positive meaning;
- positive climate;
- positive communication;
- positive relationships.

At a high level the practices he advocates are:

- Create a culture of abundance. This in essence is about looking at strengths as well as weaknesses and focusing on what works as well as what does not.
- Establish Everest goals. This is about setting big goals that motivate people to achieve spectacular performance.
- Develop positive energy networks. That is, first focus on developing your own positive energy and then actively building a network and spending time with others who have positive energy.
- Deliver negative feedback positively. This refers to the ability to use supportive communication when delivering difficult messages. This includes avoiding defensiveness, being congruent and validating the other person.

We don't yet have a definitive competency framework for leaders and EX. However, in 2011 the CIPD conducted research to identify specific management behaviours that are important for employee engagement, and we believe that this framework is entirely relevant for EX too. As you'll see from the framework, the competencies link to both the psychological element of EX that we talked about in Chapter 3, as well as specific leadership styles that impact EX outlined in this chapter (see Table 4.1).

TABLE 4.1 Summary of the 'Managing for sustainable employee engagement' framework

Competency	Brief description
Open, fair and consistent	Managing with integrity and consistency, managing emotions/personal issues and taking a positive approach in interpersonal interactions
Handling conflict and problems	Dealing with employee conflicts (including bullying and abuse) and using appropriate organizational resources
Knowledge, clarity and guidance	Clear communication, advice and guidance, demonstrating understanding of roles, and responsible decision-making
Building and sustaining relationships	Personal interaction with employees involving empathy and consideration
Supporting development	Supporting and arranging employee career progression and development

SOURCE CIPD (2011)

In the absence of a definitive competency framework for managing EX, we believe this is a great place to start. You can of course add to the framework with further competencies relevant to your organizational context. The framework could be integrated into your management development offering, or used as part of a 360-degree feedback process if you have one. In addition, the framework and associated competencies could be used within your performance management and appraisal systems, helping to not only communicate the desired behaviours, but also to reinforce the value of demonstrating them. Also, competency-based questions could be developed in line with the framework to assist recruiting managers who either have these skills already or have the potential to develop them.

Perhaps the most useful element of the framework, though, is the ability to clearly articulate to managers what good looks like. As discussed in Chapter 1, the definitions of EX are varied and wide. Communicating a competency framework enables your managers to understand the behaviours and competencies they need to help facilitate a compelling EX.

EXERCISE

Evaluating managers' competencies

The 'Managing for sustainable employee engagement' framework identifies which behaviours are helpful for a manager to engage their teams. We also believe these competencies will facilitate a positive EX. You can use the questionnaire below to assess the competencies of your managers, helping them to understand what they already do well, what they need to do more of, and what they need to do less of or stop doing altogether. The questionnaire can be used in a variety of ways:

- as a stand-alone 360 review;
- as part of your current 360 review process;
- self-assessment;
- as part of your selection process;
- pre-work for management development training.

Questionnaire

1. Open, fair and consistent

Is not overly critical of me and other team members

Does not blame me and other team members for decisions taken

Does not focus on mistakes

Demonstrates faith in my capability

Consults with me rather than tells me what to do

Allows decisions to be challenged

Uses humour and sarcasm appropriately

Does not show favouritism

Never talks about team members behind their backs

Does not criticize me and other team members in front of others

Treats me with respect

Is predictable in mood

Acts calmly in pressured situations

Does not pass on their stress to me

Is consistent in their approach to managing

Is calm about deadlines

Seems to give more positive feedback than negative feedback

2. Handling conflict and problems

Acts as a mediator in conflict situations

Deals with squabbles before they turn into arguments

Deals objectively with employee conflicts

Deals with employee conflicts head on

Uses HR as a resource to help deal with problems

Seeks help from occupational health when necessary

Follows up conflicts after resolution

Supports employees through incidents of abuse

Addresses bullying

Makes it clear they will take ultimate responsibility if things go wrong

3. Knowledge, clarity and guidance

Gives advice when required

Takes responsibility for problem-solving to senior management

Gives specific rather than vague advice

Clarifies role requirements and expectations

Is clear of their own role requirements

Demonstrates a good understanding of the role I do

Communicates whether I am on track or not

Gives adequate time for planning

Demonstrates understanding of processes and procedures

Follows up on action points

Always has time for me

Is decisive at decision-making

4. Building and sustaining relationships

Shows interest in my personal life

Checks I am feeling okay

Shows understanding of the pressures I am under

Provides regular opportunities to speak one to one

Brings in treats

Socializes with the team

Is willing to have a laugh at work

Takes an interest in my life outside of work

Regularly asks 'how are you?'

5. Supporting development

Takes time to discuss my career development

Actively supports my career development

Offers opportunities for career development

Plans or arranges time off/out for career development opportunities

Arranges development activities

There's no doubt that your leaders and managers will have an impact on EX. Intentionally designing interventions to set them up for success helps to ensure this impact is positive and makes a difference.

Takeaways

In this chapter we looked at the significant relationship between culture, leadership and employee experience and how they influence each other. In summary:

- Culture impacts EX at multiple levels and it needs to be approached in a cohesive way to deliver a joined-up experience.
- There is a recursive relationship between culture and design – with each influencing the other.
- Many culture reform management thinkers believe design is a significant element of cultural change.

- Leaders and managers have a critical role in facilitating a brilliant EX.
- Set your leaders up for success; invest in their development and don't leave it to chance.

References

Achor, S (2011) *The Happiness Advantage: The seven principles of positive psychology that fuel success and performance at work*, Random House Group Publishing, London

Buchanan, R (2015) Worlds in the making: Design, management, and the reform of organizational culture, *She Ji: The Journal of Design Economics and Innovation*. http://www.journals.elsevier.com/she-ji-the-journal-of-design-economics-and-innovation (archived at https://perma.cc/8TMZ-D4SG)

Cameron, K (2013) *Practicing Positive Leadership*, Berrett-Koehler, San Francisco, CA

Chesky, B (2014) [accessed 13 August 2020] Don't fuck up the culture, *Medium*, 20 April [Online] https://medium.com/@bchesky/dont-fuck-up-the-culture-597cde9ee9d4 (archived at https://perma.cc/B4ST-WS77)

CIPD (2011) [accessed 13 August 2020] *Sustainable Organisation Performance: What really makes the difference? Shaping the Future* [Online] http://www.cipd.co.uk/binaries/5287stffinalreportweb.pdf (archived at https://perma.cc/YBZ9-LPL9)

Coyle, D (2018) *The Culture Code*, Random House, London

Design Council and Warwick Business School (2014) [accessed 13 August 2020] *Leading Business by Design: Why and how business leaders invest in design*, Design Council [Online] https://www.designcouncil.org.uk/sites/default/files/asset/document/dc_lbbd_report_08.11.13_FA_LORES.pdf (archived at https://perma.cc/499C-J58U)

Elsbach, K and Stigliani, I (2018) Design thinking and organizational culture: A review and framework for future research, *Journal of Management* [Online] https://www.researchgate.net/publication/322550517_Design_Thinking_and_Organizational_Culture_A_Review_and_Framework_for_Future_Research (archived at https://perma.cc/86TQ-NWUW)

Gallup (2019) [accessed 13 August 2020] The manager experience [Online] https://www.gallup.com/workplace/259820/manager-experience-challenges-perk-perspective-paper.aspx (archived at https://perma.cc/W3JH-FG2R)

Glassdoor (2019) [accessed 13 August 2020] Mission and culture survey 2019 [Online] https://www.glassdoor.com/about-us/app/uploads/sites/2/2019/07/Mission-Culture-Survey-Supplement.pdf (archived at https://perma.cc/7P95-METU)

IBM (2017) [accessed 13 August 2020] The Employee Experience Index: A new global measure of a human workplace and its impact [Online] https://www.ibm.com/downloads/cas/JDMXPMBM (archived at https://perma.cc/QL77-4JHX)

Liedtka, J (2020) [accessed 13 August 2020] Maximising the ROI of design thinking, *Mural Imagine Talks*, 28 May [Online] https://www.mural.co/imagine/talks (archived at https://perma.cc/AZ45-NBSR)

McGowan, H and Shipley, C (2020) *The Adaptation Advantage: Let go, learn fast, and thrive in the future of work*, Wiley, Hoboken, NJ

McHale, S (2020) *The Insider's Guide to Culture Change*, HarperCollins Leadership, New York

O.C. Tanner (2020) [accessed 13 August 2020] Global culture report [Online] https://www.octanner.com/uk/global-culture-report.html (archived at https://perma.cc/7VYE-G7EN)

Schein, E (2004) *Organizational Culture and Leadership*, Jossey-Bass, San Francisco, CA

Shuck, B, Rocco, T and Albornoz, C (2011) Exploring employee engagement from the employee perspective: Implications for HRD, *Journal of European Industrial Training*, 35, pp 300–325

Sull, D, Turconi, S and Sull, C (2020) [accessed 13 August 2020] When it comes to culture, does your company walk the talk?, *MIT Sloan Management Review*, 21 July [Online] https://sloanreview.mit.edu/article/when-it-comes-to-culture-does-your-company-walk-the-talk/ (archived at https://perma.cc/N4KQ-AAQK)

Tims, M, Bakker, AB and Xanthopoulou, D (2011) Do transformational leaders enhance their followers' daily work engagement?, *Leadership Quarterly*, 22, pp 121–31

Walumbwa, FO, Wang, P, Wang, H, Schaubroeck, J and Avolio, BJ (2010) Psychological process linking authentic leadership to follower behaviours, *Leadership Quarterly*, 21, pp 901–14

Wright-Wasson, D (2019) *Talk the Walk: Designing a clear path to a world class employee experience*, Page Two Books, Vancouver

Xu, J and Cooper Thomas, H (2011) How can leaders achieve high employee engagement?, *Leadership and Organization Development Journal*, 32 (4), pp 399–416

Zineldin, M (2017) Transformational leadership behavior, emotions, and outcomes: Health psychology perspective in the workplace, *Journal of Workplace Behavioural Health*, 32, pp 14–25

05

EX design in action

In this chapter we'll cover:

- what we mean by EX design and why it matters;
- where EX design comes from and its links to design thinking and agile;
- the three principles of EX design – empathy, curiosity and experimentation;
- the EX design framework and how to get started with EX design;
- common misconceptions about EX design.

What is EX design and why does it matter?

Every employee has an experience of you as an employer. Their experience starts before they join and lasts as a memory long after they've stopped working for you. The question is, to what extent is it the experience they want and need, and how aligned is it with your intended EX? Only by being intentional about how you craft the many significant – as well as everyday – experiences people have of you can you hope to architect the larger, overall employee experience. That all comes down to EX design – the application of design principles, first to how we understand people and their needs and expectations, and then to how we develop, test and iterate solutions to make the experience the best it can be. 'Best' is a loose term – and deliberately so. EX is not one-size-fits-all and, in reality, it involves compromises. What best looks like is a balance between three competing and shifting demands: your organizational context, the requirements of the work and your people. Looked at in this way, it is clear EX design is *not* a phase in a development process. Neither is it making the intranet or any other tool, product or service look nice (although aesthetics may play a part). Rather, it is a continuous focus on, and intentional evolution of, the many small, medium and large experiences an employee has with you – and, as a consequence, the cumulative impact of those experiences.

In this chapter we introduce the EX design framework and explain how to get started with EX design. In subsequent chapters we go into more detail about each step and the tools involved. EX design is a lot less linear and a lot more iterative than that suggests. However, by sharing the approach in this structured way, we hope to give you the confidence to get started and flex it as much as you need.

Where does EX design come from? Introducing design thinking

To understand EX design, we first need a grasp of design thinking, a creative, human-centred approach to problem-solving used by designers of products, processes and environments. Because it does not have its own academic niche – design thinking straddles many disciplines, from design to engineering, business and technology – there are a range of definitions, interpretations and even origin stories. Here we share a popular narrative about design thinking. However, this narrative is by no means comprehensive. For example, see also Chapter 11 for a reflection on the commonalities between design thinking and Dr Brenda Dervin's sense-making methodology, a philosophically derived approach associated with knowledge management that focuses on listening to users' needs to inform the design of knowledge-sharing practices and systems (Cheuk and Dervin, 2011).

The roots of design thinking are commonly said to date back to the 1960s, when academics started to talk about design science as a method of creating something new. It also has links to human factors psychology, which looks at how things like dials and machines can be created to be easier to use. This came to the fore in the Second World War, when a range of experts came together to improve the safety of airplanes. Human factors psychology has since come to play a significant role in many areas, including computing, manufacturing, product design, engineering and even the military. Design thinking takes some of these ideas – especially prototyping and user testing – and combines them with a mindset approach and toolkit.

While design thinking began in the world of design, it has long since moved on to macro business issues, including operational problems and strategy. The ideology and language of design thinking was first widely publicized in an article in the academic journal *Design Issues* by Professor of Design, Management and Innovation Richard Buchanan in 1992. Buchanan suggested that a designer's thought process allowed them to deal with complex, multifaceted, wicked problems where creativity is required to find multiple workable solutions. This idea was taken up by the Stanford d.school, which helped to popularize design thinking as a problem-solving method across business. d.school has remained one of the largest proponents of design thinking ever since.

Design thinking is now used across businesses and functions as an effective tool for problem-solving when standard analytical methodologies fall short. Design thinking practitioners seek to think deeply about the nature of the problem based on an exploration of the needs of end users. They then deliberately collaborate with people with different perspectives to solve the problem. The approach has been widely popularized through academic institutions, including Stanford University, as well as popular businesses, such as Apple, Google, LEGO and IDEO. Tim Brown, executive chair of IDEO, describes the entire way his business works – not just how it creates new products and services – as design thinking. His 2009 book, *Change by Design,* introduced the concept to a far wider audience and has one of the most quoted definitions of design thinking:

> Design thinking is a human-centered approach to innovation that draws from the designer's toolkit to integrate the needs of people, the possibilities of technology and the requirements for business success (Brown, 2009/2019).

How does design thinking work?

Brown and IDEO's interpretation of design thinking can be summarized as: inspiration, ideation and implementation (Brown, 2009/2019). He expands on this to make the point that its success relies on empathy with the end user, integrative thinking (the ability to exploit opposing ideas to construct a new solution), optimism and cross-disciplinary collaboration.

As an approach to problem-solving, design thinking is a loosely structured and non-linear process. It is based on a collection of tools that can be used by anyone with a problem that is abstract, complex or both. Its number-one selling point for many organizations is how it allows people to take a problem that is ambiguous and complex and provide a clear and simple way to get started understanding and solving it. From there, it is an iterative process, with each iteration bringing practitioners closer to the optimal solution.

That clear starting line might be a number-one selling point, but the benefits of design thinking go way beyond that. In fact, they go way beyond the obvious outcome of solving complex problems. Jeanne Liedtka, a professor of business administration at the University of Virginia Darden School of Business, has widely researched and written about the impact of design thinking in organizations. Speaking in May 2020, Liedtka emphasized the importance of design thinking as an engaging and collaborative process that shifts innovators' mindsets and beliefs as well as their skills, builds their creative confidence, offers psychological safety and creates an openness and a willingness to try new things.

So rather than simply being an effective way of solving problems, design thinking is a form of change management, shaping those involved in the process as they shape new solutions. Some describe it as like a bug – it's a way of working that is contagious and lasting.

How design thinking and EX work together

Design thinking tools and principles are central to employee experience design. The optimism or hopefulness associated with design thinking dovetails neatly with the other core ingredient of our approach – positive psychology. In fact, we draw on the two interchangeably. However, before we go any further, it's worth noting how we have adapted one of the fundamentals of design thinking – the three constraints. Tim Brown (2009/2019) makes the point that design cannot happen without constraints. He suggests the willing, even enthusiastic, acceptance of competing constraints is the foundation of design thinking. Discovering which constraints are important and creating a framework for evaluating them is often the first stage in design thinking (see Chapter 6). The three constraints identified by Tim Brown are:

1 Feasibility – what is functionally possible?
2 Viability – what is likely to be sustainable for the business?
3 Desirability – what makes sense to and for people?

When we apply design thinking tools, we reframe these three constraints to make them more immediately relevant to employee experience. So EX design is about intentionally curating an EX that is right for:

- people's needs and expectations – what makes sense to and for people;
- requirements of the work – the technical or other requirements of the work, for instance where people are located, what equipment they have, and what processes they need to follow;
- organization context – commercial objectives as well as requirements of the culture, brand, purpose, values, etc.

We borrow and adapt from design thinking with pride. However, some designers balk at what they see as the misappropriation of the word design by non-designers (like us). After all, if someone takes up dressmaking at the weekend, it doesn't make them a fashion designer. But, when it comes to EX, the word design is apt – because it is intentional, and it is markedly different from other, more traditional approaches to human resources and related people-focused activities, such as internal communications.

Experienced designers have also been known to challenge what they suggest is design thinking's overly structured approach, suggesting it leaves little room for the skill and mastery of real designers. However, that shouldn't worry us. In fact, the structure – as loose as it is – is helpful. Given that most people involved in EX design are not designers and that many of the behaviours and activities associated with design thinking are new to them, the structure provides useful guardrails that quickly help to establish a new language and confidence.

As we've already said, our intention with the EX framework and tools we cover in this and subsequent chapters is not to be prescriptive. Our approach to EX design borrows from design thinking, but they are not one and the same. When working with clients, we flex our approach and the tools we use. We recommend you do the same. Choose EX design tools and activities and apply them in a way that makes sense to you. We'll explain more below.

DESIGN THINKING AND EX

How design thinking came of age

Design thinking as a way of approaching employee experience first got a mention in Deloitte's Global Human Capital Trends in 2015. In the report, Deloitte described how design thinking was moving HR's focus beyond building programmes and processes, to a new goal of designing a productive and meaningful employee experience through compelling, enjoyable and simple solutions. In the same report a year later, Deloitte (2016) started to evaluate the impact of design thinking on employee experience, suggesting that organizations where HR was delivering the highest value were almost five times more likely to be using design thinking.

In reality, individuals, teams and whole companies have been focusing on the experience they create for their people since long before 2015. And involving people in that process is not a new phenomenon. Emma introduced involvement as a pillar of employee engagement in the first edition of her book *Employee Engagement* in 2015 (Bridger, 2015). What's changed is that there is now a methodology and a suite of tools to support EX design. The fact that there are many principles shared between design thinking and agile methodologies (more on this below) is also helping to establish the approach and build confidence and capability. The EX Leaders Employee Experience 2020 Global Report (Kennedy Fitch and EX Leaders Network, 2020) suggests focusing on EX is now a feature of most global Fortune 500 organizations (as well as a significant number of smaller ones). Like Deloitte, it suggests that what separates leaders from the rest of the pack is design thinking capability, and we believe this will continue to be the case. The COVID-19 pandemic changed many things for every organization and their employees. It may also have sped up the adoption of an EX design mindset and approach. The pandemic has fast-forwarded the arrival of a new era of work. Our needs, expectations and attitudes towards work and our employer have changed. Employers will need to keep listening, learning and responding. Much traditional HR activity is about delivering functional solutions, often for yesterday's problems. Now, more than ever, we need to design for the opportunities of today and tomorrow.

People teams, in whatever guise, need to seek out, deeply understand, and redesign the things that really impact their people's experience. And they need to do so against a backdrop of complexity and uncertainty. EX design, with its roots in design thinking, is uniquely well placed to help – because it doesn't just deliver change; it discovers what kind of change is needed and it creates a more human-centred culture in the process.

Three key principles of EX design

When learning about design thinking, it's easy to focus on a set of tools and activities. However, design thinking is much more than an innovation recipe with steps and ingredients. Design thinking is also a mindset with curiosity, empathy and experimentation at its core. EX design borrows these three principles – principles that are inherently optimistic, rooted in a belief that it is possible to understand human experience *and* to design solutions to improve it. This is why we bring together tools and approaches from both the world of design thinking and positive psychology:

1 curiosity: being insatiably curious about people and what makes them tick as well as what is possible;

2 empathy: putting people and their experience at the heart of the process;

3 experimentation: constantly learning and iterating – testing multiple small solutions or prototypes to better understand what might solve a problem or realize an opportunity.

1. EX design and curiosity

Curiosity is fundamental to great design because it challenges assumptions and raises questions. It encourages deep and expansive thinking that helps generate more creative solutions. Writing in *Harvard Business Review* about her research into curiosity, Harvard Business School Professor Francesca Gino (2018) says when we are curious, we are less susceptible to confirmation bias – looking for information that supports our beliefs and ignoring evidence suggesting we are wrong. We are also less likely to slip into stereotypes and so make fewer broad judgements about individuals and groups.

Curiosity is powerful for another reason as well. When we ask lots of questions, we become more comfortable acknowledging we don't have all the answers. This is important as, particularly in HR, people are rewarded for their expertise and it takes a mental shift to look for answers, rather than simply provide them. Curiosity also prompts us to find and work with the people who have the insight or skills we lack. The best designers know that it takes people from all backgrounds and experiences to truly understand a problem and find a solution. Only a fraction of the employee experience is made up of HR products and services, and HR should only be one part of the design team. Great EX design requires new connections, partnerships and conversations across the organization. Writing in *Strategic HR Review* in 2017, Josh Plaskoff, director of organizational effectiveness at Anthem, Inc., calls this 'radical participation' – meaning extensive, broad, multi-level and egalitarian:

> Not only does this create more robust solutions, as it brings together diverse perspectives and expertise from across the organization, but it also reduces resistance to change and increases ownership, engagement and commitment, since participants who feel empowered to enact change are less likely to reject their own solutions (Plaskoff, 2017).

2. EX design and empathy

Human-centred design is rooted in empathy for the people you're designing for – the ability to stand in someone else's shoes and see the world through their eyes. Empathy is the route to finding the right answers to our questions. It challenges our preconceived ideas and forces us to set aside our sense of what we think is true, in order to discover what's really happening for someone else.

Empathy is all about human connection, how we connect with other people in order to travel into and explore their internal world. Doing so means we can spot and seek to solve previously unseen problems and realize new opportunities. If we don't go deep when it comes to EX design, we get stuck at the level of beer Fridays and football tables. These office perks are nice to have, but they don't touch the sides when it comes to creating and sustaining emotionally enriching human experiences (see Chapter 3). Empathy doesn't just require us to stay close to the people we're designing for; it requires us to design with our people. This is radical participation in action, and for many organizations, it is a paradigm shift in how solutions are specified and developed – a significant shift, but also a hugely beneficial one, as we will explore in subsequent chapters.

3. EX design and experimentation

It's easy to think of experimentation as an action and not a mindset at all. But experimentation all starts in the head – with a commitment to trying things out in order to learn. When we try new things, we are rewiring our brains by creating new neural pathways. Conversely, our old habits and regular ways of doing things have strong, well-worn neural pathways, which is why these things come easy and why we often fall back on them. In everyday life this can be useful. But if we want innovation, or new, or different ideas, we have to be intentional about experimentation. Adopting an experimentation mindset forces us to do this and try new things rather than fall back on our old habits or ways of doing things.

An experimentation mindset is playful. It's what children instinctively do to learn. But too often we lose our experimental drive. However, the most design-oriented businesses have a playful experimental approach, not just to problem-solving, but at the core of the culture. LEGO, for example, shuts down the business one a day year to focus solely on its values of play and help turn more of its people into play ambassadors in their communities.

An experimentation mindset in EX design steers us away from solutions that are over-specified, take years to develop, and then fail to land. Instead, it encourages a bias for action, for continuous experimentation, and rapid learning. Great EX solutions are always in beta because they're always being built on and improved. EX design is by its nature evolutionary and an experimentation mindset helps drive it forward.

Agile and EX design – complementary approaches

If it hasn't already, agile is coming soon to an HR team near you. That might mean a number of things, because agility, a concept born in software development, is used to describe a wide range of concepts, systems and processes. In her 2017 book *Agile People: A radical approach for HR and managers*, Pia-Maria Thorén describes agile as a way of moving forward and creating value. For HR, this means improving processes and driving efficiency. It can also mean embracing a bottom–up approach and empowering team members to make decisions faster, reducing bureaucratic structures, simplifying operations and culling unnecessary processes, systems, reports and checklists.

But HR transformation is only part of the picture. An agile transformation is about organizational culture as much as it is about any one function. Thorén describes agile as a 'mentality that allows people and groups to meet challenges, learn quickly, and respond to change' (Thorén, 2017). So agile clearly has consequences for employee experience. An agile organization where individuals are empowered and supported to do the right thing and at pace has a big impact on people's experience of work. There are also implications for how an organization approaches EX design. There are many overlapping principles between EX design and agile – not least the focus on the end user, on experimentation, rapid prototyping, and making incremental improvements. Both also rely on collaborative, cross-functional teams.

Developing EX design capability is often easier where agile is already established. On the other hand, agile transformations that are incomplete or implemented ineffectively may have a detrimental impact on employee experience and the organization's ability to design EX. The consequences of a failed agile transformation can be disastrous, with systemic complexity leading to confusion, depressed engagement, declining performance and high turnover of people.

CASE STUDY

EX and agile in practice

How the two approaches worked together at Roche and River Island

Nebel Crowhurst – people and culture director of Roche UK, and formerly head of people experience at River Island – has led agile transformation in two organizations while also focusing on the principles of employee experience. Here she looks at the relationship between agile, employee experience and employee experience design and how they fit neatly together.

From tech to HR transformation

River Island is a high street fashion retailer with a 70-year heritage and more than 12,000 employees internationally. In recent years the shift towards creating an online shopping experience for customers has resulted in a large-scale tech-driven transformation, where the benefits of agile were obvious. However, it was when we started building agile capability more broadly across the organization that things really started to change.

For HR, agile allowed us to update our practices to better meet changing employee expectations. Beyond simply being keepers of policy and process with a largely reactive and operational approach, we started to develop a much more people-centric mindset. This meant a shift in both mindset and practice, away from the transactional towards the transformational.

The importance of mindset

The idea of delivery through iterations is deeply embedded in agile philosophies, and this concept is one of the first that needs to be understood and adopted in order for people to appreciate the benefits of working in this way. That's where mindset comes in. It's human nature for people to want to stick with what they already know, often within our comfort zones, but having an open mind and a healthy dose of curiosity is what helps to begin the transformation.

Fundamentally, what is needed is a 'growth mindset', in which people have a desire to want to learn and experience new approaches. But how can we make that happen? How can we positively influence those people who feel uncomfortable with change and how can we leverage those that are eager to want to change? The answer is: slowly and gradually. This isn't a mindset shift that happens overnight; it is something that is developed and grown collaboratively – in essence, using the agile principle of iterations.

You have to be completely committed when embarking on a transformation of this scale, and know that to truly reap the benefits, there are a good few years of work and careful planning ahead. What you can't do is just say to people: today we are an HR team, and tomorrow we are a progressive EX team. There is more to it than that, not least the need for people to understand the why – the story behind the change. This is where you begin to truly value the skill of communications and the ability to bring people on a journey to understand and appreciate the progress forward. Only once people have an understanding of the why and the growth mindset to work in a new way can you begin to introduce the idea of a new identity for HR.

Retail to pharma

For River Island, the concept of 'people experience' was born, along with a newly defined team and a new approach to delivery. No more long-winded and old-fashioned project plans – instead we introduced an iterative approach that meant continually listening to feedback from the business to ensure new innovations were in line with people's needs. We began eliminating waste and improving efficiency.

I'm now on a similar journey with Roche. The HR transformation is part of a broader organizational agile transformation that is transitioning to a culture that empowers nimble decision-making, fosters bold innovation and celebrates experimentation. This requires a mindset shift for our people – an appetite to experiment, be bold, to reflect and learn, to take accountability and decisions. The same advice applies, though, regardless of the organization. Consider the approach, work on defining the why, create a compelling narrative to inspire people to want to come on the transformation journey, and only then begin to introduce the new identity of HR – which for Roche is 'people and culture'.

A great example of how we are bringing together the principles of agile, EX design and EX is through the delivery of a modernized onboarding programme. Onboarding is something that never goes away and requires continual improvements and nurturing. However, it often falls to the bottom of the pile, and before we know it our onboarding 'process' is fundamentally broken and providing few, if any, meaningful experiences for our people.

In our Roche UK team we realized we needed to work on how we improved our onboarding approach and early on made a decision that agile principles would enable us to deliver something that really aligned with the needs of our people. The early stages sat in the realms of 'design thinking' or 'human-centred thinking', appreciating what the current end-to-end experience looked like, where there were broken links, and what people felt they needed and expected from an onboarding experience. This is where the element of empathy comes into play. All too often in HR we believe we know all the answers, we know best and know what people want and need – but the reality is, unless you are continually engaged in a dialogue with your people and open to feedback, you can't really ever know. Our approach included speaking with line managers, people that had recently joined our business, and people that were due to join in the next three months. This gave us a much richer picture of where we needed to place our efforts.

Anyone with experience of delivering onboarding knows the complexities and layers of touchpoints are vast, so when you begin to unpick the current process and define a prioritized backlog of work, the task ahead can feel mountainous. This is where agile comes into its own. Breaking down workload into manageable chunks through agile sprints, keeping the work momentum going by having regular sprint stand-ups, and managing the workflow through a simple kanban tracker enables the teams working on this type of project to feel motivated by the progress rather than daunted by the volume of work ahead. On the topic of teams, this is another key consideration when working in an agile way. Agile removes many layers of hierarchy and encourages a culture of co-creation and shared collaboration – again, another positive approach but one that comes with a need for a more progressive mindset.

By working in this way, we have been able to design an employee experience that we know will deliver the desired results of an onboarding approach that provides personalized moments that matter for every new employee who joins our business. What's important, though, is that we continue to keep the feedback loop open to ensure the experience keeps on being refined and improved.

Bringing people on the journey and sharing the story are critical. We need to tell a story about why we are making the change, what is the benefit to people, departments and the business and what will be different.

We can't do it alone. We need to use the shared voice of people within the organization to help make the shift. We need to listen to our people, work with them and bring a new culture of collaboration to life.

A framework for EX design

So far we've focused on the principles of EX design. Now we are going to look at the tools and activities that underpin both a strategic approach to employee experience, as well as the development of people-oriented, prototype-driven solutions to EX challenges and opportunities.

Introducing the Design Council Double Diamond

The UK's Design Council has codified the steps in any design or innovation project – irrespective of the methods and tools – in the Design Council Double Diamond, created in 2004. This simple representation of design steps – discover, define, develop and deliver – is now part of design language worldwide. The two diamonds are often labelled as problem space (where you discover and define the problem) and solution space (where you generate ideas to solve the problem and then develop and test prototypes). For the purposes of EX design, we prefer to call the first diamond the opportunity space, as it encourages a more optimistic or strengths-based mindset. The double diamond model also demonstrates the thinking that is happening at each step. The diamond is wide to represent divergent thinking, where new information is being sought or new ideas created. It narrows to represent convergent thinking, when the design team is defining the problem or opportunity they've discovered, and defining solutions to address it.

The Stanford d.school model is another commonly cited approach. This method has been reproduced widely with many companies, including IDEO, using it as a template for their own design thinking method. The d.school model suggests five groups of activities – empathize, define, ideate, prototype, test. This is the model we build on, introducing a range of tools and activities at each stage. Each activity creates a clear output that the next activity converts to something else until there is a solution to test and implement. This process can be used to design a wide variety of solutions, from new HR tools and processes, to L&D, internal communications and beyond. It can also be used in many related projects, not just obvious EX design tasks. For example, we use it to design workshops. And it is widely used in career coaching and more besides.

Introducing a third diamond for EX design

When we're talking about employee experience, we work in a third space as well – the scoping space – the diamond to the left on Figure 5.1. This is the area where we take a more strategic focus on EX and EX design, evaluating at a strategic level the competing and aligned needs of people, the work, and the organization. As with the other two diamonds – opportunity and solution – there are both discovery and defining activities in the first diamond. Depending on where you're at and what you're trying to achieve, you may not spend time in this space. It's a great place to be if you're looking at the overarching EX and trying to understand where to get started. You can also use the activities in this diamond (see Chapter 6) to define the overall experience you're trying to create.

An overview of the EX design framework

SCOPING SPACE

Discover   Find out what your EX should be to meet the needs of your people, the work and the organizational context – and where it is and isn't delivering.

Define   This is about defining your intentional EX as a result of your discovery activities. This might be expressed in the form of a

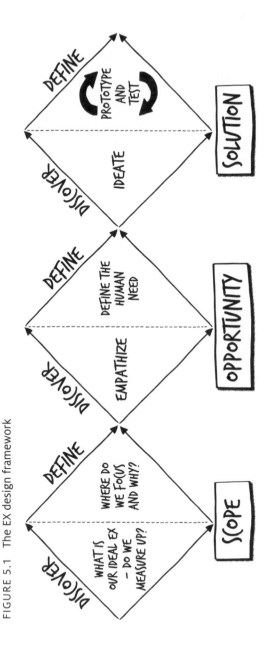

FIGURE 5.1 The EX design framework

statement of your intended EX, as an employee value proposition, or a people vision. It really doesn't matter. What does matter is setting a vision of what overall experience you're trying to achieve and using that to prioritize where to focus design efforts.

OPPORTUNITY SPACE

Discover   This is where you put curiosity to work and use empathy to broaden and deepen understanding of the issue you're working on. It involves speaking to and spending time with people who are affected by the issues – not simply looking at survey and other data.

Define   Using insight from the discovery phase, you then redefine the problem or opportunity through your people's eyes. This problem or opportunity definition creates the focus around which ideas are generated and solutions developed.

SOLUTION SPACE

Develop   This is where you generate ideas – lots of ideas – to solve the problem or realize the opportunity, eventually focusing on one or more to develop and test.

Deliver   Ideas are turned into rapid, small prototypes to test and get feedback. By testing different solutions at a small scale, you can reject those that don't work and learn about and then develop the ones that will.

CASE STUDY

EX design in action

How InVision redesigned its onboarding programme

InVision is the leading product design and development platform for teams building world-class digital products. In addition to a rapidly growing team, InVision is also 100 per cent remote and globally distributed – there are no headquarters and no offices. Manager of employee experience design Marie Kretlow describes how she and her colleague, Dennis Field, took a design-led approach to design a new onboarding programme at InVision.

InVision is unique in both culture and how it operates. Our employee onboarding should reflect that. We believe in crafting employee onboarding with intention and maintaining it with care. As such, onboarding is an experience that requires design – design as a practice of solving problems by deeply understanding our users, building solutions to meet their needs, and testing and iterating those solutions until we get it right.

Discover the problem/opportunity

Our first step in redesigning the onboarding process was to discover who our audience was and fulfil one of the cardinal rules of design – having empathy for our users. We did this by bringing stakeholders together to map out the current onboarding experience, from a new hire signing their offer letter, all the way through their first 30 days in role. This service blueprint of new-hire actions, support team actions, and our onboarding process and tools revealed gaps in the new-hire experience. To add depth to our understanding, we added real-world context to the map with direct feedback from our employees through surveys and one-to-one interviews. To better understand the information we collected, we sorted it into major themes. We then overlaid those aggregate themes right onto the service blueprint to demonstrate what new hires were thinking and feeling.

Define the problem/opportunity

Now that we had knowledge of the current-state end-to-end onboarding landscape and our users' individual needs and experiences, we were able to frame up the greatest problems that needed to be solved. We did this by analysing the end-to-end map of the experience to highlight strengths, weaknesses and opportunities, and framed these as user stories:

1   As a new hire, I want to learn the company culture so that I understand where and how I fit in our remote community.

2   As a new hire, I want clearly defined expectations so that I know what's most important for me to do today, next week and beyond.

3   As a new hire, I want my onboarding experience to be handled with care so that I feel valued and prepared for my role.

4   As a new hire, I want to easily get started so that I can focus on my new team and role, rather than system and tool issues.

Once our problem set was well defined and the opportunities within that were recognized, we began exploring what this programme could be. We went on a journey to define our north star and illustrated the ultimate vision for onboarding through storytelling. With this being the first company-wide onboarding programme at InVision, we wanted to define the vision to ensure that both our immediate team, as well as our leadership team, understood the direction we were headed with the programme. To support and evangelize that vision, we outlined a specific mission statement, our design principles, brand concept and key elements of the experience. We weaved all of this together through a story of onboarding told through the eyes of a new hire. Together, this is what made up our company-wide onboarding 'pitch deck' to sell the vision to the wider team.

Develop ideas

Our opportunities, design principles, and mission also served as our anchor and outline through rounds of ideation and concepting. As we're a fully remote team, we leveraged our own digital whiteboard tool, Freehand, to synchronously brainstorm 'how might we...' for each user story we identified. We also spent time individually ideating and providing feedback asynchronously with the commenting feature in tools like Google Docs and InVision as we explored ways the onboarding programme could emulate our company focus on 'people, practices and platform'. After much debate and scrutiny, we were able to whittle our solution down into a single, testable minimum viable product (MVP) – or MLP, most lovable product, as we like to call it. We synthesized our ideas down by evaluating what was absolutely essential to the foundation of the programme (tools, format, content, etc) through the lens of user impact, business necessity, and feasibility of our team being able to quickly build out the programme.

Develop a solution – overview of the MVP

- Tools – for our MVP, we chose to use tools that new hires were already using (like our pre-boarding tool) and tools that they would need to use throughout their journey as employees (like video-conferencing, instant messaging and our learning management system).

- Format – the day-one experience is critical for any company, but particularly so for fully remote organizations. We designed a five-day programme for a new hire's first week that included daily live, facilitated sessions of our core content, plus ongoing 'homework' of onboarding tasks, like security training and benefits enrolment, that was tiered out over 30 days. Our goal was to run the programme every other week to best align to new-hire start dates.

- Content – our framework for the core onboarding content was focused on people, product and practices. The goal was to create a safe space for new hires to learn, connect with one another and their teams, and get them set up for success at the company.

Test a solution

With a defined scope and shortlist of things we wanted to learn, we built a prototype of the MVP programme and launched our first pilot test to a small group of employees in our customer-facing department. To learn what was working well and what could be improved, we asked our pilot group to give us daily feedback in the form of a survey, as well as feedback at the end of the week and 30 days in role. We learned that the core components of the onboarding process were a success, with room to refine our content delivery and live class engagement.

Iterate the solution

Since our pilot test in 2018, we've made countless improvements, both big and small, and remotely onboarded hundreds of new InVisioners. They consistently exit onboarding feeling highly knowledgeable, engaged and connected to our InVision community. We're currently on our third major version of the programme, refined through feedback, and it's proving to be the best yet.

The solution – our latest and greatest onboarding programme

We now run our week-long onboarding programme once a month. It gives new hires a solid foundation of knowledge about the company culture, community, remote life and, of course, design. And while we believe that the information we share is important for all employees to know, there is one thing that trumps it – their sense of belonging.

To that end, our onboarding class is hosted in a way that feels real to 'InVision life', where new hires are welcomed as whole human beings and are invited to break through the screen as their most authentic selves. Our greatest hope is that by the end of the week, new hires feel connected, engaged and confident to take on their role. There are a few fundamental pieces of this programme design that define the experience:

- Flip the script: Instead of presenting content in a traditional lecture format, we ask our new hires to learn about the next day's content ahead of time and show up to class prepared to discuss. Bonus – at the end of the week, each small group reflects on their biggest takeaways and presents a 'show and tell' to the greater class. We have been blown away by the creative and thoughtful presentations we've seen thus far.

- Real-time co-creation: Class discussions are facilitated through Zoom, a video-conferencing tool, and Freehand, one of InVision's own products that acts as an infinite whiteboard. We set a goal and outline for each day, but let the conversations lead us where we need to go. Everyone writes, draws and doodles together – each class's Freehand is unique.

- Small group discussion: We intentionally assign small groups to be cross-departmental. By creating a smaller, more intimate space free of onboarding hosts/facilitators, new hires can have open and honest conversations and build bonds that will last throughout their time as InVisioners.

- All-in attitude: To get the most out of the programme and really tune into InVision's culture, we ask that new hires show up and do the following:

  1 Be bold – throw out your questions and 'bad ideas'. They're never as bad as you think.

  2 Say 'Yes, and...' – collaborate. Build on each other's ideas. Help create the community you want to be a part of.

  3 Lean in – commit! The more you put into the week, the more you will get out of it.

About the process

Without truly and intentionally designing our new-hire experience, by first deeply understanding who we are serving, we would not have been able to create a programme like the one we have. This onboarding programme was our first venture in leveraging design to craft people programmes, and we have used it as an example in much of our work since then. We'll continue to listen to our customers, iterate to meet their needs and do what's right for the business as we grow and scale. Good design is never done – right now, we are yet again reviewing the end-to-end candidate and new-hire journey to look for ways to level up and create an even more delightful and seamless experience.

   Find out more about the activities and tools InVision used:

Journey mapping – Chapters 6 and 7

Interviewing – Chapter 7

Insight and user stories – Chapter 7

'How might we...' questions – Chapter 7

Misconceptions about the EX design framework

It's a linear process

On paper, the three diamonds suggest a neat, linear process. In reality, it's much more flexible than that. EX design is a creative, practical suite of activities that draw on the principles of curiosity, empathy and experimentation – but not necessarily in the order you'd expect. For example, when you're creating a new solution, it is possible to understand something new about the problem at the prototyping phase that can send you back to the beginning to start all over again. It's equally possible to create a basic prototype to explore people's needs and behaviours when you're scoping a possible programme of work and need to generate insight to validate the programme. The activities don't need to be sequential and they can be repeated. Think about the diamonds as different thinking modes, rather than consecutive steps. The key is to be clear what mode you are in and why. Keep your experimentation mindset in play and remember this is an iterative process – you might go through several loops before landing on a solution.

It's all about design sprints

While multi-day design sprints – everyone in a room together (or, increasingly, a virtual space) for consecutive days to rapidly work through the design process – may be a commonly understood picture of how designers comes up with solutions, in our experience they're not that common in EX. That's not to say things can't move fast – they can and do. However, for an EX design team – especially one just starting out – getting the commitment from a diverse team of collaborators to invest a number of days can be tricky. So while some teams get together and crack through a design challenge in this way, in reality, activities are more likely to be spread out over a number of weeks or even months.

Everyone needs to be in the same room

There's a lot to be said for a design team working together side by side to create a shared view of the problem and then find solutions. It creates a lot of energy and alignment. But it's not always essential or possible. In fact, for some people you may want to involve, it might even be preferable to collaborate remotely. For example, remote interviews can allow a much broader range of input. And working virtually as a design team through the solution space can be liberating for more introverted personalities, who might find face-to-face brainstorming approaches don't enable their best thinking.

We need an EX team to get started

You don't. In fact, you can start incorporating EX design tools into your work right away. It's surprising how quickly asking a different set of questions can start to change a conversation and approach. The tools we share in the following chapters are a practical and easy way to start experimenting on a project, or even just to shake up meetings or workshops. They are flexible and creative. Apply them in ways that make most sense to you and your team.

We can stand in for our people

There's a reason empathy-based discovery activities are there, however fuzzy and personal they can feel to teams used to working solely with the supposedly more rational inputs of survey data or requirements documents. Empathy is all about connection. You can't connect deeply to people by proxy. However well you know your employees, there will always be new things to be discovered and undetected needs to surface. Whatever role you are in, you too are of course an employee. But that doesn't mean your needs are the same as everyone else's. You cannot stand in for them; you need to stand with them. Making the case to involve employees can be an uphill battle. But it's worth winning.

It's all about brainstorming

Ideation, where you get to generate lots of ideas, is fun, but don't rush here. Einstein is supposed to have said: 'If I had an hour to solve a problem, I'd spend 55 minutes thinking about the problem and five minutes thinking about solutions.' Make this your mantra. Only by truly exploring the problem or opportunity through the eyes of your people can you hope to find solutions. Meaningfully solving problems relies on divergent thinking, not racing to the finish line or converging too quickly on a single solution.

Getting started with EX design

EX design tools and activities flex to adapt to local conditions and take advantage of local intelligence. However, they can and often do challenge established ways of doing things. For many teams and organizations, the move to designing with as well as for employees, for moving fast and always being in beta, is a significant change. As a result, EX design can feel strange and different – especially where there is no culture of design in the organization. Introducing an EX design approach can be a lot easier in a software company used to working in agile, iterative ways, for example, than in a more top–down organization, such as an investment bank or law firm, that values more traditional, analytical approaches. Where EX design is successfully embedded, it is often a complementary discipline to other established approaches, such as lean, agile, even behavioural economics and more. And it is well suited to such combinations. How you start to embed an EX design approach will look different in every organization depending on size, design orientation and these cultural and business factors. But there are some common features.

Start small

In most instances, the best way to start is to start small. For a new head of EX in a global bank, it was about mapping one journey in one market and working on that. For a large US software company, a pilot EX programme run by one HR pioneer tackled 15 small and varied projects in its first year. Elsewhere, it is simply introducing personas and journey maps – sometimes with learning borrowed from a customer experience team – to change the focus in meetings and planning sessions. Such was the route taken by one UK pub company and a UK health authority. For another lone champion, it was simply spending time with employees and asking lots of questions to explore their experience and then sharing those insights with the team to challenge established thinking.

Find a low-risk project

A bolder step is to take on a small project. In her blog, Sarah Corney (2020), head of digital experience at the Chartered Institute of Personnel and Development, suggests 'Trojan mice' projects – small, low-risk initiatives that operate under the radar to test out new ideas and experiments. She suggests gradually leveraging small wins to make a case for more radical change. One EX lead in a global oil company suggests a group of just six to eight people – a mix of end users and stakeholders – can often get to 80 per cent of an EX solution really quickly.

Find sponsors and allies

When it comes to scaling the approach, securing sponsorship and bringing stakeholders on board from across the business is critical. Design thinking has a reputation for layering on the buzzwords, which puts people off. Even the word 'design' can be problematic, so use what works. One EX design lead talks about being in the 'problem definition business' rather than EX design. Jason Cyr (2019), director of design transformation at Cisco, says the first job of any evangelist is to create more. He recommends championing the principles, rather than the process, and being thoughtful about who you bring into the conversation. Put another way: use empathy to understand and work with your stakeholders, allies and collaborators.

Frame it in the familiar

EX can be hard to get your head around due to the potential size of the task. Chuck in a new method and things can quickly start to feel alien to would-be collaborators. One way to help the conversation is to frame it in the context of what people already know. If you have a strong customer experience culture, start every conversation about EX with a reference to something that person will be familiar with, eg journeys, touchpoints, etc. One music industry EX pioneer found they made a lot more headway when they could spell out the parallels between EX and talent experience. It's all human experience at the end of the day.

Believe in the process

If this all sounds like hard work, don't be put off. Developing an EX design capability, no matter how nascent, will always pay dividends. However, sometimes the impact is not where you expect. The effective use of design thinking tools can lead to a great EX solution. But it also has an effect on organizational culture, spreading, according to one global head of L&D, like a virus. So rather than people waiting to see this sort of human-centred change coming their way, you will find pioneers starting to be the change they want to see. Design thinking is a form of change management that people want to be part of. Sometimes the process is just as important, if not more important, than the product.

EX DESIGN
Pathways to maturity

EX design capability is developed and scaled in different ways depending on the context of the organization. However, there are a few common stages that we often see. We have described these below, with some tips for developing the approach at each stage.

Experimenting

Individuals and teams are experimenting with EX design tools.

Evidence:

- EX is becoming a talking point.
- EX design tools appear in a limited fashion in offsites and workshops.
- There are exploratory discussions with customer experience teams.

How to develop the approach:

- Use data-driven insights around an element of EX to open new conversations and thinking.
- Model and talk about the principles of empathy, curiosity and experimentation.

Equipping

EX design tools are regularly used across people projects.

Evidence:

- Design tools are used frequently, with data and insight helping to develop understanding of different journeys.
- User research and testing starts to become a regular way of working.
- Collaboration between functions, eg HR, IT and facilities, becomes more frequent with a focus on solving obvious problems.

How to develop the approach:

- Build design thinking capability by investing in training.
- Bring in external help and support, such as facilitators.
- Plug user research and testing into more activities.

Delivering

EX design methodology is consistently used in people projects.

Evidence:

- There is investment in new EX teams, roles and capability.
- Agile, cross-functional teams regularly work together to find EX solutions.

- The impact of newly designed and iterated solutions is routinely measured and reported.

How to develop the approach:

- Recognize and celebrate the impact of design initiatives.

- Create a design thinking centre of excellence and recruit and equip a network of design thinkers to more widely champion new ways of working.

Scaling

There is a clearly articulated EX vision and constant innovation to deliver on it.

Evidence:

- The focus of EX design moves beyond what are traditionally considered HR products and services.

- Design capability is embedded across many teams.

- Many people and functions are involved in the EX design process.

- Design thinking is a core L&D focus across the business.

How to develop the approach:

- Rigorously document and review successes, especially where EX design has helped strengthen the company brand.

Takeaways

Employee experience design is the application of design principles, first, to how we understand people and their needs and expectations, and then to how we develop, test and iterate solutions to make the experience the best it can be. In this chapter we introduced the EX design framework and explained how to get started with EX design. In summary:

- What best looks like is a balance between competing and shifting demands – organizational context, requirements of the work, and what people need and expect.

- EX design borrows tools and activities from design thinking, a form of human-centred design.

- Design thinking allows us to understand the complexity of the system in which EX occurs, but it also provides easy ways to get started.

- EX design has three principles borrowed from design thinking: empathy, curiosity and experimentation.

- The relationship between EX design and organizational culture is two-way – each impacting the other. A culture rich in empathy, curiosity and experimentation will support an EX design approach. And by adopting an EX design approach, the people involved and broader culture will become more empathic, curious and experimental.

- EX design happens in three spaces – scoping space, opportunity space and solution space. Different activities produce outcomes that feed into the next activity, eventually creating solutions.

- Organizations get started with EX design in different ways and for different reasons. It often goes hand in hand with another transformation, often an agile transformation.

- Without (even with) sponsorship, pioneering EX design activities can meet resistance as they challenge the status quo to look for new data points and new possibilities. This can feel very different and uncomfortable. Starting small and securing quick wins can help.

References

Bridger, E (2015) *Employee Engagement*, Kogan Page, London

Brown, T (2009/2019) *Change by Design, Revised and Updated: How design thinking transforms organizations and inspires innovation*, HarperCollins, New York

Buchanan, R (1992) [accessed 8 August 2020] Wicked problems in design thinking, *Design Issues* [Online] https://web.mit.edu/jrankin/www/engin_as_lib_art/Design_thinking.pdf (archived at https://perma.cc/FHT8-GDU6)

Cheuk, B and Dervin, B (2011) Leadership 2.0 in action: A journey from knowledge management to 'knowledging', *Knowledge Management & E-Learning: An International Journal*, 3 (2), p 119

Corney, S (2020) [accessed 18 July 2020] Transformation by stealth: Trojan mice and design thinking [Blog], *CXNoodlings*, 21 February [Online] https://cxnoodlings.wordpress.com/2020/02/21/transformation-by-stealth-trojan-mice-and-design-thinking/ (archived at https://perma.cc/RFA6-HUKS)

Cyr, J (2019) [accessed 14 June 2020] Designing the organizational conversation, *The Conversation Factory Podcast* [Online] https://theconversationfactory.com/podcast/2019/11/15/designing-the-organizational-conversation (archived at https://perma.cc/Z36T-VHP4)

Deloitte (2015) [accessed 6 June 2020] Global human capital trends 2015: Leading in the new world of work [Online] https://www2.deloitte.com/content/dam/Deloitte/au/Documents/human-capital/deloitte-au-hc-global-human-capital-trends-2015-301115.pdf (archived at https://perma.cc/M7KD-XQQD)

Deloitte (2016) [accessed 6 June 2020] Global human capital trends [Online] https://www2.deloitte.com/us/en/insights/focus/human-capital-trends/2016.html (archived at https://perma.cc/J3DM-ZMT2)

Gino, F (2018) [accessed 18 July 2020] The business case for curiosity, *Harvard Business Review*, September–October [Online] https://hbr.org/2018/09/curiosity (archived at https://perma.cc/28TN-CA7W)

Kennedy Fitch and EX Leaders Network (2020) [accessed 18 July 2020] Employee experience 2020 global report and case studies [Online] https://www.exleadersnetwork.com/wp-content/uploads/2019/12/EX-2020-Report-by-EX-Leaders-Network.pdf (archived at https://perma.cc/5WY2-MNCD)

Liedtka, J (2020) [accessed 18 July 2020] Maximising the ROI of design thinking, *Mural Imagine Talks*, 28 May [Online] https://www.mural.co/imagine/talks (archived at https://perma.cc/QJ73-ZL8U)

Plaskoff, J (2017) [accessed 18 July 2020] Employee experience: The new human resource management approach, *Strategic HR Review* [Online] https://www.deepdyve.com/lp/emerald-publishing/employee-experience-the-new-human-resource-management-approach-eeg6sXKuBA (archived at https://perma.cc/B6J4-UWEQ)

Thorén, P (2017) *Agile People: A radical approach for HR and managers (that leads to motivated employees)*, Lioncrest Publishing

06

Scoping the employee experience

In this chapter we'll cover:

- what we mean by scoping the employee experience and how it fits with the EX vision and goals activities in Chapter 2;
- tools and activities to explore the gap between your intended EX and your people's lived experience;
- EX design tools and activities to help you define where to prioritize to start to address the gap, including personas, the employee life spiral, journey maps and moments that matter.

What do we mean by scoping the employee experience?

Employee experience can feel huge. If it doesn't start off like that, by the time you've begun to explore the levels of experience (see Figure 1.3), it soon will. And that quickly gets overwhelming. This tends to send EX teams down two paths. They try to do too much or, at the other end, they get to work on a project level but then find it hard to connect with the big picture and fail to scale the approach. This conundrum is the reason we've introduced a third diamond into the EX design framework at the beginning. While design thinking encourages practitioners to begin by exploring the demands of user desirability, commercial viability and technical feasibility, we wanted to be really explicit about what's happening here. So here, in the scoping space, it's about working at the big picture or strategy level to discover and define a vision of what you're aiming for with your EX. And then discover and define where to prioritize. This will ensure you are working on the things that matter and will give you the wins you need to scale the approach.

In Chapter 2 we looked at how to define your EX vision and align EX objectives to your strategic business priorities. In Chapter 3 we looked at using appreciative inquiry to create this vision of the future and find the gaps between where you are now and where you want to be. Now we've introduced you to the EX design framework (Figure 5.1), we can be more explicit about saying these activities all sit in the first diamond.

In this chapter we now build on the tools and activities introduced in Chapters 2 and 3 and suggest ways to help you discover more about the employee experience you are delivering and the gap between this and your intended EX. We also introduce a range of EX design tools and activities to help you define where to prioritize to start to address the gap. This is about taking a strategic approach to EX. However, in advocating a strategic approach, we don't want to raise the bar and prevent you just getting started. It's possible to start an EX journey in other places, not just with strategy. So even if you're not responsible for developing your EX strategy, do give this chapter a read as the tools we introduce here are core to the whole EX design approach – developing strategy *and* developing specific EX solutions. We'll talk about the tools some more in the following chapters, where we look in more detail at developing EX solutions.

Why take a strategic approach to EX design?

Everyone we speak to is at a different stage with their EX design maturity. Some organizations have whole teams (albeit small); for others, there's a lone champion on the fringes of a people team. We've written this book to offer flexible and practical help no matter where you are on that journey. And wherever that is, it's worth taking a big picture or strategic perspective. Why?

- Ensure strategic alignment – it is easy to find opportunities to improve experience. However, unless they are aligned to organizational goals, they might fail to make a meaningful contribution to the business. This lack of strategic alignment can create brilliant orphans – amazing solutions that never go anywhere because no one wants to own them.

- Create an impact – the best way to scale an EX approach is to create wins. If you don't deliver something, the theatre of the approach – the Post-It notes, language and fun whiteboard sessions (whether that's in the room or on a virtual platform) – will generate expectations that fail to deliver. As a result, you will create detractors when what you need is collaborators.

Discovering the gap between your intended and lived experience

So, you've defined your EX vision (see Chapter 2) and you know why and how it aligns to your strategic objectives. But how does your experience measure up? One way to explore this is through the three EX lenses. In Figure 6.1 we suggest some elements of your people's experience you might want to explore – from the work they do and how they do it; to the culture and values of the organization; to their relationships with leaders, teammates, partners and customers. These examples are not meant to be prescriptive, but to bring to life the different elements of EX and where and how you might begin to discover your people's lived experience. Use these lenses as a starting point and add the elements that are most relevant for your people, the business and the work.

FIGURE 6.1 Three EX design lenses with examples

Core EX design tools

In the rest of the chapter we introduce a set of core EX design tools you can use to discover more about people's experience and define where to prioritize your focus. These aren't the only tools in the EX design toolkit (we'll introduce more in subsequent chapters), but they are the most widely used, so it's important to get to know them so you can use them across the whole of the EX design approach.

Personas

Personas (see Figure 6.2) are fictional characters representing a group of employees. A key design tool, they consolidate quantitative and qualitative data to create better understanding of the needs, experiences, behaviours and goals of employees. Personas can be used by anyone involved in the EX design process to see things from the perspective of employees. They are used continuously and in multiple ways across the design process, ensuring a multi-dimensional

FIGURE 6.2 Personas

'NO WAFFLE WILL'

'I JUST WANNA KEEP MY HEAD DOWN, HAVE AN EASY LIFE AND COLLECT MY PAY CHEQUE AT THE END OF EACH MONTH'

WHERE DO THEY WORK?	MANAGER OR NON-MANAGER	ACCESSIBILITY	TOP CHANNELS
FACTORY		OFFLINE	FAVOURITES ARE: • 1-2-1s • FACE TO FACE

A BIT ABOUT 'NO WAFFLE WILL'...

WILL'S BEEN HERE FOR FIVE YEARS. HE'S HAPPY IN HIS JOB AND GETS ON WELL WITH HIS TEAM AND MANAGER. HE'S RECOMMENDED OTHER PEOPLE TO JOIN THE COMPANY BECAUSE HE SAYS IT'S A GOOD PLACE TO WORK, IT FITS IN WITH HIS FAMILY LIFE AND WE LOOK AFTER HIM.

GOALS

WILL ISN'T LOOKING TO PROGRESS. HE'S HAPPY IN HIS JOB, HE'S GOOD AT IT AND FEELS VALUED BY COLLEAGUES. HIS MAIN GOAL IS TO DO THE JOB WELL. HE IS MOTIVATED BY KNOWING IT'S A JOB WELL DONE.

CHALLENGES

WILL IS WORRIED ABOUT HIS FUTURE AS HE'S HEARD STORIES ABOUT TAKEOVERS AND CLOSURES.

CONSIDERATIONS

WILL NEEDS TO KNOW THE ESSENTIALS. HE DOESN'T ACTIVELY SEEK INFORMATION SO MANAGERS AND PEERS ARE THE MOST EFFECTIVE WAY TO GET MESSAGES ACROSS.

SKILLS

WILL HAS A LOT OF KNOWLEDGE AND UNDERSTANDING OF HOW THINGS WORK. HE'S A GREAT PERSON TO SUPPORT NEW STARTERS.

approach to any task. Personas are also used increasingly in a range of related activities. For example, a transformation team in a large financial services organization used personas to explore and plan for the human impact of a large-scale platform migration. As well as helping to create a more human-centred approach to the change programme, the personas were also a powerful way to help the executive team understand and prioritize the human experience.

Creating personas is a common first step in building EX design capability. And they can be a great place to borrow some expertise from a customer experience or marketing team. However, when starting out, don't over-complicate things. Think of personas as a thinking tool, a way to support your human-centred design approach. Unless you have a team of data analysts on hand or a lot of time to do a lot of deep interviewing, they are unlikely to be as scientifically robust as those found in CX or marketing. We like to approach persona development in stages. You might start off representing roles, tenure, level, etc, before using interviews to add more attitudinal and behavioural aspects. The key is to keep your personas alive and keep revisiting them. And, where possible, if there are multiple sets – internal communications, L&D and HR may all end up with different personas – try to rationalize rather than ending up with an unwieldy number. Creating a single set of high-level personas and enabling local teams and functions to build on the personas with additional details to support their own projects allows flexibility and helps to keep personas up to date. At the same time, they stay relevant to the work in hand.

HOW TO USE PERSONAS

While scoping your EX, you can use personas in a variety of ways, including:

- Discover more depth of insight about the employee experience when using any of the tools in this chapter.
- Define priority personas in line with a specific business need, such as a talent shortage or high levels of attrition. That's not to suggest one group of employees is more important than another, rather that starting with a persona that is relevant to a key business priority will help to gain collaborators and demonstrate the value of the EX design approach.

Employee life spiral

The employee life spiral (see Figure 4.1) is a thinking and conversation tool. The spiral represents the overarching employee experience, from excitement before joining, to leaving and becoming an alumnus. The difference between the spiral and the classic linear employee life-cycle with which you may be more familiar is that the spiral makes the employee and their experience the focal point – rather than the focus being the prescribed stages executed by the employer, eg recruit-ment, onboarding, etc. It's a small, but significant shift that really changes how people think and talk about employee experience. But the benefits don't stop there.

Because the spiral is not linear, it also gives more focus to often overlooked areas of employee experience, including ones with signif-icant strategic impact, such as internal mobility and people rejoining the organization. In doing so, it encourages us to think of careers as cobwebs, rather than one-way ladders, which, again, opens up a different dialogue and more innovative ways of addressing EX.

HOW TO USE THE LIFE SPIRAL

The spiral can be used in a number of ways. We use it as a conversa-tion tool to subtly introduce the empathy principle that is so critical to a human-centred approach. While scoping your EX, use the spiral to:

- Make a shift away from lifecycle thinking in meetings and work-shops to put the emphasis on the employee experience.
- Introduce employee experience to stakeholders for the first time.
- Discover data and insight gaps by exploring what is and isn't already known about different parts of the employee experience.
- Take a holistic view of the whole experience to discuss and prioritize problem areas (see activity below).

EXERCISE
Employee life spiral SWOT

What this is: This is an activity combining a SWOT analysis (strengths, weaknesses, opportunities and threats) with the life spiral to prioritize EX focus areas and/or define an EX strategy or plan.

Why use it: Using a SWOT analysis alongside the life spiral will help you define your priorities based on the needs of the business, the work and your people.

How to use it: Circulate and review relevant data (engagement surveys, HR data, etc) in advance to provide context. Run the session as a workshop – with plenty of Post-It notes.

Who to use it with: We recommend running this activity with your people team, plus stakeholders from the business.

Background: When creating a plan of action for EX, you need to do more than simply discover areas where your EX is failing to deliver – or where there's an opportunity to do something better. You need a way to prioritize.

Facilitator instructions

- Explain the objectives of the session (to prioritize the EX plan) and why you are using the spiral (to ensure the focus is on the employee experience rather than HR activity and to make non-linear journeys more visible).

- Explain the EX vision (if you have one) or frame the EX opportunity in some way, ie why is EX important to your organization?

- Kick off with an open discussion to get people talking and ensure they understand the process. Start by asking: 'What are our EX strengths – what are we known for doing well (both inside the business and externally)?' The latter might include candidate feedback, industry comment and Glassdoor reviews.

- Collect all the ideas – one on each Post-It – and then start to add them to the spiral, explaining what you're doing (use a printout or a representation of the spiral on the whiteboard). Use green Post-It notes to distinguish them from the next part of the activity. If weaknesses, opportunities or threats come up – park them for now. If a key part of the employee experience isn't represented on the spiral, add it in.

- Now look at weaknesses. Ask the group to write on red Post-It notes responses to the questions: 'Where are we failing to deliver?' 'What are we known for doing badly?' One thought per Post-It note. Add them to the spiral.

- Now the discussion looks at why this matters. As a group (or you could do this in pairs or small groups), work your way around the spiral. As you go, ask the group to explore the opportunity for improving or amplifying an experience. Why is it important to our people, the organization or the work? Then ask them to consider the threat. 'What is the risk if we don't improve this experience – to our people, the organization or the work?' Capture the key points on a new colour of Post-It note and add to the spiral as a record.

- As a result of the discussion around each area, agree as a group the priority level:
  ○ Now – this is a priority to work on immediately.
  ○ Near – this is a priority to work on next.
  ○ Far – we need to keep a watching eye, but not prioritize this for now.
- Revisit the rankings at the end to ensure you have a spread across the three priority levels. To prevent everything being a 'now' priority, agree in advance how many areas of EX will go in each band.
- To conclude, check in with the group for alignment and agree next steps.

Journey maps

Journey maps are a visual representation of an experience from the point of view of an individual or group. They are one of the most widely used EX design tools, deployed to visualize, analyse and then improve the employee experience. Journey maps can be used to capture or identify:

- steps taken – the things employees do either inside or outside of the organization in pursuit of a particular goal;
- touchpoints – interactions employees have with the organization, including its tools, systems and people;
- pain points – steps or touchpoints that don't work and have a detrimental impact;
- moments that matter – emotionally charged moments in the journey that have a disproportionate impact on the experience (see below).

Journey mapping typically starts with identifying the steps someone goes through, then looking at each step from different angles – for example, what is someone thinking, feeling and doing at each step? This might draw on quantitative data from surveys, qualitative data from observation, participation (ie going through the process yourself), interviews, or group discussions. The result is a picture of an experience represented on a map. This can be visualized in different ways, from simple lines and text to infographics and even an artistic style.

TYPES OF JOURNEY MAP

It is possible to map the overarching employee experience, or any number of shorter journeys, such as returning to the workplace after parental leave or becoming a first-time manager. Mapping the onboarding journey is a popular starting point for new EX teams because it offers a lot of potential for quick wins. It has also become a priority during the COVID-19 crisis as more organizations seek to learn how to welcome new joiners into entirely virtual workspaces. Because onboarding is owned by a range of people and teams, it is a good place to start breaking down silos and introducing an EX approach to multiple teams at the same time. The act of getting a group of people together to build or reflect on a journey map can have a big impact, helping to switch from a process (business-centred) to an experience (people-centred) mindset.

The list of EX journeys is long. To make it more manageable, more established EX design teams categorize and then prioritize journeys. For global organizations, the initial focus is often on one market, with solutions developed and then scaled to others.

We categorize journeys in the following way (see Figure 6.3):

1 Join: Journeys related to joining the organization.

2 Work: Journeys related to an employee's current role and responsibilities.

3 Live: Journeys related to personal life events, employee and family wellbeing.

4 Grow: Journeys related to an employee's learning and development.

5 Leave: Journeys related to leaving.

6 Sustain: Journeys related to the alumni experience.

7 Rejoin: Journeys related to rejoining the organization (including after leaving or a period of absence such as parental leave).

FIGURE 6.3 Journey map categories

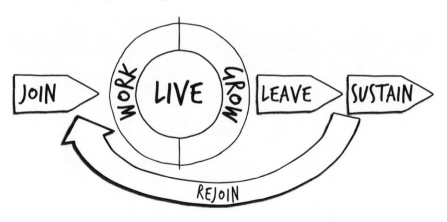

HOW TO USE JOURNEY MAPS

Journey maps can be used in multiple ways across EX design. While scoping your EX, use journey maps to:

- Collate and visualize insight about a journey for one or more personas to identify peak points (where you're delivering) and pain points (where you're not) and prioritize where you will focus activities.

- Compare the journeys of different personas, geographies or business units to discover inconsistencies in the experience you're delivering and then amplify peaks and address pain points.

- Visualize the 'as is' *and* the 'to be' experience – as suggested by your vision, EVP, or similar – across a journey to highlight and scope EX projects.

EXERCISE

A journey mapping workshop with employees

What this is: A journey mapping workshop to run with employees. In Figure 6.4 we've illustrated a journey map focusing on the new joiner experience, but the same approach can be taken with any journey.

FIGURE 6.4 Journey mapping activity

	LOOKING	APPLYING	INTERVIEWING	ACCEPTING	WAITING	STARTING
THINKING	☐	☐	☐	☐	☐	☐
FEELING	▦		▦		▦	▦
DOING	◼	◼	◼	◼		◼
GOALS	FIND OUT WHAT'S OUT THERE	QUICKLY HAVE A GO	LEARN ABOUT THE BUSINESS	LEARN AS MUCH AS POSSIBLE ABOUT WHAT'S NEXT	KNOW I'VE MADE THE RIGHT DECISION	FIT IN, FIND MY PLACE, DON'T MESS UP
EXPERIENCE	😐	😐	🙂	🙂	😕	😕

Why use it: This activity will shed light on the experience of a journey from the employee's perspective. This insight will help you prioritize where to focus to improve the experience.

How to use it: Be clear in advance that this is a judgement-free zone. Be sure that your employees are comfortable in the process. Brief your people team and stakeholders to only ask questions and prompt, not justify, challenge or explain.

Who to use it with: Mapping the journey with a relevant group of employees together with a people team and stakeholders will create not just insight, but energy and buy-in across the group. You will want to involve four to five employees (or more) to gain a breadth of input.

Background: It's possible to map almost any people process, and journey maps are a simple way to inject a bit of human-centred design thinking into any project. They are revealing and energizing and often help to generate commitment to a project among a mixed group of stakeholders.

Facilitator instructions

- Set your room up in advance. Ideally you want a space with at least one wall where you can add a 'swim lane' style journey map (see Figure 6.4). This can be done with Post-It notes and masking tape. At the top you may choose to label specific areas of the journey to help get the team started. But be clear, these are just suggestions that can be changed as you work through the process. The 5Es are a helpful guide for thinking about how to break down and label a journey; use them as a prompt for yourself or as you facilitate the team process:
    - Entice – How are people drawn in? What's the trigger?
    - Enter – What is the threshold event that brings them into the experience?
    - Engage – What are people doing during the experience?
    - Exit – What is the end of this journey?
    - Extend – What happens next?
- Run an ice-breaker activity to help people get to know each other and relax.

- Brief the group about the task and why you're doing it.

- Remind the group of the different roles in the room. The employees are there to share their experience. The people team and other stakeholders are there to ask questions and prompt the exploration. If they have relevant experiences to share, that's fine, but they should not lead, justify or challenge.

- Walk the group through the map in the first instance, perhaps telling your own or someone else's story to bring it to life.

- Then begin the process by asking the employees in the group to share their goals at the first stage of the journey – what were they trying to achieve and why? Capture this on Post-It notes and add to the map.

- Then ask them what they were thinking, feeling and doing at the first stage. This may include things outside of the organization, such as talking to family and friends, reviewing Glassdoor, etc. Write thoughts, feelings and actions on different colour Post-It notes and add to the map.

- Don't rush, and keep asking 'what else?' and 'why?'

- When you've finished exploring each step, ask them to recall how they felt at the end of that step. Add a smiley, neutral or sad emoji. If you have a group, rather than an individual, you might want to ask them each to choose an emoji silently and individually before adding it to the map to avoid group think and build a more complete picture. If there is a range of results, explore that – what worked for some people, but not for others?

- Repeat this process for each step.

- At the end, ask a group member (not one of the representative employee group) to walk through the map, telling the story as they go to ensure they've understood what has been shared. Check with the employee representatives if they've got it right and if anything is missing.

- Depending on how far you want to take this activity, you could choose to work with the same group to identify the most critical pain points to solve by asking people to vote using stickers in response to the question: 'Which part of the experience would you change to create the biggest impact?'

HOW IT WORKS ONLINE
Running a virtual journey mapping session

Journey mapping can be done virtually using a range of inexpensive tools and online whiteboarding platforms. To manage this, have a smaller number of participants in the group and repeat three times to ensure you have a valid picture of the experience, not just the story of one person's experience.

Moments that matter

Moments that matter aren't really a design tool, rather they are a way of flagging critical points in a journey – highly emotionally charged moments with a disproportionate impact on experience and engagement, either positive or negative. Moments that matter are often discovered during the journey mapping process and may include:

- specific moments – such as a first day at work, or meeting a team for the first time;
- ongoing moments – such as regular check-ins with a manager;
- created moments – such as an awards event;
- broken moments – everyday or routine moments (such as looking for information on an HR topic, accessing IT equipment or submitting 360 feedback) that escalate into something more significant if the experience is not frictionless.

New moments that matter have emerged as a result of the COVID-19 pandemic and existing ones need to be revisited. For example, becoming a manager for the first time feels very different when you don't see your team face to face. And returning to work after parental leave is a different experience when the office no longer exists, or you have to travel to work in a face mask and the coffee areas are closed.

HOW TO PRIORITIZE MOMENTS THAT MATTER

Prioritizing moments that matter is a useful way to break the EX design task into something more manageable. There are different ways to do this. You may choose to vote during the journey mapping stage or use a card sort exercise, with groups of employees ranking in order which moments have the biggest impact on their experience and where they think the business should focus.

Alternatively, when a number of moments that matter are failing to deliver the experience, we use a simple two-by-two grid made up of two axes to help the team identify quick wins. To do this, simply add two axes to a whiteboard – one vertical, one horizontal. Label one 'high impact' / 'low impact' and the other 'easy to solve' / 'hard to solve'. Then get the team to plot the moments according to two statements:

- If we solve this, it will have a high/low impact on our target persona (or entire employee population).
- It will be easy/complex to solve this problem.

Important quick wins will be in the easy-to-solve/high-impact box. Give special attention to the hard-to-solve/high-impact box and choose the key ones to focus on.

Another way to prioritize moments that matter is to select some criteria and give each a mark out of 10. We have listed some potential criteria you may wish to include:

- People have a strong emotional response to this moment.
- This moment impacts a large number of people.
- This moment occurs frequently.
- This moment is strongly aligned to our strategic people goals – for example, to improve the leadership pipeline or the employer brand.
- This moment is strongly aligned to our culture and brand values.

CASE STUDY
Big picture EX in action

How Repsol uses its EX framework to get started

With 25,000 people across more than 25 countries, Repsol has made EX a priority not only for its HR function, but a way of doing things across the organization. The approach goes hand in hand with its digital transformation and emphasis on customer experience.

The approach is all about learning and doing, explains employee experience and employer branding manager Esther Poza Campos. 'We're copying all the CX techniques – not inventing anything new.' Central to that is design thinking, which is helping to generate a culture of design centred on the employee experience. Starting in HR, the focus is now moving into the wider organization. 'We looked at journeys and pain points and prioritized the work from there,' Esther explains.

Every process has an owner and connecting with them is a big part of the role. It's also, Esther says, where she faces the biggest challenge. 'It's about approach – design thinking is a new mindset and can feel very different. It's also about breaking down silos and process owners can be sceptical about our intent.' This is where Repsol's EX framework comes in. It provides a context for the conversation with process owners by answering the question: 'What is the experience we want to deliver to our people?' The EX framework draws on Repsol's four cultural pillars – efficiency, respect, anticipating and adding value.

Co-creation sessions with process owners alongside employees then help to align perspectives and departments. Esther explains:

> In the onboarding process, for example, there are many departments and process owners. All of them were working with the best intentions, but working as a silo. Applying design thinking with co-creation sessions with them and inviting new employees and managers helped them realize the impact of their part of the process and see the whole picture.

The learning? Even where EX is a strategic priority, you still need to sell it:

> We're modifying systems, programmes and ways of doing things. And we're taking a different approach and mindset to do it. We need to be bold and build each step with confidence, but we also need to find ways to take people with us. The EX framework helps. We also need to be very close to the business strategy, because EX is about creating a good experience for our people *and* delivering on the company strategy.

CASE STUDY
Big picture EX in action

How the digital workplace helped Adeo bring EX to life

Adeo, the home improvements business, employs 130,000 people globally. It is on a transformation to become a platform company, which will have a significant impact on the organizational culture, supply chain and customer approach. The Digital Workplace Community (DWC) is at the heart of that transformation. Here EX and digital workplace leader Carlos Erazo-Molina and colleague Romain Quicq, lead UX designer, explain how they're using design thinking to change the conversation about the employee experience and define where to focus to make the biggest impact.

The DWC is made up of predominantly HR and IT colleagues from across the group, and also includes store managers, marketing and other managers with responsibility for how well the business is doing. We were originally tasked with looking after internal tools for communication and collaboration. However, we soon realized that there was something much bigger at stake – the whole employee experience. From the moment someone hears about Adeo, to how they apply, collaborate, change jobs – every touchpoint. To widen our focus, we developed a map identifying all the touchpoints across the journey. We're using it to support conversations and explain the scope of the community to HR and IT leaders across our companies. It helps us collaboratively identify priorities, propose solutions and set budgets.

It's also helping us think about the future architecture of the digital workplace – mapping objectives and key results across the different moments on the map, then finding out if we have the training, tools, integration and culture necessary to create the best experience at those moments. It's a way to imagine the future system based on the experience we would like to offer to employees.

The DWC is now working to find the most significant moments, or the moments that matter, across the journey. We're doing this by identifying moments that are associated with our objectives and key results (OKRs). Whenever we find a connection between an OKR and a moment, we start to look at the two views in parallel. What is the business need and what is the human need? For example, there is an OKR to reduce by 25 per cent the attrition rate of employees leaving the business within their first 12 months. To achieve this, we are focusing our efforts on three moments: 'pre-boarding', 'my first day in the company', and 'I know my mission, my role and my company'.

Because our team has UX design experience, taking a user-centred approach to EX has been very natural. For us, design thinking is more than a process; it is a method of creativity, based on empathy, co-creation and iteration. You can use this method in any context and for any subject. For any project we undertake, we first identify end users, then meet them to understand their needs and work with them as part of the team to imagine solutions to solve their problems. We test with them and evaluate solutions before developing them. This saves us time and money because we can quickly test a solution before launching a large or expensive project.

Takeaways

In this chapter we built on the tools and activities introduced in Chapter 2 to suggest ways to help you discover more about the employee experience you are delivering and the gap between this and your intended EX. We also introduced a range of EX design tools and activities to help you define where to prioritize to start to address the gap. In summary:

- Considering the big picture helps to ensure your EX design efforts have the biggest impact, that you can gain stakeholder backing and scale the approach.

- The ideal EX is unique to your organization and sits within the intersection of what your people want and need, the organizational context and the requirements of the work itself.

- There are many tools to help you define your EX priorities, including: the three EX lenses, personas, the life spiral and journey maps.

- Moments that matter are highly emotionally charged moments that have a disproportionate impact on experience and engagement – but they don't always start off that way.

07

Empathy and the opportunity space

In this chapter we'll cover:

- empathy as a principle in EX design and how to put it to work in the opportunity space;
- discovery activities to learn about the truth of people's experience;
- what is insight and why does it matter;
- how to turn data from discovery activities into insight;
- how to redefine the opportunity from the employee's perspective and make it actionable in the next phase of the EX framework.

In this chapter we enter the second diamond in the EX design framework – the opportunity space. There are two sets of activities in this space. First, it's about taking an empathic approach to better understand the human experience – this is divergent thinking because we're broadening and deepening our knowledge about the issue. Then it's about turning that knowledge or data into insight to work with and refining it down to a definition of the problem or opportunity to be solved or realized. This is the convergent thinking end of the diamond. This process ensures we design for real needs, problems and opportunities, not our assumptions. Defining an opportunity can be an iterative process. You are likely to learn more still about an opportunity at the prototyping and testing phase and that might send you back to redefining it again. If it does, embrace it; don't ignore it. You'll only find the right solutions if you've nailed the right opportunity. Trust in the process and you are much more likely to reach a solution that delivers.

What is empathy?

Let's start by getting clear on what we mean by empathy, which is at the heart of the process. To do this, meet a boy and a lost penguin. In his beautiful storybook *Lost and Found,* Oliver Jeffers (2006) tells the story of a boy who finds a penguin and puts all his energy into rowing the penguin back to the South Pole. But, when they get there, the penguin is still sad. The penguin, it turns out, wasn't lost; he was just lonely. He didn't need a boat. He needed a friend. Here's the thing. The boy made a good guess at the problem. But he didn't get close enough to the penguin to get to the real need. This is a common problem. To take a real example, a company's engagement survey suggested people didn't feel recognized, so HR spent six months and a lot of money designing an employee of the month programme, a new platform to support it, and a glittering event to celebrate winners. However, in the next engagement survey, the score was still rock bottom. It turns out, all people really wanted was for someone to say thank you for a job well done.

So, if empathy is a way to uncover people's real needs, what is it? We like to think of empathy as the ability to stand in someone else's shoes and see the world through their eyes. It challenges preconceived ideas, forcing us to set aside what we think is true, to discover what's really happening for other people. From there we can create solutions for the things that really matter to people, not the things we *think* are important.

Psychologists debate precise definitions of empathy. Most agree, however, that empathy is not one thing, but many. It is a collective noun for a range of ways people respond to other people's feelings. Indi Young, author of *Practical Empathy for Collaboration and Creativity in Your Work* (2015), likens it to a roll of tools. When we unroll our kit, we have a choice about which empathy tool to pull out. That choice activates different brain systems that are useful at different times in how we connect with others:

- Emotional empathy is when we take on the emotions of others: the little boy felt sad because the penguin was sad. Sad stories and movies make us sad. Emotional empathy connects us not just with the story, but with each other. This is really powerful in EX design, helping to fuel ideation and create the energy to see the process through to final solutions.

- Cognitive empathy helps us identify and understand other people's perspectives – like walking in their shoes. It helps us get to the core needs and motivations of the people we're designing for and overcome our own assumptions and biases.

- Empathic concern goes beyond understanding others and sharing their feelings. It inspires us to take action. It is a useful energy when it comes to solving problems, as well as a helpful characteristic in leaders, managers and colleagues.

Empathy isn't a fixed trait. In individuals, teams and organizations it can be nurtured and grown. And like a muscle, empathy strengthens the more it's put to use. This is powerful information. Simply knowing that it is possible to build empathy can inspire individuals towards empathy, according to Jamil Zaki, associate professor of psychology at Stanford University and author of *The War for Kindness: Building empathy in a fractured world* (2019). And we are more likely to exercise empathy if we have a sense of belonging or connection with another person or group – or we're seeking to create it. This tells us a lot about how we should be constructing and working with our mixed EX design teams and end users – employees.

Cultures that openly value and reward empathy also help to nurture it. Some organizations are focusing on creating moments and opportunities to nurture and celebrate empathy among their teams. IDEO, for example, encourages employees to set aside time to help colleagues, and considers generosity during hiring and promotion (Amabile *et al*, 2014). And many organizations have taken the recent changes in ways of working ushered in by COVID-19 as an opportunity to upskill leaders and line managers in emotional intelligence (EQ), the foundation of empathy. EQ is the ability to identify, understand, manage and use emotions in positive and constructive ways, recognizing our own emotional state and that of others. Just as empathy is not fixed, neither is our EQ: we can develop and improve it and so develop our ability to empathize. EQ involves being able to first identify our emotions, and then manage and regulate them.

Developing our EQ enables understanding of not only what other people are feeling, but also why they are feeling that way.

Empathy-based EX design discovery activities

Empathy is of course a principle of great EX design across the whole approach, but it really gets put to work in the opportunity space – the second diamond in the EX design framework. Here we work our empathy muscle to discover new information to broaden and deepen our understanding of an issue – to uncover not only *what* the problem or opportunity is, but *why*. Sometimes initial understanding of an issue might come from a survey or other quantitative data indicating that something is up, for example 75 per cent of people leaving within their first three months of joining. Or, on the other hand, you might have an ill-formed hunch about an issue and start with empathy-based discovery, going deep with a small group of people to work out where the issue lies, before then validating it with quantitative data – perhaps then going back to explore more with those affected. Whichever way you come at it, the empathy discovery process is an essential component. It means speaking to and spending time with people who are affected by the issue, not simply looking at survey and other data. Cognitive biases – unconscious assumptions our minds use to process information – influence how we interpret information and make decisions without us realizing it. Building empathy into the discovery process helps overcome these biases and ensure a better outcome (see Chapter 3 for more on the psychology behind employee experience and employee experience design).

However, it takes resolve to invest the right amount of time and energy in this part of the process. Rose Tighe is an innovation coach in the innovation lab of a large media and telecoms company. Having previously focused on external customer experience, she also now helps the organization explore challenges and opportunities around new ways of working necessitated by COVID-19 and more broadly. Whether the focus is customer or employee experience, she says it's vital to spend time exploring the problem or opportunity with the people directly impacted. However, this often means challenging teams' eagerness to skip to solutions too quickly. Lack of time, space and methodology, coupled with a strong bias to action in many large organizations, means teams often under-invest in their understanding of the problem or opportunity space, she says. Under pressure to deliver a plan, teams end up launching solutions that don't shift the dial, because they're 'addressing the superficial symptoms of a problem and missing the less obvious, gnarly, often paradoxical truth that lurks beneath'.

When it comes to success in EX design projects, it all starts with bringing together different knowledge and perspectives and providing an inclusive space to hear diverse voices. But it's not just the findings and making new connections between disparate bits of information that is so powerful; it's also the process itself. The process of discovery helps to build team alignment about what problem needs to the solved (or opportunity realized), and how successful outcomes will be measured. Research, Tighe suggests, *is* alignment.

University of Virginia Darden School of Business's Jeanne Liedtka (2020) describes this stage of the design process as immersion and says it has a significant impact on the design team, creating an emotional connection, shifting perspectives and revealing new ways of doing things. It's powerful and the benefits for the team often go way beyond the project in hand.

Types of discovery activities

Whatever the size or scope of your project and team, your first step will be discovering more about the problem or opportunity. Rather than a traditional HR approach that may at best collect data from a survey to inform the design of the solution, in EX design you get to spend time exploring the issue at a deeper level. You do this by combining different discovery activities to meet the needs of the project. Broadly, discovery activities fall into three categories:

1 observing what's happening;
2 exploring the experience with individuals or a group in interviews or focus groups/workshops;
3 living the experience for yourself.

How you choose activities will depend on a number of factors:

- how much it will reveal about people's real needs, attitudes and beliefs;
- how many stakeholders you need to involve;
- how many end users, ie employees, you need to involve;
- how much time you have;
- where your people are and how accessible they are.

Like the entire EX approach, empathy-based discovery is an iterative process. So your first discovery activity may well reveal new information that suggests you need to explore more in another way. That's why rapid, iterative research techniques are so useful. It's about bringing in users and experts at the right point and threading that learning through the rest of the project. For example, a team at a large company was asked to look at what could be learned from the rapid switch to virtual working during the COVID-19 pandemic. What from these new ways of working could and should be retained and expanded as the option to return to the office became available? The whole discovery process happened virtually. The team used one-to-one interviews with executives to get an honest perspective from the top of the organization. They issued an employee survey, then started group exploration sessions with employees. However, the content of the conversation was more sensitive than they had imagined and there were a number of unexpected questions raised. To help the team interpret this, they brought in experts to explore these findings before moving to the next stage of one-to-one interviews with employees. Armed with the additional perspective from these subject-matter experts, the design team was in a better place to generate deeper learnings from their one-to-one conversations. All of this was documented and captured along the way to help with the next step of turning data into insight.

1. HOW TO OBSERVE PEOPLE

Observing is simply watching people and their behaviour in their own environment – for example, watching how someone uses your careers website; navigates your new office; uses new collaboration or social spaces in your redesigned office hub; or how well they adjust to hot-desking. Observation should, on the face of it, be straightforward. However, it's easy to fall into some traps if you're not careful. When practising observation, try the following:

- Be curious about what people are doing and why. Look at how they interact with each other, with objects and what they're frustrated by.

- Look for compensating behaviours or modifications they've made. This is where the person knows what job they want to get done, but there is no existing solution to help them do it – so they innovate. For example, a new starter creates a checklist on their phone to make sense of the overwhelming volume of information they receive on day one.

- Log exactly what you see, not what you expect to see or why you think you're seeing it (ie don't make assumptions). When making notes, make them specific and detailed and don't summarize.

- Take lots of photos, make sketches, create videos, etc (without impacting what the people you are observing are doing), so you can replay with your team.

- Work in pairs (or more) and compare notes; seeing and hearing for yourself and agreeing on conclusions is a critical part of the process.

- Follow up with interviews to ask questions about what you've seen.

2. HOW TO INTERVIEW PEOPLE

Engaging directly with the people you are designing for is the most powerful way to reveal new insights and generate an emotional connection to the end user and their needs. If you need to take stakeholders on a design journey, get them involved too – remember, emotional connection is a powerful thing. There is an awful lot written about interviewing in the design process, and we only touch the surface here. But if you do nothing else, try to:

- Have more than one person on the interview team and assign roles, eg asking questions, watching for body language, taking notes.

- Work up questions to keep the conversation on target, but allow for spontaneity in exploring things that come up.

- Build rapport and don't let anything get in the way, eg don't try and take detailed notes if you are interviewing on your own. And don't dive into questions too soon; spend time getting to know your interviewee. Make it clear to your interviewee that this isn't a test, that you're interested in their experience.

- Remove yourself and your opinions from the conversation – your aim is solely to hear from them.

- Challenge vague or abstract summaries that the interviewee might offer for brevity by asking the interviewee to tell a story about their experience. For example, if they start a sentence with 'we usually...' or 'generally...' or 'in my team we do...', try bringing them back to the real activity by asking questions such as: 'Tell me a time when...'.

- Try asking why five times in a row to really dig into someone's motivations around an action, especially when you think you know the answer. For example, your question might be: 'Why did you do x in that way?' Follow up their answer with: 'Why did you decide that / think that / do that?' And then again with: 'Why did you decide that / think that / do that?' If you do this five times, you are more likely to get to the root of the human need.

- Practice makes perfect. Talking to people on an emotional level is very different from analysing a survey. You'll get markedly better at it after a third or fourth interview. So practise on friends and family before you go into the wild.

INTERVIEWING REMOTELY
Tips for video-based interviewing

Using live video calls and vox-pops (pre-recorded video interviews) lets you quickly accelerate and expand the number of voices you bring into the process. Video-based feedback can be commissioned at speed, and auto-generated subtitles make content accessible regardless of language barriers.

> When it comes to observing these interviews, group observation offers a lot of benefits for team alignment. Ask every team member to make notes and review them after each interview. Duplicate observations can be removed, disagreements aired and resolved. Seeing and hearing for yourself, and collectively agreeing on conclusions, is a critical part of the process.

3. HOW TO LIVE THE EXPERIENCE FOR YOURSELF

Living an experience can provide great insight into an opportunity to improve it. For example, if you are a returning mother, why wouldn't you use your experiences in a design project seeking to improve the experience of returning from parental leave. We know of a company with a new office building who wanted to create the best manual for its employees by living the experience of working in the office to identify what information people would need before the move. In another example, when a not-for-profit organization needed to rapidly move people to remote working, it made sense for the EX team to use their own experience to spot problems in the process – number one being you couldn't contact the IT helpdesk unless you were logged on to the system, but you needed the helpdesk because you couldn't log on to the system. It was the first of many small but significant issues they discovered and were able to respond to.

So, lived experience counts. But treat proxies – or stand-ins for end users – with extreme caution. Don't use them as an alternative to real engagement with employees unless you can help it and it really makes sense. Your experience may not reflect the experience of your employees. One of the biggest challenges new EX design teams often face is convincing HR to step out of this role of proxy and start real dialogue with real people. It slows the process down and creates new hurdles, they argue, so why would we? The answer is clear: you can't discover the real needs and motivations of people if you don't talk to them. If you can break this cycle and get the team to spend time with employees, the revelations will come thick and fast.

EXERCISE
Empathy at work

An activity to practise listening skills

Listening is a fundamental skill of the empathy-based discovery process. Indi Young, author of *Practical Empathy for Collaboration and Creativity in Your Work* (2015), describes effective listening as getting past the layer of explanations, preferences and opinions to start to unearth intention and why. The problem is that most people don't listen at a very deep level. And that is very often the case at work, where we tend to listen for the minimum of what we need to know so we can move on to the next task. In the book *Co-active Coaching: Changing business transforming lives*, the authors describe three levels of listening (Kimsey-House *et al*, 2011):

1 Internal – listening primarily to ourselves. We listen to the words of the other person, but our attention is on what it means to us, our own thoughts and agenda.

2 Focused – focusing on what the other person is saying, their expressions and emotions, as well as what they're not saying.

3 Global – sometimes described as environmental listening, this includes everything you can observe with your senses – what you see, hear, smell and feel, the tactile as well as emotional sensations. Stand-up comedians, actors and trainers all have this ability to sense what is going on or 'read the room'.

Operating at these deeper levels of listening is new to most of us. It requires practice, lots of it. Matt Matheson, founder of coaching and facilitation consultancy Improvising Change, shares an activity he uses with groups to develop listening skills and put them in touch with their own emotions in order to develop their empathy muscle.

How does it work?

- Two people take part in this conversation.
- A topic or location (of any sort) is given to the pair to discuss.
- Person one delivers a line of dialogue. For example: 'Today, I plan on going to the shop, to buy a cucumber, lettuce and a bottle of gin for the weekend party.'
- Person two responds, by first inserting the line of dialogue: 'When I hear you say that, it makes me feel "X" because...' For example: 'When I hear you say that, it makes me feel anxious, because I know how rowdy the party got last time and it cost me a lot of money to clean up the apartment!'

- Person one then responds in the same manner – starting by saying how they feel. For example: 'When I hear you say that, it makes me feel frustrated, because I put so much time into organizing these parties, and it feels like all you are worried about is how clean the apartment is.'

- Continue this for two to three minutes, inserting, 'When I hear you say that, it makes me feel... because' after each response and until a natural conclusion or time is called.

This exercise tunes you into the feelings and emotions of yourself and your partner through the direction of the conversation. In stating your feeling, empathy is built, and through adding 'because', insight into what has generated that emotion emerges. With two people following this framework, a conversation based on human emotion, rather than transaction, emerges. This can be practised using a fun topic, or a work topic. Either way, enjoy the process and allow your conversation to go wherever it ends up – as well as practising a skill, you're flexing a muscle that deals with emotional awareness.

What is insight and how to get there

Discovery activities give you data about the issue. But the data itself is inactive and lacks context – it just is. To use the data to inform the design, you need to make it active. This is the task of turning data into insight – insight that will fuel the ideation process and lead to solutions. In his new book *How to be Insightful: Unlocking the superpower that drives innovation* (2020), friend and collaborator Sam Knowles defines insight as 'a profound and useful understanding – of a person, a thing, a situation, or an issue – that truly effects change'. Insight, he explains, takes us from 'what does this mean?' to 'what should we do as a result?' (Knowles, 2020).

Insight needs to inspire and motivate the design team and stakeholders and make them feel something. Feeling something is a great way to fuel creative juices, generate energy and remove roadblocks. Feeling something is also a good test to see if what you have distilled is merely a research finding, or if it is a genuine insight. Don't worry if this distinction feels hard to get; the more you do it, the more you'll start to feel the difference.

For example, a finding might look like this:

New starters ask a lot fewer questions and miss out on vital information when joining a virtual organization and working remotely.

This is valuable information to have found, but until we understand what causes the behaviour, it is difficult to design to improve the situation.

An insight looks more like this:

New starters working remotely are so nervous about doing the wrong thing, looking stupid, and bothering teammates and their managers, that they ask far fewer questions and miss things as a result.

The latter is more actionable as it highlights the underlying behaviour – the why. If you can't find the underlying behaviour or emotion from your notes, it might be that you didn't ask 'why' enough times to get there. Make a note of this and reflect on how you'll do your next interviews.

As well as making you feel something, insight should also be simple and memorable so the team can keep returning to it and checking in against it to ensure solutions are on target. And it should be easy to pass on, because not everyone in the design team will be involved from beginning to end.

There isn't a perfect formula for an insight, but challenge yourself and the team to see if you have arrived at a genuine insight by asking:

- Does it inspire? Does it make you want to create something to solve the problem or realize the opportunity?
- Is it relevant? Is it related to the employee experience you are investigating?
- Does it have a story? When you explain the insight, is there a human story to bring it to life?
- Is it new? Is it something that surprised you when you first discovered it? (New can also be the result of making less obvious connections between bits of data.)
- Is it actionable? Will it inform your design and thinking?

The challenge of sense-making

Great insights don't just appear magically out of the data generated in the discovery activities and the notes, sketches, photos, videos, etc. To understand and think about the issue not just more completely, but more clearly, you need to organize and interrogate the data you've collected. In human-centred design this process is called synthesis – an exercise in organizing, pruning and filtering data to find relationships or themes and uncover hidden meaning. In the language of Sam Knowles (2020), it's about answering the 'What does this mean?' question. IDEO design director Matt Cooper-Wright (2015) describes synthesis as a foggy process of:

- sense-making;
- sharing stories and prioritizing;
- creating a coherent summary of what you know so far.

With the goal to develop:

- consensus across the group;
- a clear journey of evidence for design.

Navigating potentially a lot of data to get to this point isn't without its challenges and it's not something most of us are trained to do. In a world dominated by PowerPoint, the temptation to be reductive is overwhelming – we are used to simplifying a landscape so it can be communicated more easily. When it comes to synthesis, however, that means we instinctively want to hone in on the strongest themes and exclude signals that don't fit the emerging narrative. But, beware of this urge. Returning to the experience of Rose Tighe: 'It's the less obvious connections, the outliers, the contradictions, the signals in our peripheral vision that often lead to the most interesting insights.'

Getting the team to this point without them feeling overwhelmed requires a lot of structure and some careful facilitation. Matt Cooper-Wright (2015) explains:

> It may feel overwhelming at the beginning as you wonder if you'll ever be able to distil down the mass of evidence into something actionable and inspiring to design. The trick is to become comfortable with the ambiguity and take small steps – try not to worry about the ultimate goal. If your

research was good you'll find the answers you need, synthesis will help you get the value from the notes you recorded when out in the field.

Below we share different ways to turn data into insight depending on the scale of the project, the volume of the data you've collected, and when you want to involve stakeholders. You might want to do these activities in a single workshop, or in a series of sessions. These activities can be run face to face or virtually using a collaborative whiteboard platform. You can cherry-pick or combine the activities to suit your needs. There is value in the whole team working through this process together; however, for a small project, it is equally possible for a sub-group, or one person, to do all or part of it for the purposes of speed or other practicalities.

Research safari (also called a gallery walk)

This is a popular way to make sense of data. By bringing in stakeholders uninvolved in the discovery process, it removes the risk of the design team being unduly influenced by their own biases. This has the added benefit of bringing the opportunity to life for stakeholders and helping to ensure their commitment.

A gallery walk has two stages:

1 The first step is for the design team to select the most important data. Write it down on large posters, complete with pictures of employees you have interviewed and quotations. Hang the posters around a room.

2 Invite stakeholders to tour the gallery and write down on Post-It notes the data they see as essential for the solution. Then put stakeholders into small teams to share their observations, combine them, and sort them by theme into clusters. The whole group then mines the clusters for insights. A healthy discussion should ensue where conclusions and assumptions can be challenged and insights emerge. Aim for a handful of insights only.

Sense-making workshop

A sense-making workshop is ideal for navigating large volumes of data in a short space of time. Rather than the team selecting data in advance, all the data is explored in the workshop. The aim is to reach a consensus around the most compelling insights and consistent problems and to create a story about why they are related. Because this is a collaborative process, it quickly aligns people around the key insights.

STEP 1: GET IT OUT THERE AND BRING IT TO LIFE

Get the data into the open. Putting it all in one place – ideally on a large whiteboard where you can revisit and play with it – creates a mental picture of everything that's been learned. Never skip this step. If the content is hidden, you limit the team's ability to make sense of it. Moving pieces of the picture around – ie notes, photos, etc – is a powerful part of the sense-making process. If possible, try and do this while memories are still fresh, as it's harder to make sense of data if too much time lapses.

STEP 2: TALK ABOUT IT

Ask people involved in the discovery process to share their stories and talk about what they've learned. Encourage everyone to explore and share what surprised them, what moved them, and what they are curious about. This discussion will identify new connections between seemingly unrelated bits of data and help the team remember new things to share, things that previously might not have been obvious or seemed relevant.

STEP 3: FIND PATTERNS

Now organize the data to find patterns and themes. At this stage, it is not the individual bits of data that are important, but the relationship between them. Write individual data points on Post-It notes – observations, quotes, interpretation, stories, drawings and photos – and add to a new wall. It's not about recapturing everything, but finding the stand-out points, surprises and revelations. Move the items into clusters of related themes. Don't worry about the exact nature of the groups; allow your collective instinct to lead. Ask the group to look for themes and patterns. If a sticky note relates to more than one group, create a duplicate. Rearrange the groups as you go along, removing some altogether as stronger patterns and connections emerge. If an idea doesn't fit, create a new group or simply park it and revisit it later. Continue until you have a manageable number of clusters you can agree on. If at any point the group gets stuck or runs out of energy, ask someone to tell a story (any story will do) from the notes on the wall.

STEP 4: FIND THE MEANING

Now you have clear groups of related themes, it's time to find the meaning. Take the groupings you identified and give them a name – don't overthink this. It's just about making themes easier to navigate. Then, for each theme, create an insight statement to transform a theme into a core insight of the research. The richest insights are supported by multiple research activities with data points, quotes, photos and observations all pointing to the same thing. Be wary of drawing insights from only one or two interviews as it may not be broadly applicable. Remember, a good insight statement should be simple and tell an emotional story to inform the design. Aim to identify anything between three and eight insights. Less might suggest you didn't speak with enough people. More suggests you've not been thorough in your sense-making and might be expressing the same insight multiple times.

Journey maps as a sense-making tool

If you have a manageable amount of data and a narrow focus, you might choose to make sense of your data, create or share your insight using a journey map. To do this create a journey map (see Figure 6.4) and populate it using the data from your discovery process. Things to add to the journey include:

- What are people thinking and feeling at each stage?
- What are the high and low points?
- What are the moments that matter most in this journey?
- How does one experience in the journey impact the next?

Don't forget to generate the insight statements as a result or you won't have what you need for the ideation phase.

Empathy maps

Empathy maps are a way to collaboratively visualize and articulate what is known about a particular persona's experience across a journey or a moment that matters. We split our empathy maps into four areas to focus on what the person: thinks and feels, says and does, sees and hears (see Figure 7.1). From that, it's possible to deduce pains they are trying to avoid or overcome and gains they are seeking. Creating empathy maps for your personas is a great way to interrogate, make sense of the data, create and share insights. Not only do empathy maps help to externalize knowledge about employee needs, but they help ensure a shared understanding across the design team that will be vital in the next stages of the process. Keeping empathy maps at hand throughout the rest of the process helps to keep the team oriented around the problem you are trying to solve and the people you are solving it for.

FIGURE 7.1 Empathy map

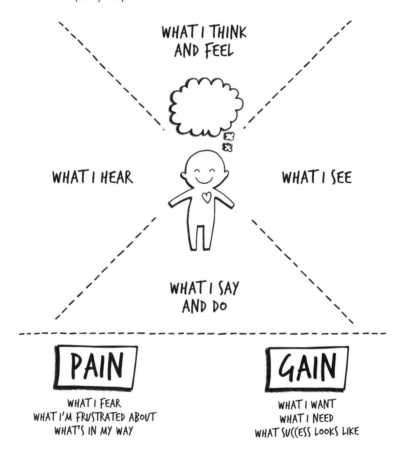

Redefining the opportunity

At the end of the synthesis process your understanding of the problem or opportunity you are trying to solve is expressed in a small number of insight statements. The task now is to define what needs to be solved or realized from the perspective of the employee. This is the springboard into the next diamond – the solution space.

In design thinking what is created at this stage is known as a problem statement, but you can equally think of it as an opportunity statement. You might choose to create this in the sense-making workshop or afterwards.

User stories

One method of formulating and presenting opportunity statements is through user stories. They are a simple and easy way to articulate what a user will do with a part of the EX system. User stories will be familiar to people in technology-related industries where they are widely used in product and software development. User stories deliver the 'who', 'what' and 'why' of user requirements in a format that can be easily understood. They help chunk up a big opportunity into smaller, more manageable areas.

It works like this:

> As a __[user description] __, I want _[need/verb] ___ so that _
> [compelling insight] ___.

The design team at InVision, our case study in Chapter 5, created user stories to frame the biggest problems that needed to be solved in its redesign of the onboarding process:

> As a new hire [user description], I want to learn the company culture
> [need/verb] so that I understand where and how I fit in our remote
> community [compelling insight].

If you're doing this in the sense-making workshop, try bringing a pack of blank cards and getting people to write a range of user stories the group can then discuss and agree on. Alternatively, you might do this with an employee group. Collecting all the requests and then sorting them into themes and prioritizing them can help employees feel heard and involved.

SYNTHESIS IS A STICKY PROCESS
Tips for getting unstuck

- Cut yourselves some slack – no matter how many times you've done it, it's not easy work.

- Trust in the process – wandering around in the fog is part of the process. Don't react to the murk; embrace it.

- Ask for help from the outside – invite in someone less close to the project to give you perspective (this is why the gallery walk is such a great tool).

- Bring in an interrogator – find someone to ask questions of you. By explaining an insight area, you'll help yourselves to make sense of it.

- Shift the focus – give yourself a more structured, generative task, such as asking 'How might we...' (HMW) questions of each theme. HMW questions are used to drive the ideation process, framing the task as an opportunity to be realized rather than a problem to be solved. It's a subtle difference that helps to create and sustain energy and optimism around the task.

- Take a break.

CASE STUDY
Navigating the sense-making process

How the CIPD's research safari synthesized data

The Chartered Institute of Personnel and Development (CIPD) wanted to learn more about the reflective learning practice of its members to understand how it could help them regularly and easily learn and reflect on their learning. Sarah Corney, head of digital experience at the CIPD, explains the discovery and synthesis approach and why it was vital to the successful design sprint that followed.

Research

Our ethnographic research focused on the gap between the CIPD's benchmark for best-in-class reflective practice and what members were doing to support their personal development through reflective learning. We gathered feedback through diary studies from people professionals about their current reflective practice activities, including whether they are doing it and if they record it and, if so, how. We also explored the impact that providing a framework of prompt questions and supporting information about reflective practice has on the likelihood to do reflective practice. Additional interviews and focus groups gathered further data on any wider barriers to reflective practice and surfaced ideas that might make it easier and more likely to become routine. As a result of the research, we had 19 data-rich user stories.

Synthesis

The task then was to synthesize the data so we had clear insights to inform the opportunity we'd be working on in our design sprint. We did this through a research safari (similar to a gallery walk) as part of a pre-sprint workshop. Taking over a room, we covered the walls in the notes and outputs of the research. Participants then spent time immersed in the research, answering a number of pre-prepared questions to help guide their thinking. To ensure all participants had an equal 'voice' in the process, each team member wrote up their top five findings on separate Post-It notes. They did this 'silent and solo' before coming together as a team to post their notes up on a wall, each person reading their notes out aloud as they posted them up. Similar insights were clustered and duplicates removed. The team then agreed on the final top five insights by using sticky coloured 'voting' dots.

Opportunity statement

The session was followed up with the creation of personas and journey maps tracking each persona's actions, pains and gains across a typical week showing how reflective practice fitted within their week. Following this we were able to craft an opportunity statement to take into the sprint.

I chose this synthesis approach because it's such a rich and energizing way to engage people in research that they haven't been part of and to help them empathize with the end users they're designing for. Synthesizing data can be hard work – the structure of the safari session ensured everyone was comfortable and able to play a part. By taking part in the synthesis process, they really had to interrogate and internalize the data. Not only did that ensure we were able to create the insight needed to craft our opportunity statement, but the team was also really engaged and inspired to work on finding solutions that met real users' needs.

Takeaways

In this chapter we looked at empathy as a principle in EX design and how to put it to work in the opportunity space through a range of activities designed to learn the truth of people's experience, and then how to turn data into actionable insight. In summary:

- Empathy means a number of things. For the purpose of EX design, it's worth simply thinking of empathy as the ability to stand in someone else's shoes and see the world through their eyes.

- Empathy is not a fixed trait – like a muscle, it can be built up the more it is put to use.

- Discovering the true nature of the human experience before starting to design solutions is fundamental to successful EX design. Taking an empathic approach ensures we design for real needs, problems and opportunities, not our assumptions.

- Insight is a profound and useful understanding of someone's experience that effects change. It should be simple, memorable and inspire people to action.

- Turning data into insight involves a process of synthesis and sense-making. This is a foggy process that can leave people feeling overwhelmed. Take it slow, keep it light and take lots of breaks.

References

Amabile, T, Fisher, CM and Pillemer, J (2014) [accessed 25 September 2020] IDEO's culture of helping, *Harvard Business Review*, January–February [Online] https://hbr.org/2014/01/ideos-culture-of-helping (archived at https://perma.cc/6TWC-TCYS)

Cooper-Wright, M (2015) [accessed 12 August 2020] Design research from interview to insight, *Medium*, 12 September [Online] https://medium.com/design-research-methods/design-research-from-interview-to-insight-f6957b37c698 (archived at https://perma.cc/CF43-CVEZ)

Jeffers, O (2006) *Lost and Found*, HarperCollins Publishers, London

Kimsey-House, H, Kimsey-House, K, Sandahl, P and Whitworth, L (2011) *Co-active Coaching: Changing business transforming lives*, Nicholas Brealey Publishing, Boston

Knowles, S (2020) *How to be Insightful: Unlocking the superpower that drives innovation*, Routledge, Abingdon

Liedtka, J (2020) [accessed 18 July 2020] Maximising the ROI of design thinking, *Mural Imagine Talks*, 28 May [Online] https://www.mural.co/imagine/talks (archived at https://perma.cc/E3ZQ-49LC)

Young, I (2015) *Practical Empathy for Collaboration and Creativity in Your Work*, Rosenfeld Media, New York

Zaki, J (2019) *The War for Kindness: Building empathy in a fractured world*, Little Brown, New York

08

Ideate

In this chapter we'll cover:

- how to prepare for perfect ideation and the six steps to ensure a successful ideation session or sessions;
- different ideation tools and techniques and some critical brainstorming rules;
- how to make choices about which ideas to develop into prototypes.

What is ideation?

Ideation is where we move into the solution space, the third diamond in the EX design framework. This stage of the EX design framework involves a number of activities as we look for ways to solve problems and realize opportunities. Ideation is the process of generating and developing new ideas – lots of new ideas. If it's not obvious already, ideation is another divergent thinking mode (that's why it's in the part of the diamond that gets bigger). Ideation is about going broad – or, as IDEO's Tim Brown puts it, creating choices (Brown, 2019). It is not about looking for the single best solution, but for multiple potential ways of realizing an opportunity. And that's important, because often it is only by going beyond the obvious that you can address needs in ways that make the biggest difference. Or as famed twice Nobel Prize Winner Linus Pauling is said to have remarked: 'The way to get good ideas is to get lots of ideas and throw the bad ones away.'

Successful ideation activities push people to think beyond the limits of the usual way of doing things to unlock new possibilities. Even though more out-there options are rarely chosen, big ideas often pave the way to more practical solutions.

Who to involve in the ideation process

Employees

If you're wondering who the most important people are to involve in your ideation process, the answer is simple – employees. If you're looking to change their experience, why wouldn't you do it with them? EX design is all about designing with and not for your people because it simply creates better solutions that are more likely to land. End users bring a unique perspective to ideation activities while also helping to keep the challenge real for other team members. They are also the people most motivated to get things moving when they get stuck and so bring a vital energy. So involve them. This might be the employees you got to know in the discovery activities, or for practical reasons you might work with another group.

It's worth noting that involving employees in an EX design process doesn't just benefit the process. According to a report into the application of design thinking to create an experience for employees going through an organizational change programme, involving employees increases employee engagement and feelings of inclusion (Richards, 2019). It's an all-round win that we've seen played out time and time again. Employees want to get involved, they love the experience of being involved and the benefits last long after the project has finished. People take the skills and tools back to their teams. One NHS client even introduced design thinking to her scout group.

Diversity

Sometimes the team tasked with generating the solution is different to the team that did the initial discovery work – this may be for practical reasons, for example the first group doesn't have the time to continue, or because you want to bring in specific skills and perspectives. Alternatively, there may be a core design team of one or two people that do the bulk of the work and then bring in collaborators at key points. Whatever way you structure your team, think carefully about who to involve at the ideation stage – it is a good opportunity to spread the net. A diverse group brings with it the opportunity to mix different ideas, perspectives and ways of thinking.

Multiple functions

It is useful to involve people from different functions, employees who can talk about feasibility and make the necessary changes to systems, processes or communications. This unlocks ways to rapidly test ideas. For example, when a luxury retailer wanted to create opportunities for its employees to surprise and delight customers, one idea was to give shop floor team members store cards to cover the cost of these 'gifts'. While the idea was quickly dismissed in the room as untenable due to the potential for misuse, a finance person was able to spot a work-around and the idea quickly got to testing. Involving different teams and functions creates collaborators and ambassadors for when it comes to rolling out solutions.

Senior stakeholders

The senior stakeholders to include in ideation activities – and when – is something to consider on a case-by-case basis. The upside of including senior stakeholders is that it can give the team confidence in the business's support for the process, and open doors to testing. But senior people can also suppress quieter voices and have a disproportionate impact. This can be problematic if they've not bought into the need for ideation and instead push too soon for a single solution. More out-there ideas need a safe space to grow and form and this can feel risky if there is someone senior in the room heavily invested in the status quo or one particular route. One option is to involve senior stakeholders at regular check-in points rather than across the whole ideation process. They can be useful for their gardening skills – tending, pruning and harvesting ideas – and this will minimize the risk of solutions failing to get past gatekeepers at a later point. We've sometimes seen great projects fail when ideas go back into the business. It's critical to address this re-entry up front, both through the relationship with business units before, during and after the project, and by crafting a specific role for the executive sponsor.

Getting ready to ideate

This stage of the EX design framework involves a number of steps, not one single idea-generation activity. Before you get to the ideation process itself, you need to prepare. Think of this in two steps: sharing the challenge or opportunity with the group and then framing the ideation task. The first is about bringing the insight to life and the second about being clear on what the work needs to deliver.

Sharing the challenge

The opportunity is the focal point for ideation, expressed in a simple and memorable statement (see Chapter 7). To do the work, the team needs to understand the insight that sits behind the opportunity statement. Even if the team was involved in the discovery activities, it's worth refreshing everyone on the insights.

In sharing the insights, the aim is not only to convey the facts, theories and interpretations *about* employees, but to create empathy with them. Bringing the people and their stories to life through photos, drawings and videos is a good way to connect the design team to the heart of the challenge they will be working on. Doing this in advance of the ideation session will save you time on the day and give people longer to think about it. Research suggests the outcomes are better if participants have longer to think about the experience of the people they're designing for (Richards, 2019).

Framing the ideation task

Now it's time to move from understanding the opportunity to setting up the ideation session(s). A classic design approach we like to use is to create 'how might we…' questions (HMW). HMW questions frame the task as an opportunity to be realized rather than a problem to be solved. It's a subtle difference that helps to create and sustain energy and optimism around the task:

- 'How' suggests optimism that the challenge is solvable.
- 'Might' suggests multiple possible solutions.
- 'We' reminds the team that this is a collaborative effort.
- Following this up with 'in order to' keeps the team focused on outcomes.

It can take a while and some practice to craft the perfect HMW question – and that's fine. Be prepared to revisit it so that it is right for the task at hand. If you're short on time, it can be worth crafting your question in advance of an ideation session, rather than eating into time when everyone is together. However, it is also a really useful way to create alignment if you can do it with the group who will be ideating. The HMW question will have a significant impact on the outcome of the ideation session – too broad and people will get lost, too narrow and their thinking will be constrained. Beware also hiding the solution in the question or you will be directing people to one solution rather than opening up the possibility of finding many. If you're not sure you've got the right question, ask the group for feedback and keep revisiting it.

Let's return to the example in the previous chapter: a project looking at the challenges of onboarding when everyone is working remotely.

Problem statement: People who are onboarding in a virtual setting are more fearful and anxious and need more care to help them connect to their role, their team and the organization.

How might we question: How might we create a meaningful virtual onboarding experience that helps people feel truly welcomed and confident in order to hit the ground running?

Notice that we didn't suggest a solution in the question – we weren't leading the discussion that we would have been if we'd said: 'How might we create a new onboarding website / app / buddy system, etc…' Keeping things open in this way allows ideas that go beyond usual ways of thinking to be brought to the surface and discussed.

EXERCISE
Warm-up for ideation sessions

An activity to get in the zone

Creating the right atmosphere, connecting people to each other and freeing their creative spirit are vital ingredients of a successful warm-up. Here we share one of our favourites from collaborator Matt Matheson, founder of Improvising Change, an improv-based coaching and facilitation consultancy.

This activity is a way to practise collaborative listening, building on and combining ideas. In this activity, we listen to what has been provided, pick out what we like from it and build upon it – the essence of collaboration. In doing so, we acknowledge the areas of strength in our partner's offer, rather than focusing on what we don't like. The activity puts us into a positive and collaborative state of mind, helping people stay curious, listen actively and respect others' ideas while also bringing their own.

How to do it:

- Two people take part in a conversation about a challenge related to any topic or location (the facilitator or the group can provide this).

- Person one delivers a line of dialogue offering an idea, eg: '*I had an idea about how we might improve the office. I think the best way to tackle this would be to bring everyone together, every Friday and Monday, and listen to their suggestions.*'

- Person two responds by saying what they like about the idea and adding to it, eg: '*What I like about that is* bringing everyone together and hearing their voice. *I wonder if we could* go one further and have them submit their ideas before presenting, so we can learn sooner?'

- Person one then responds in the same manner, saying what they like before adding to the idea, eg: '*What I like about that is* submitting sooner. I have an excellent tool called Google Forms we could use, and I could let our teams know during the manager catch-ups. This would bring the management team on board too.'

- The conversation continues for a few minutes, until a natural conclusion arrives or the facilitator calls time on the activity.

In this activity, a number of things are happening:

- You are practising consciously listening to the exact words the other person is saying, identifying detail and nuance.

- In repeating the last sentence, you are consciously responding directly to what the last person said, moving the focus onto them and their ideas rather than your own agenda.

- You experience how conscious listening can feel – you feel heard, listened to and understood.

The six steps for perfect ideation

Many variables impact how you choose to run an ideation process – whether that's face to face, online, one session, multiple sessions over a course of days or a few weeks. Rather than being prescriptive and suggesting a single workshop format that might not meet your needs, here we share six steps to structure your ideation session or series of sessions (Figure 8.1). As with every element of the EX design framework, this is a flexible and iterative approach, so adapt it to make it work for you. For example, try shifting the channel – you might do some activities as a whole group face to face, such as generating ideas in a brainstorm, and some online as a smaller group, such as developing ideas and selecting which to prototype. The key is to be clear about where you are in the process – idea generation or idea selection – and what you need to do there. And stick to the rules we outline here.

FIGURE 8.1 Six-step ideation process

1. Generate ideas

This is about generating ideas, lots of ideas. While brainstorming is arguably one of the most popular and powerful ways to do this, it is also an often misunderstood method. In a brainstorm, groups bounce ideas off each other and then combine ideas and build on them in various combinations of individuals, pairs and group work. However, common misuse of the term means it is often seen as just another form of discussion: a meeting with Post-It notes. In truth, brainstorming is a specific activity with clearly defined rules of behaviour designed to maximize the volume of ideas and choices generated.

How to do it:

PREPARATION

- Find the right space so people are comfortable, there is room for group and individual work, walls or whiteboards for ideas and tables for people to sketch or even create models.

- Choose a few brainstorming activities to suit your group (we outline our favourites in an upcoming section). You might not use them all, but having some up your sleeve will help to keep things moving if the group gets stuck.

- Gen up on the rules. If this is your first time facilitating a brainstorm, why not have a few practice runs with your team, family or even friends. It will pay dividends on the day, giving you confidence in the process and helping you champion the rules.

ON THE DAY

- Make sure you run a warm-up activity. Never skip the warm-up or think you don't have time (we're speaking from experience).

People never think they are 'ideas people', but we all are – it can simply take a while to get in the zone. If you skip this step, you'll go slower, have fewer ideas, and they will be a lot more ordinary.

- Explain the brainstorming rules clearly and repeatedly. Print them out and have them in the room as a reminder after you've introduced them. It's really important the facilitator upholds the rules throughout the time. This doesn't have to feel dictatorial; find a variety of ways to gently and overtly remind people of the rules. For example, simply joining a group for a while will remind people of expectations. And encourage people to call themselves out when they're not following the rules – make it fun, and not political.

- Use a mix of activities that include some quiet reflection time to give different personality types the space to work in the way that is best for them.

- Use energizers when the group needs a lift. For example, add in new constraints, such as halving the amount of time or doubling the amount of ideas you're asking for. Or, if you have multiple groups, try swapping people in and out of them. You can also ask the group to try combining ideas as an energizer. You might end up reviving an older idea or thinking of a fresh angle on an existing idea.

BRAINSTORMING ACTIVITIES

Reverse the question   In this activity you take the 'how might we' question and replace the positive outcome you're seeking with a negative. It's amazing where this can take you. It's guaranteed to lift the energy and fun factor. Use this as a warm-up or to re-energize a group when they are stuck.

How to do it:

- Ask individuals to answer the question in silence – one idea per Post-It note. Set a time limit – five or ten minutes – and ask them to come up with as many ideas as possible.

- Ask people to share their ideas, adding them to the whiteboard.

- After each individual share, ask who has similar ideas and group them together on the board (this saves time).

- At the end of the process, try looking for the workable ideas. Discuss as a group what can be flipped to create a new idea. Alternatively, ask people to work in pairs, giving them a number of ideas to flip.
- Prune, grow and select ideas in line with the six steps.

Personality swap   To get the group to step out of the limits of their own thinking – and the context of the organization – try replacing the 'we' in the 'how might we' question with a brand or celebrity – How might IKEA, Apple or Patagonia…, Or how might Bill Gates or Oprah Winfrey…. You can use this activity at any point, including as a warm-up or to inject some energy if people get stuck.

How to do it:

- Give every individual a brand or celebrity to focus on. Try putting these on cards and getting people to pick one from a box.
- Ask individuals to answer the question in silence through the lens of that celebrity or brand – one idea per Post-It note.
- Set a time limit – five or ten minutes – and ask them to come up with as many ideas as possible.
- Ask people to share their ideas, adding them to the whiteboard.
- At the end of the process, prune, grow and select ideas in line with the six steps.

1-2-4-All   This involves everyone simultaneously in generating ideas and solutions, quickly reviewing and sieving them. It works with groups of all sizes. It starts with the 'how might we' question and individual reflection, before discussion in pairs, in fours and then the whole group (hence the name). The entire process takes no more than a few minutes and can be repeated multiple times. This activity comes from Liberating Structures. For full details on how to run it (as well as lots more brilliant workshop activities) visit the Liberating Structures website (www.liberatingstructures.com).

2. Connect and combine

At the end of the brainstorm, there may be potentially hundreds of ideas on Post-It notes – that should be your goal. You need a way to navigate them. Clustering similar or connected ideas together helps people see what's there and creates a smaller number of areas to work with. Be careful, though; you are not yet judging or selecting ideas, simply arranging them into themes. This is still part of the idea-generation stage, so more ideas may emerge – stay open and expansive.

How to do it:

- Ask people – solo and silent – to move Post-It notes with the individual ideas around the whiteboard to create themes. This is a collaborative process as people will need to notice and respond to what others are doing.

- If an idea needs to be in more than one theme, create a duplicate Post-It note.

- This could go on indefinitely, so set a time limit and call time wherever you are in the process.

- Ask the group to discuss broadly what they see and acknowledge any ideas that are as yet without a theme.

- Look at each theme in turn. Ask individuals to share why they put things together – this will surface more context about the ideas and how they connect.

- Label the themes to help the team see what's there.

- Now ask people to look at combining ideas. This isn't an essential step; it may arise organically earlier in the process, or you can add it in earlier as an energizer. The aim is to create new and different ideas. You could do this by giving pairs two themes and use an ideas collision approach to see if they can combine random ideas within and across the themes. Ask one person in each pair to close their eyes and randomly point to two ideas and then combine them.

3. Prune ideas

The task now is to reduce the number of ideas and themes to something more manageable. As you start to judge ideas, politics and personalities will come into play, so be sure to stick to the rules. You may end up further combining ideas, but beware of doing this as a substitute for losing weaker ones.

How to do it:

- Discuss and agree which ideas or themes to develop and which to leave behind.
- Do this through dialogue or dot voting (give people a limited number of stickers and ask them to vote on which ideas to develop).

4. Grow ideas

You now want the team to get deeper into the remaining ideas – exploring and developing their potential. You may want to continue combining similar or related ideas at this point.

How to do it: As with idea generation, there are many techniques for developing ideas. Storyboarding is one of our favourites (see Figure 8.2):

- Ask individuals, pairs or groups to draw pictures in cartoon-style boxes to bring their idea to life.
- Use speech and thought bubbles to create a narrative of what's happening to the employee and what other people, tools or systems are doing.
- No artistic skill is necessary – yes, *no* artistic skill is necessary. Nevertheless, this activity will generate chat about not being able to draw – that's fine and it can lighten the mood. However, don't let it derail the session. A good way to avoid this is to have a sketching activity in the warm-up. Why not get people to sketch their superpower as part of the introduction or check-in at the beginning of the session (see Chapter 9 on prototypes for alternative warm-up activities to get people drawing)?

FIGURE 8.2 Storyboards

5. Probe ideas

At this point there will still be a number of competing ideas – some more attractive and feasible than others. A useful way to find the strongest possible ideas is to surface the assumptions that sit beneath them. Over-optimism, confirmation bias and attachment to first ideas – especially our own – can all creep in and sabotage the process if not kept in check. This technique cuts through biases that might see a weak idea progressing too far.

How to do it:

- Look at the ideas you now have in front of you. Ask of each idea in turn: 'What needs to be true about the world for this idea to work?'

- Get the originator and the group as a whole to answer the question. Remember, you're looking for positives: 'what needs to be true' not 'why won't this work'. The answers will clarify the conditions needed for a solution to succeed.

- Make a note of them next to the ideas.

- You might want to remove ideas if the conditions for success are too challenging.

6. Select ideas

At the end of this process you should have a number of well-thought-through ideas. Unless there is scope to test all the ideas (unlikely), you'll need to choose the idea(s) to take into a test. This may involve a number of steps, including prioritizing and voting. We often use a simple two-by-two grid – high effort/low effort versus high impact/low impact (see Figure 8.3).

How to do it:

- Create the prioritization grid (Figure 8.3) on the whiteboard.

- Ask people – solo and silent – to plot the remaining ideas in the grid. They will need to create new Post-It notes to do this.

FIGURE 8.3 Prioritization grid

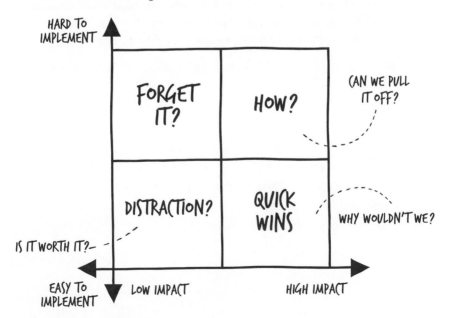

- As a group discuss what is there and if everything is in the right place.

- Depending on the context, the group might easily come to a decision to select an idea that is high impact and low effort – ie a quick win. Or an idea that is higher effort but higher impact. Or both.

- If it is unlikely a consensus will be reached, use dot voting where individuals add stickers to their favourite ideas. You could also try dot voting without using the prioritization grid.

HOW IT WORKS ONLINE
Running a virtual ideation process

Getting people to think beyond the usual way of doing things to unlock new possibilities can be harder when separated by a screen. Harder, but still very achievable. Virtual ideation often has the benefit of being able to plug in a more diverse group of people where it might not have been possible due to distance. If you have a blended group of in-person and virtual, put the virtual people into the same sub-groups.

Preparation

- When it comes to virtual ideation, much of the preparation is the same. Virtual whiteboarding platforms are your friend, providing a way for people to generate, combine, prune, grow, probe and select the best ideas. Get it set up in advance and give people a chance to have a go at using it.

- Choose a range of activities and be prepared to flex. Many listed in this chapter work well, eg reverse the question and personality swap. As with a face-to-face session, there are many ideation activities to choose from, so do your research or ask around.

- Have a practice run. Get your team, friends or family to go through the process with you. Everything works a little bit differently online, so don't leave it to chance. And do have a producer on your team – someone who can make sure the tech does what it needs to and people are happy using it. That way you can focus on the people.

On the day

- A warm-up activity is more important than ever when people are remote, as not only are you crossing mental barriers, you need to cross physical ones too. Never skip the warm-up. The ideation warm-up above can work well in a virtual setting if you put pairs into breakout rooms to do it. Similarly, you can try the 'family portrait' or 'draw something about you' warm-up activities from Chapter 9.

- To mix up the flow, when you are asking people to work individually, give them the option to write their ideas on physical Post-It notes and then share a picture of what they've done. Having a pen in your hand sometimes unlocks a different thought process from writing on a keyboard. People love adding their virtual Post-It notes on whiteboarding platforms, but having a mix of approaches can keep the energy up.

- Build in lots of breaks and suggest people get out of the house to find inspiration. For example, if you are in the idea-generation phase, ask people to spend 10 minutes outside to find five or ten new ideas to bring to the discussion.

CASE STUDY
The ideation process in practice

How a luxury department store used ideation to work around ingrained challenges

Niall Ryan is an employee experience practitioner who has worked as an independent consultant and for several well-known global brands. Here Niall explains how as director of employee experience at a luxury department store, he used ideation techniques to find new ways to overcome blocks to people doing a great job for customers at every opportunity.

This was particularly important as the customer experience is a key brand differentiator. Much work had been done to design training, reward and recognition programmes that were aligned to driving customer-focused behaviours and enhance the customer experience, all of which had been tracked and showed proven causality for improving customer net promoter scores as well as higher sales.

As is the case in many organizations, some ingrained cultural challenges were getting in the way of employees doing their best for customers at every opportunity. This mainly came down to bureaucracy – often described as 'it is difficult to get things done around here'. A lot of energy was being spent getting around the system and taking shortcuts. Other people were simply resigned to it.

To explore the challenges and start to shape solutions, we pulled together a change network of 14 passionate people from different functions, grades, skillsets and perspectives. The network had executive sponsorship, was supported by a culture change facilitator and design thinking consultant, and had a budget to explore ideas, proof of concepts and pilots.

With some principles and ways of working defined, the network began by prioritizing issues and identifying quick wins to rapidly show impact and build a reputation. These revolved around creating a better experience for customers at key touchpoints. Ideation was really important in finding new ways to solve these challenges and overcome established ways of thinking. To help, we worked through a number of steps.

First up was getting the right mix of people in the three teams to work on the three challenges. We mapped out the skills people brought from their professional and personal lives and interests. Individual contribution was determined by skills, not seniority, and the people best suited to the problem were chosen to lead on the challenges. We also mapped the skills and resources the network could call on for additional support. With this information, we split the network into three teams, each with a mix of skills, working styles and attributes. When it came to the ideation, we used a number of techniques to unlock new ideas and ways of thinking.

Generate: personality swaps to shift perspective

Members of the network had experienced or knew of the challenges already, but they were prone to see them in the current cultural context. We needed them to see the issues differently. We used a personality swap exercise to help teams reframe the problem and provoke new ideas. We began by asking each group to describe the problem as a type of person, eg an entrepreneur. We then asked them to think of three entrepreneurs they knew, eg Virgin Group's Richard Branson, SpaceX's Elon Musk and Gymshark's Ben Francis. Each group then picked one and were tasked with exploring how that individual would tackle the problem – their approach, risk levels, etc. The exercise proved a great way to think from a different perspective and tap into people's creativity. The range of ideas was much wider and wilder as a result.

Combine: ideas collision

Now we had ideas, we wanted to see if we could generate more. So, we wrote the ideas down and carried out random combinations to see how many new ideas could be created from either all or the component parts of two separate ideas. Not only did this throw up new ideas; we also discovered potential solutions and quick wins for other lower-priority issues.

Grow: constraints

We had previously discovered that problem statements usually describe things you could not do, ie constraints. We decided to play with that. The teams were tasked to ask what, if anything, they would do differently if the constraints were different. They turned the constraints on their head by asking: was the constraint a perception and could it be changed, removed, etc? We also applied new constraints to the existing ideas. For example, what if you had double the budget? Half the budget? If you had the freedom to remove all constraints? We tried many options and this generated more possibilities, but also led to dialogue about how constraints are not always a negative, but a necessary part of business. This meant that the ideas that were developed were not reckless, but considered reasonable business sense and protected the brand.

Probe and select: selecting ideas and defining solutions

The network was more than a change network. This was a group of change influencers who needed to demonstrate focus, sound business thinking, common sense, customer focus, etc. When it came to sorting the ideas, the network looked for what could be realistically achieved and credible. But also for ideas that did not reflect the status quo, presented an opportunity to challenge stakeholders and where the outcome would have a significant positive impact for the customer and employees. The problem statements we started with were rewritten as solution statements supported by business cases, which detailed key stakeholders, resources required, process maps, customer journey maps, timeframes, budgets, pilots and so on.

Brainstorming rules

A brainstorming session should be fun, creative and collaborative – it can also, however, get political, personality-driven and sticky. Getting it right takes careful facilitation. It will help to build people's confidence if you make the rules clear and help the group keep to them. When we run a brainstorm, we borrow from d.school at Stanford University:

- Defer judgement – switch off your inner monologue and outward critic. You'll have plenty of time to evaluate ideas after the brainstorm.

- Encourage wild ideas – wild ideas don't mean you have to have a wild solution. Just-right ideas are right next to the overly hot ones (remember Goldilocks and the three bears' porridge).

- Build on the ideas of others – more minds make better work, so listen and add to the flow of ideas. Use the language of 'yes, and' rather than 'yes, but'.

- Go for volume – the best way to have a good idea is to have lots of ideas.

- One conversation at a time – keep momentum by saving off-topic conversations for outside the room.

- Make it a headline – capture the essence of a point quickly and move on. Don't stall the group by going into long-winded ideas or explanations.

CASE STUDY

Brainstorming rules in practice

How an NGO found the answer to its performance management challenge on TV

Lucia Abugattas (2020), consultant and author, was working with an NGO in the education sector, when an ideation process led to the team adopting an idea from a TV dating show to improve its performance management process. Here she explains how it happened.

We were looking at the way the organization approached and delivered performance management. Within the HR journey, performance management was one of the things the organization had struggled with the most. Feedback surfaced during interviews included criticism that it was simply a 'once a year' process, 'system heavy' and 'based only on the line manager's view'. The problem was defined as: 'How can we design a better performance management experience for our teams according to their needs and preferences?'

For the ideation process, we split participants into three teams, making sure each team had people from different areas and different roles within the organization. Once in their teams, they were given time to think individually about ideas they would like to implement that would help solve the problem and be enjoyable for employees. Among their ideas, each person had to come up with at least one crazy, judgement-free idea. I love using the phrase 'this is a safe sharing space!' when doing this exercise.

Individuals started coming up with ideas within their teams. Having this individual activity up front helps every participant have accountability of the outcome and ensures everyone gets a say in the process. Ideas included physical mailboxes for employees to receive feedback weekly, coffee catch-ups with their teams and managers, 360 surveys four times a year, speed-dating-style feedback and even drones to deliver feedback letters within the office.

After this, every member shared the headline of their idea and the teams started discussing and building on each other's ideas. This is where the beauty and value of ideation comes to life through co-creation. Sharing with others opens the door to 'yes, and...' conversations, where ideas get better and stronger with all the team's input.

The winning idea started as a chance to get feedback speed-dating style. The participant that proposed this had seen the movie *Hitch* the night before the workshop, where there is a scene on speed dating. Through collaboration and co-creation – and deferring judgement, which might have shut down this idea at the very beginning – SpeedFormance was born. This idea tackled the employees' needs and preferences from three different angles: easy to implement during monthly team meetings; a large face-to-face component to build rapport and sharing within the team; and a 360 feedback approach that can be included within the formal performance review.

Takeaways

In this chapter we explored the steps to generate a successful ideation session or sessions, different ideation tools and techniques, and how to make choices about which ideas to develop into prototypes. In summary:

- Ideation is the process of generating and developing new ideas – lots of new ideas.

- This stage of the EX design framework involves a number of steps, not one single idea-generation activity.
- Successful ideation activities push people to think beyond the limits of the usual way of doing things to unlock new possibilities.
- The most important people to involve in ideation are employees – EX design is about designing with, not for, employees.
- Involving people from across the business will help to develop more achievable ideas and unlock blockers to testing and implementation.
- Involve senior stakeholders judiciously to minimize the risk of blocks further down the line while ensuring the design team has a safe space for ideas to grow and form.
- Preparation is key to a successful ideation session or sessions.
- To set up the ideation process you need to share the challenge and frame the task with the group.
- The six key steps for successful ideation are: generate, combine and connect, prune, grow, probe and select. Separating idea-generation and judging activities will make the process stronger.
- Brainstorming rules are your friend and your guide:
  - Defer judgement.
  - Encourage wild ideas.
  - Build on the ideas of others.
  - Go for volume.
  - One conversation at a time.
  - Make it a headline.

References

Abugattas, LB (2020) *Beyond Llamas, Rainbows and Year-End Parties: Effective and collaborative HR throughout the employee journey*, published by author

Brown, T (2019) *Change by Design, Revised and Updated: How design thinking transforms organizations and inspires innovation*, HarperCollins, New York

Richards, AW (2019) *Improving the Employee Transition Experience: A practical business application for design thinking*, Dissertation, Georgia State University [Online] https://scholarworks.gsu.edu/bus_admin_diss/116 (archived at https://perma.cc/G8UJ-6P8L)

09

Prototype, test and iterate

In this chapter we'll cover:

- what we mean by prototypes and prototyping and its role in EX design;
- some simple tools and techniques to start to create and learn from early-stage prototypes;
- how to approach more developed prototypes – and how to test them;
- how to make prototyping a powerful habit in your team or the wider organization.

Prototypes and their role in EX design

By now we are reaching the end of the third diamond in the EX design framework. This is where we create prototypes to test our ideas, learn from them and iterate. It's where the diamond converges as we start to narrow in on final solutions. However, don't be tricked into thinking this is the end of the story. Rather than being a dash to the finishing line, EX solutions often continue to evolve over weeks and months, even years, as more is learned about an issue. Equally, testing prototypes can result in new opportunities to improve EX being discovered that can send us back to the beginning of the process. Writing in *Strategic HR Review*, Josh Plaskoff (2017) describes how EX solutions 'iteratively unfold' rather than being designed in total once and for all, and that means they are 'flexible, adaptable and well-suited to the organization's and the employees' needs'. This gets to the heart of why prototyping matters – because it leads to better solutions.

In this chapter we look at what we mean by prototypes and prototyping. While EX prototypes take many forms and are developed and tested in a wide variety of ways, we suggest some simple tools and techniques to start to create and learn from early-stage prototypes, as well as how to approach more developed prototypes. We also look at how to make prototyping a powerful habit in your team or the wider organization.

What is a prototype?

A prototype is the first design of something from which other forms are copied or developed. Prototypes come in different shapes and sizes and become more detailed and refined as they are iterated during the process. A first prototype – perhaps the first few iterations – is often a very rough execution of an idea. It's more likely to be a sketch of an idea or a storyboard of an online experience, rather than a website or functional process. Rough and ready is the key. We've worked with teams who have created prototypes in LEGO, through role play, as well as with a bunch of craft materials. There's nothing like building something together to drive team bonding, boost energy and create a shared sense of where you're heading.

The word prototype is often used interchangeably with the phrase 'minimum viable product' (sometimes called minimum lovable product). However, the two are not the same. A minimum viable product is a version of a product or solution with just enough features to satisfy early users and provide feedback for it to be developed. A prototype, on the other hand, is an earlier embodiment of that idea. So it doesn't matter if prototypes are a bit rudimentary. Prototypes are not created to *sell* a solution; they exist to communicate an idea sufficiently well as to learn something new. So prototypes have two critical features – they communicate an idea and enable feedback.

Take NixonMcInnes, one of the first social media agencies in the UK and well known as pioneers, including its focus on team happiness. The team wanted to understand more about the nature of happiness in the business and its impact on the work. As a tech-oriented business, it would have been logical to jump to a digital solution for measuring and tracking happiness. But something was easier and quicker still. The first prototype, or version 0.1, of the NixonMcInnes happiness measure involved buckets and tennis balls. Every day on leaving the office, team members simply put a ball in one of two buckets – happy or unhappy. This was subsequently iterated to three – happy, meh, unhappy. What did the team learn? Yes, people would use them. It was possible to map levels of activity in the agency to the collective emotional state. And there was an optimum point between busy and super busy (tracked on agency time sheets) where happiness peaked. And all this was learned with a quick shopping trip and a budget of little more than a few coffees.

What is prototyping?

The task of prototyping is developing a prototype (or multiple itera-tions of a prototype) and then using it to generate insight about the issue you're solving, catch problems with the design and find other opportunities to improve an experience. What we are actually doing at this point is exploring a hypothesis – if we do this, then that will happen. Usually this is a well-informed guess about what employees want and what they will value. Creating prototypes featuring only the elements you need to test at that point means you can move quicker, figuring out the finer details later. Rapid prototyping, as it is known, provides the means to place small bets on a hypothesis and test it out before investing too much time, money and energy. Rapid prototyping is an exercise in non-attachment. The team behind a solution have to have emotional distance from it in order to hear and act on feedback. It's good to practise that early and often in the process.

So prototyping pays dividends. Unfortunately, they're not always realized. Why? Because too many teams fall in love with the front end of the design process and don't do testing. This happens for a number of reasons – the team loves the solution too much; they've invested too much in sunk costs; they run out of time; or the energy switches elsewhere. That is a mistake, because prototyping leads to better solutions. So make a commitment to prototyping and build it into the plan from the start. Keep it simple by testing one idea at a time. And iterate and add to your prototype one step at a time. Although this may seem to take longer, you will learn a lot more along the way and end up with a solution that needs fewer workarounds. You'll also have a more receptive audience because they have been part of the process.

Still not convinced? Let's look at an example from a small US business of 50 people and one HR person. Given its size, it would be easy to assume the process of building and testing prototypes would be out of reach. In fact, the company created a compact process that goes from identifying an opportunity from survey data, to prototyping a solution within a couple of weeks. The trick is treating everyone in the business as potential collaborators to generate ideas. This is done in regular team lunches. After facilitated idea-generation activities, the whole company votes on the ideas there and then. The winning idea immediately moves to prototype stage, with people asked to volunteer to be part of that process. The prototyping sessions are then facilitated by trained volunteers – in a recent case, members of the diversity and inclusion group.

A recent example of a prototype developed in this way is a 'community contract' – covering meeting norms, behaviours and accountability. This was developed in response to an inclusion survey finding that women in the business feel less confident voicing contrary opinions without fear of negative consequences. The prototype led to a 10-point improvement in the next survey and feedback was used to further develop the contract. (This is one of many examples of design thinking transforming HR processes found on the Talent Tales podcast created by Nicole Dessain, founder of HR.Hackathon Alliance. Details are in the references (Talent Tales, 2020).)

Moving from ideas to prototypes

At the end of the ideation process, you will have one or more ideas you want to prototype. You may even have the beginnings of a prototype in your sketches or storyboards from the ideation session.

You might create a prototype immediately after the ideation process, or during one or a number of prototyping sessions over the following weeks (even months).

The first step in creating a successful prototype is getting the team in the right frame of mind. Prototyping is sometimes described as building to think. The challenge is that most of us are conditioned to think, think some more, put it into a PowerPoint, have some conversations about it and then build nothing. To get people into the right mindset for prototyping, you need to do something to break that cycle. We're not talking here about shifting a cultural love affair with PowerPoint presentations – that is a much bigger task – rather about quick interventions that help people tap into their innate, but often buried, desire and ability to create. We have a few activities we like to use at the beginning of a prototyping session to get people comfortable with just creating something.

Workshop activities to get into the prototyping mindset

FAMILY PORTRAIT

This is an improvisation activity that gets people to quickly think and work together to communicate an idea using just themselves (no words). It's a human sculpture if you like. It's quick and fun.

How to do it:

- Create groups of five or six people.
- Give each group a title of a family picture, eg a family of dentists, cobblers or librarians.
- Give the group(s) 10 seconds to create a portrait based on the title – each person needs to be in the picture doing something to bring the theme to life (remember, no talking).
- At time, shout freeze and take a picture of each group.
- You could award a prize for the best family portrait.

Options:

- Get different groups to do it consecutively and guess what the other groups' pictures are. Guesses are usually fairly accurate, and it makes the point about how possible it is to build to communicate an idea.

- Run this as a virtual session, either in breakouts or as a whole group. Take a screen shot of the video windows as time is called.

HUMAN MACHINE

A similar activity to the family portrait involves giving the team the task of creating a human machine. Think of it as creating a moving picture with action and sound. This is great for groups who are more comfortable with each other and more extrovert, as it's lively and loud.

How to do it:

- Ask the group to randomly shout out a series of nouns and then verbs – capture these on a flipchart or whiteboard.
- Randomly combine these words to describe your machine, eg a spaghetti-making box, chair-painting horse.
- Give the team a machine and 60 seconds to create it using movement and sound, but not words (they might bring in props from the room).
- Suggest to each team that one person starts with an action and/or noise and that others then join. This can work in a much larger group of 20 or more people.

SINGLE-HANDED PLANE

In this activity, teams build a paper plane – but there's a catch. Each team member can only build with one hand. Not only does this exercise get people building; it also demonstrates that it is possible to improvise and iterate even with significant constraints.

How to do it:

- Break into groups of three or four people.
- Ask everyone to raise their dominant hand and then put it behind their back (and keep it there).
- Give groups five minutes to work together to build the plane.

- Encourage the teams to have test flights and iterate their designs (give them more time to encourage this).

- At the end, have a flying competition to see which plane will go furthest.

DRAW SOMETHING ABOUT YOU

This is a simple activity to use at the start of a prototyping session to get people comfortable with drawing and allow them to discover how easy it is to communicate an idea or experience.

How to do it:

- Ask people to draw something in response to the question: 'What's one thing people probably don't know about you?' You could also make this question directly related to the problem or opportunity you are working on, eg: 'What's one thing I learned in the discovery activities that took me by surprise?'

- Get people to briefly explain their drawing to a neighbour or the whole group.

- Put the drawings on the wall to remind people of what they've learned about each other, or the problem, and their ability to communicate through drawing.

How to facilitate a prototyping session

Now you've got people ready to flex their build muscles, it's time to start creating some prototypes. Early stages of the design process require quick and dirty prototypes that can be rapidly tested. These initial, rough representations of an idea are described as low-fidelity. You might create a low-fidelity prototype in as little as an hour and quickly get feedback within two. Creating low-fidelity prototypes requires no technical or specialist skill and next to no resources. A high-fidelity prototype, on the other hand, more closely resembles a final solution and takes more time and resource to build. They usually appear later in the process and typically have a more involved testing regime. However, there are no rules and sometimes low-fidelity prototypes go the whole distance and never become high-fidelity.

An early-stage prototyping session is usually lively, collaborative and fun. However, it may also feel decidedly different from how work usually gets done. Both the process and the outcomes may be new for people. As a facilitator, be sure to set expectations, emphasize the role of simplicity in a great prototype and keep the energy up.

SET EXPECTATIONS

When facilitating an early-stage prototyping session, manage the team's expectations about what is expected by sharing examples of other low-fidelity prototypes. You could share examples from your own early-stage prototypes from different design processes or find examples online. Another great way to set expectations is to produce a bag of craft and modelling materials and put it in front of them. A tiny bit of theatre will help the group understand that something different is happening in the room.

KEEP IT SIMPLE

During the prototyping session, keep the team focused on creating the simplest version of their idea, and encourage them not to over-complicate things. Remind them that the aim is not to wow, but to learn. And they can only achieve that if the prototype simply communicates an idea in a way that generates feedback on the idea.

STOKE THE ENERGY

If you have multiple teams and the energy starts to lag, try trading people between teams to add more creativity to the group and recharge. Being on a timer and having upbeat music playing can also help with the fast and fun tone of the room.

THINK ABOUT THE TEST

As they build, remind people of the point of the prototype – to test and gather feedback. Remind them to focus on what they are seeking to learn from the prototype and how they will get that feedback and when.

Early-stage prototypes

What low-fidelity (low-fi) prototypes lose in resolution, they make up for in flexibility. Here are some of our favourites, most of which can be created in as little as an hour:

- Sketches are a visual way to make an idea more tangible. You don't need any artistic skills to create shapes, stick people and speech bubbles.

- Storyboards are a series of sketches or pictures that demonstrate an end-to-end solution. We use cartoon strip boxes to help people think through a scenario. Storyboarding is a great way to ensure the employee experience is at the heart of the solution.

- Paper interfaces are a way of creating a real interface where people can pretend to tap and click as if they are on a screen. They are useful for prototyping digital products. You can create paper interfaces by sketching, or by drawing and cutting out usable parts of a user interface (eg text field, or navigation such as dropdown menu). They can equally be used to bring a physical object to life, such as a book.

- Modelling is a fun, playful experience that people love. LEGO and Play-Doh are popular ways to create early prototypes which can be shared, and are versatile as the models can easily be tweaked or changed completely.

- Role play, or experiential prototypes, are where you re-enact scenes and situations you are trying to improve, for example a new starter's first day. While the thought of role play might fill you with dread, we are always surprised by groups' willingness to embrace this as a way to communicate their idea. Not only is it a way of getting feedback from end users, but the experience of being in the moment can also create new energy and often provides insight around the problem for the design team. You can add levels of detail to the role play, including simulating a physical environment with props.

FIGURE 9.1 Early-stage prototypes

- Wizard of Oz prototypes sit halfway between a low- and high-fidelity prototype and create an illusion of the functionality you want to test, without actually providing it. It's about smoke and mirrors. A team we worked with came up with an idea for an interactive map to support virtual onboarding. The idea of the map was to show new starters, their buddy and the line manager where everyone was in the process and automatically suggest prompts and ideas to keep people connected and moving on the right lines. The end solution was to incorporate the interactive map into the company's online collaboration platform and automate the prompts and reminders through the platform. The first prototype was a video using mocked-up screens to suggest the user experience. After getting feedback, the team planned to create a Wizard of Oz prototype of the map as a PDF that the HR team could manipulate while also sending the new starter, buddy and manager reminders and prompts through the collaboration platform.

CASE STUDY
Low-fidelity prototyping

How Expedia Group explored what people thought about its survey

When travel company Expedia Group wanted to understand what people thought about the online employee survey, it opted to use a low-fidelity prototyping method to find out. Here, former senior director of talent programs Lindsay Bousman PhD, explains why and how they did it.

We had been trained in design thinking methods as well as other experimentation strategies and were supported in applying these methods to our HR products and services. After looking at our talent management roadmap, we decided to use a low-fidelity prototyping method to truly listen to our employees about the online employee survey and reporting experience and see if we could reinvent it with their guidance.

The challenge was that the annual survey was revered as a 'flagship product', and over time we had stakeholder feedback requesting somewhat conflicting changes. So we narrowed the options to a set of features, mixed them up and took it to the people. Through a series of live and virtual sessions with randomly selected groups of employees from various personas (or audience types), we gathered their input. We chose to use poster-size storyboards to help illustrate the series of combinations of the features we had heard were valuable. To make it interactive, we handed out stickers, markers and small self-stick notes for them to mark up the prototypes.

The process

We asked participants to roam around the room (when virtual this was more structured), and we listened and observed reactions. They noticed right away some of the trade-offs in different options through the 'Prototype Walk The Walls', and when everyone had finished their walk, we would ask attendees to vote with their stickers on their most preferred and least preferred options, those that might have surprised and delighted them and those that were disappointing. This forced-choice voting isn't a decision, but another way to instigate conversation about design. Many attendees wanted to create hybrid options, the best of several features in their mind. This is a desired part of using design thinking and a prototype process, listening and co-creating in the moment, writing notes on the posters, evolving the design.

As expected, the trade-offs in features were sometimes controversial, but allowed the participants to organically take the 'seat' of one of the stakeholder groups and develop empathy for the myriad combinations available. For example, managers could see that their needs as a report receiver might differ from their needs as a survey respondent, and we were able to talk through their ideas for solving it. We ended up taking inputs from participants and applying several new features to our employee survey programme, not choosing any of the prototypes as-is, but rather taking the nuggets of ideas and creating two new features entirely: more transparency in reporting directly to employees and a separate rotating pulse survey for longer-term change initiatives.

Why it worked

Some may argue that in-person testing or iterating is best, and some may argue it is impractical, but what matters is that it can be beneficial and also can be done virtually. Making some adjustments was necessary to do this virtually, but it still worked. Asking for input, using whatever method you can, is always better than not asking at all.

The benefits to in-person as well as virtual sessions are that you can see the facial expressions of the participants as they look at or interact with the prototype. You can probe those expressions or verbal moments of 'huh' with a quick question or statement: 'What made you say that? You look puzzled/ confused/pleased. Why? Tell me more.'

Acting as a researcher or anthropologist of your own work may lead to a new idea you didn't think of, or an unintended consequence or assumption made which you can address in the design or the support materials. In some cases, you may opt to reset the problem itself as you uncover a secondary or related problem that may lend itself to solving first. This organic interaction provides a moment to co-create, build upon and further iterate.

An additional benefit is that you are able to build trust and credibility with employees. They see the care and thoughtfulness you are putting into the product or solution and, in turn, it has the tendency to reflect positively on their general overall employee experience. You can even use the time to solicit employees to be part of a longer product-creation process.

Designing the employee experience in a practical way doesn't have to be expensive or complicated, but it should be thoughtful and involve simple ways like prototyping for employees to participate.

HOW IT WORKS ONLINE
Virtual prototyping isn't as hard as it sounds

Prototyping is often an energetic, messy and collaborative affair. So virtual prototyping doesn't feel like a natural option. However, like its spiritual parent, design thinking, EX design works within constraints all the time. Remember the three lenses of work, people and business – all suggest constraints of one form or another. So if you need to work virtually, there is always a way to do it.

We have found online whiteboarding platforms a huge help. They can support the entire design process and can be used in a wide variety of ways to develop prototypes, from simply hosting a Post-It note session, to collaboratively creating a prototype using words, pictures, even video. Other collaborative online tools include storyboarding platforms. There is also a growing number of really simple prototyping platforms that allow you to quickly and easily create apps and basic web pages with few technical skills.

There are two routes to choose from or combine when facilitating virtual prototyping sessions – parallel and collaborative prototyping.

With parallel prototyping, group members work individually in parallel with the same brief. People then develop their own prototypes and share with each other before combining them into one. It's a useful process as you can see where people design the same thing and where there are nuances or differences. This in itself throws up interesting conversations. Parallel prototyping is a great choice if people are in different time zones or you want to draw out where the team is and isn't aligned on what the solution is. It's also a good way to ensure all voices – including quieter voices – are able to contribute.

Collaborative prototyping, as the name suggests, is where the group works on the prototype together. This is useful where the team is aligned and clear on the solution and where things need to move fast.

Virtual prototyping needs clear facilitation with well-defined instructions and summaries at either end of the session so people know what the expectations and the constraints are. The brief for the prototype and testing regime needs to be really well understood and re-articulated at the beginning and end of each session to help people stay on target.

Creating higher-fidelity prototypes

Creating and getting feedback on a solution using low-fidelity prototypes is often a rapid affair. However, as prototypes are iterated and more details added, the feedback you're looking for becomes more specific. For this reason, it is important that prototypes are purposeful, ie that considerations around how feedback will be sought and what you are testing are factored in from the start. If they are not, you might end up with a great looking prototype and nowhere to go with it.

In 2019 a group of academics and design practitioners shared a paper highlighting studies showing that without a clear purpose, prototypes can end up as a function of the design process, rather than a function of the design (Lauff *et al*, 2019). These findings motivated the creation of a prototyping canvas, a tool to help designers create purposeful prototypes by identifying the critical assumptions and questions the prototype needs to address. The tool, which can be downloaded for free (see link in the references), can be used to help groups plan prototypes in a workshop or other setting.

After you have nailed the number one thing you need to discover (eg what assumptions have been made about the opportunity or the design? What questions are still unanswered?), you need to consider a few other factors before creating your higher-fidelity prototype:

1 The build – what is the simplest way to build and test our critical assumption or question?

2 Resources – what materials, money, people and time are available and what can we get hold of to build or test the prototype?

3 Testing plan – how will we test our assumption/question using the prototype? Where, when and with whom?

4 Stakeholders – who are our stakeholders, including end users, project sponsor, functional or other heads? How will we involve them or keep them informed?

5 Insight – how will we capture, reflect on and work with the insight we generate in the testing process?

So far we have looked at what we mean by prototypes and encouraged you to get started with some simple prototyping approaches. So you've got your prototype – what next?

Testing your prototype

In the ideal process, end users will be involved in creating your prototypes. However, for testing, you will want to get additional, neutral feedback from beyond the design team. Testing can take many forms depending on the solution you're creating and the fidelity of the prototype.

Testing low-fidelity prototypes

With low-fidelity prototypes you may simply do a show and ask with your prototype – showing people a mock-up or sketch of your idea and then asking questions. To get the insight you need, follow four rules:

1 Make the person you're speaking with feel comfortable and ensure they know you want and welcome honest feedback (not edited feedback).

2 Introduce, but don't sell the idea.

3 Give enough information about the idea so the prototype makes sense, but don't explain the thinking or reasoning behind the solution.

4 Practise non-attachment – don't defend ideas in the face of feedback.

CAPTURING FEEDBACK

However you're testing, it's important to be clear on what you're trying to learn and stay open to whatever comes up. Capture the feedback to ensure you don't lose anything. To achieve this and bring it to life for team members not involved in the testing process, a feedback grid can be useful (see Figure 9.2). Use it to capture feedback in the moment and share it afterwards. Either complete it yourself or ask your end user(s) to complete it with your support. The simplest way to do this is to create the feedback grid on a whiteboard and give people Post-It notes to write on (one thought on each Post-It). You could similarly do this on a virtual whiteboarding platform.

When you've collected your feedback, reflect on what you've heard with the team, highlighting insights and documenting any new

FIGURE 9.2 Feedback grid

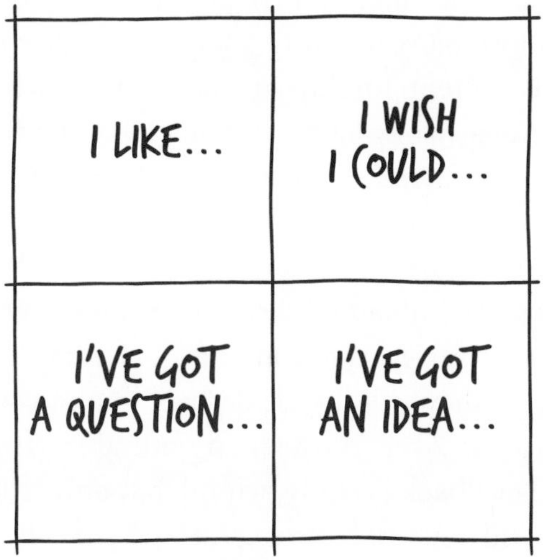

assumptions and questions that arise. This may lead to the next prototype iteration or development of an entirely new concept to prototype.

Testing higher-fidelity prototypes

How you test your higher-fidelity prototype will depend on a variety of factors, as covered above. It might involve a small or large number of people, a short or long time window. This is where it pays to have people from across different functions involved. Their knowledge of the business's tools and systems and their ability to influence what happens across the business will make it easier to have the right testing approach. Of course, you can't just chuck things out there. You may need to bring a range of stakeholders into the process so they know what you're doing. If you're clear about your intention to learn – not sell – you'll get a much better reception. Different testing scenarios we have seen include the following, sometimes in combination:

- AB testing is a method for comparing two versions of something against each other to discover which is the most successful. You'll see this demonstrated in the upcoming Asurion case study, where AB testing was used to determine the effectiveness of a new approach to performance management.

- Employee trials with quantitative metrics are another route to get feedback. A company recently took this approach to test and develop new content for line managers who were adjusting to supporting teams working from home. The first prototype was simple wellbeing-focused content shared directly with managers. Feedback was collected from managers to see what was useful. With this insight, the HR team developed more tailored content and monitored download data to understand what was working. This approach moves the concept of feedback beyond what someone thinks they will do – ie do they think they will access the content – to discover if they do indeed access the content. Quantitative feedback is really helpful, but only tells you so much. A next step will usually be to explore why people are or are not accessing the solution, how they are using it, and what the impact is. Never make assumptions.

CASE STUDY
AB testing

How Asurion prototyped and AB-tested to iterate the performance process

Pierre Delinois, senior manager of HR product design, explains how the Nashville-based technology company Asurion used prototyping and AB testing to create and iterate a new annual performance process to better meet employees' needs.

Asurion's HR team had redesigned the annual performance process with the goal of better helping employees grow, perform and thrive. The HR team had used internal and external research to inform the new approach, which was a conversation-driven process with quarterly touchpoints between managers and employees. Before launching, the HR team wanted to test the solution. That's where the HR design team got involved.

To explore the effectiveness of the new process, the HR design team recommended an AB testing route. This meant testing the process with a pilot group of about 500 members, plus a control group of 350. The control group was selected based on similarities to the pilot group across several criteria: engagement score, role type, organizational structure and tenure. The control group experienced the standard annual performance process and were not notified of their participation in the test.

Testing a hypothesis

To start the work, the HR design team captured and expressed the problem statement behind the redesign of the performance management process as: the previous approach to performance management does not help employees stay aligned to strategic priorities, grow and perform. The pilot then sought to test the following hypothesis: the new performance process will help employees have more clear performance expectations, helping them thrive and grow.

The test was carried out over the course of a year, during which time the pilot and control group experienced their versions of the performance process. Both were sent surveys over the course of the year to understand their experience across the programme and test the hypothesis.

At the end of the test, the pilot group reported statistically significant increases in clarity about their performance objectives and growth opportunities. They also reported a better experience of the process than those of the control group. To understand what contributed to the strong results, the HR design team conducted interviews and focus groups with 70 pilot group participants.

Through these discussions, the team learned that frequent conversations helped employees grow and course-correct continuously over the year. However, along with their positive take on the experience, pilot participants also shared a shortcoming – they felt their ability to make the most of the new programme was limited by how their teams set and tracked goals. This was an insight the HR design team recognized as an opportunity to help leaders and employees improve goals management.

Creating new prototypes

To explore the opportunity, the HR design team facilitated a three-day version of the Google Ventures design sprint – a rapid problem-solving process involving discovery, design, prototyping and testing. During the sprint, a cross-functional HR team discussed the research insights, identified possible opportunities for impact, brainstormed a large number of possible solutions and defined two prototypes: goal-setting skills training and enhanced goals management technology.

Following the sprint, the HR team upgraded training to support the new process. Meanwhile, the HR design team created and tested a wireframe prototype (a visual guide that represents the skeletal framework of a website) of a new goals management system. The feedback was used to source an external product that, after further testing with employees, was embedded into the conversation-driven performance management process. The process and technology are now in use across the organization and the HR team continues to monitor and make improvements, in support of employee experience.

The benefits

The prototype, test, iterate approach worked really well for us. If we had taken a traditional approach, we would have rolled out a well-intentioned process to employees that didn't fully address their needs. This would have been disruptive to the organization and would have produced less benefit.

Testing allowed us to truly understand the emotions and experiences of employees based on their actual experiences with a prototyped solution. This produced rich insights that allowed us to better understand their needs. The end result is more than a new process – it's an integrated experience for employees that helps them perform, grow and thrive.

How to make prototyping a habit

Design-centric companies aren't shy about playing with ideas in public. And they tend to iterate rapidly on their prototypes. This is a huge mindset shift, moving away from perfect and launch, to test and learn. But the more you do it, the easier it gets. Idris Mootee, writing in *Design Thinking for Strategic Innovation* (2013), suggests that companies fall into the trap of trying to innovate the 'right' way 'by spending so much time, energy and resources on getting it right and avoiding failure, not enough time, energy and resources are dedicated to playful, experimental creation'. If you want to make a change in how your organization approaches EX, think more expansively about where prototypes show up – it's possibly the most pragmatic thing you can do to build your EX capability. Challenge yourself and your team to be constantly bringing ideas to life and testing them, not burying them in PowerPoints.

One suggestion we've come across is to never go to a meeting without a prototype – which feels like a tall order. So what about setting up a weekly 'share and learn' to make it more of a regular routine? One digital agency we know had a monthly Showtime where they did just that – complete with MC and glitter ball to share new ideas and unfinished projects and get feedback. The message of Showtime: we're always in beta. Not everyone works in a creative agency where such inventions land. But everyone can choose to find new ways to make ideas tangible more quickly and get feedback. Do it often enough and it will become a habit.

CASE STUDY

Testing without a prototype

Just putting something out there

Sometimes you don't need a prototype to test an idea. This was the case for an EX design team at a large energy company. The team was tasked with finding out why participants in a leadership programme were not returning to the assessment centre to take advantage of the coaching sessions on offer and why satisfaction scores were declining.

The team began to explore the problem in a series of workshops – for people who had taken full advantage of coaching; those who had attended a few coaching sessions; and those who had never returned. The workshops uncovered a number of things that could be done to improve the experience. One of those focused on the breaks, which, it turned out, were moments that mattered, especially as the assessments lasted a few hours and were typically intense. Taking an assessment in a building you are not familiar with can be stressful. Participants were also disappointed that there were not any snacks or food available.

The following week participants were given refreshments and different catering options were tested. The result? Participants immediately began returning for their coaching sessions and satisfaction scores significantly improved. And it hasn't stopped there. The insights have led to a complete redesign of the assessment centre with new elements of the design being tested and incorporated over time.

Takeaways

In this chapter we looked at what we mean by prototypes and proto-typing and shared some simple tools and techniques to start to create and learn from early-stage prototypes, as well as how to approach more developed prototypes. In summary:

- A prototype is the first design of something from which other forms are copied or developed.
- Building time into your EX design process for prototyping leads to better-quality solutions.
- Prototypes are not about selling an idea – they're about communi-cating a concept sufficiently well so as to generate new insight.
- The task of prototyping is developing a prototype (or multiple iterations of a prototype) and then using it to generate insight around the issue you're solving, catch problems with the design, and find opportunities to improve an experience that have been missed.
- In EX design, a first prototype is usually a rough or low-fidelity representation of an idea and requires little time, no specialized skills, and few resources to create.
- Prototyping sessions should be fun, energetic, and collaborative – that can be achieved online with careful facilitation and the right tools.

- Prototypes start low-fidelity and often gain more features and details (becoming high-fidelity) as the process of testing and iteration continues.

- Thinking more expansively about where prototypes show up is a good way to build EX design capability.

References

Lauff, C, Menold, J and Wood, K (2019) [accessed 8 August 2020] *Prototyping Canvas: Design tool for planning purposeful prototypes*, Cambridge University Press, 26 July [Online] https://www.cambridge.org/core/journals/proceedings-of-the-international-conference-on-engineering-design/article/prototyping-canvas-design-tool-for-planning-purposeful-prototypes/A535E9D0DFC923B7F41C6288FA0AF3E1 (archived at https://perma.cc/FS5D-AR3G)

Mootee, I (2013) *Design Thinking for Strategic Innovation: What they can't teach you at business or design school*, John Wiley & Sons, Hoboken, NJ

Plaskoff, J (2017) [accessed 18 July 2020] Employee experience: The new human resource management approach, *Strategic HR Review* [Online] https://www.deepdyve.com/lp/emerald-publishing/employee-experience-the-new-human-resource-management-approach-eeg6sXKuBA (archived at https://perma.cc/7TFJ-67ST)

Talent Tales (2020) [accessed 13 October 2020] Hacking diversity: A conversation with Sittercity's Kelli Koschmann [Podcast], 1 March [Online] https://podcasts.apple.com/ae/podcast/hacking-diversity-conversation-sittercitys-kelli-koschmann/id1461677062?i=1000467199114 (archived at https://perma.cc/7PBV-LGMV)

10

Measuring employee experience

In this chapter we'll cover:

- what we are measuring, and why your definition of EX is so important;
- why measure – using return on experience to make your case and prove your worth;
- how to measure EX;
- running an EX survey;
- demonstrating your impact.

EX – what are we measuring?

To measure effectively, we first need to be clear about what it is we are measuring as well as what we are trying to achieve. In previous chapters we introduced our levels of experience model, which is a good place to start when considering these questions (Figure 10.1).

At the broadest level you might want to measure the overall experience your people have in your organization: the 'umbrella' EX. We discussed in Chapter 1 that there is no single universal definition of EX – you need to figure out what it means for your organization and why you're focusing on it. These questions will help you to understand what you are going to measure. Definitions of EX are wide-ranging – some are useful to help us determine what we need to

FIGURE 10.1 Levels of experience

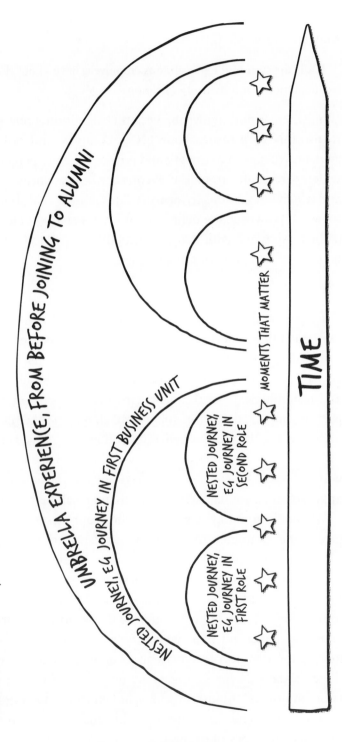

UMBRELLA EXPERIENCE, FROM BEFORE JOINING TO ALUMNI

NESTED JOURNEY, EG JOURNEY IN FIRST BUSINESS UNIT

NESTED JOURNEY, EG JOURNEY IN FIRST ROLE

NESTED JOURNEY, EG JOURNEY IN SECOND ROLE

MOMENTS THAT MATTER

TIME

measure, others less so. For example, let's consider this definition from Maylett and Wride (2017):

> EX is the sum of the perceptions employees have about their interactions with their organization.

While there is nothing wrong with this definition, understanding how to use this to measure your EX is complex and not immediately evident. We'd need to understand how to measure perceptions, decide which perceptions to measure, consider how to measure interactions and which interactions to measure. This is achievable but not straightforward. However, the definition of EX we shared in Chapter 1 from a client we work with is more straightforward and it's easier to see how we would go about measuring this:

> EX is all about enabling our people to have more good days at work.

Off-the-shelf definitions and approaches to EX can be flawed given they may not be relevant to your organizational context. For example, Jacob Morgan's (2017) model, as shared in Chapter 1, involves three environments that matter most to employees: the physical, cultural, and technological environment. However, a focus on technology as part of your EX definition and approach may not be relevant to your organization, therefore why would you bother measuring this?

When seeking to measure the overall experience your people have with your organization, we recommend developing your own approach. The content within this chapter will help you to do this.

Of course you may wish to measure your 'nested' experiences: we give some examples of these in our levels of experience model. Measuring a specific EX is much more straightforward, given we have already answered our first question: what are we trying to measure? For example, it could be the onboarding experience, or a return to work experience after furlough or maternity leave, or your performance management experience, the exit experience, or perhaps the first 12 months in role experience. You might also want to measure the everyday EX for your people, or you may want to understand your employees' mindset, which can help facilitate a great EX. We'll set out approaches and advice in this chapter to help you measure these specific types of experience.

When planning your measurement approach it is also important to make the distinction between the experience itself, eg was it good or bad, and the desired outcomes of the EX, eg reduced employee turnover at the end of the induction programme. Remember that EX is not an outcome itself, but something which we believe will help us to achieve the outcomes we are looking for. Getting clear on what it is you are looking to measure and the outcomes you are hoping for is the starting point for your approach.

Corine Boon, associate professor at the University of Amsterdam and director at the Amsterdam People Analytics Centre, recommends making the distinction between EX intentions, what is actually implemented, employee perceptions and outcomes. Put simply, it can be summarized as follows:

- Intended: what are we trying to do, eg provide a brilliant induction programme.
- What is actually implemented: an induction programme.
- Perceived: this is essentially the experience, and how your people experience what you offer, eg that was a fantastic induction experience. You can evaluate how near or far the reality of the EX is from the intended EX.
- Outcomes: what happened and what was the result? For example, employees are more likely to stay now we have this new induction and their engagement is higher.

Your EX measurement approach should ideally look at both the umbrella EX as well as specific 'nested' experiences, given the dependent nature of the two. We know that experiences do not happen in isolation and there are many factors that contribute to the overall EX your people have. Contemplating how we measure the overall EX can feel quite overwhelming, but it doesn't have to be. We'll share some recommendations to help you to achieve this, but first let's consider why we should bother to measure EX in the first place.

Why measure EX – a look at return on EX

CEOs know that company culture matters. In a study of over 1,300 businesses, HR Wins and Culture Amp (2020) found that 65 per cent of CEOs believe that company culture has a direct financial impact on their business. Demonstrating a return on investment (ROI) or return on EX (ROX) is helpful for a number of reasons. It demonstrates the value of EX to the business, enabling us to better understand where to target often limited resources. It also helps to elevate EX to be viewed by the business as a strategic priority.

ROX seeks to measure the impact that EX activity has on the bottom line. ROX is about understanding which experiences facilitate the results you want. There is no single approach to ROX. It typically involves gathering insights from a range of data points, often both internal as well as external. The starting point though for any ROX calculation is understanding the outcomes you are looking to influence with your EX efforts. For example, we might be looking at outcomes such as employee turnover, productivity, absenteeism, customer satisfaction, or more. Let's take a worked example and focus on employee turnover.

Glassdoor state that the average cost per hire is almost $4,000. Add to this the time it takes for new recruits to get up to speed in their new role, plus the costs of onboarding, and pretty soon you reach estimates of some $12,000 every time you take on a new employee. And some estimates are far in excess of this figure. Hiring people is a significant investment, so you want to ensure your people stay once they join. You might discover that there is a 'flight risk' of new recruits within the first three months and as such you make a decision to focus on the onboarding EX. In this example it is pretty straightforward to make your business case. By improving the onboarding EX you hope to reduce turnover by X per cent, which you can attribute a cost saving to. You can then monitor employee turnover figures when the new onboarding programme is in place, and if turnover reduces, you can demonstrate ROX.

Though this example looks relatively simple, in reality, demonstrating ROX can be challenging. Although the business case for focusing on EX is compelling, understanding exactly how EX contributes to the bottom line is sometimes more tricky. What can help to pull your investment case together, and then monitor ROX, is to review some of the external ROX examples that exist. Here, we've summarized some key data that may be helpful when setting out your ROX case:

- Google improved their onboarding EX by sending a checklist to managers the week before the new hire started. This resulted in a reduction of 25 per cent less time for the new hire to get to full productivity (Bock, 2016).

- Organizations with a good onboarding EX improve new hire retention by 82 per cent and productivity by over 70 per cent (Peterson, 2020).

- Recruiting has a significant impact on revenue. Research shows that good recruiting practices, which include the EX, contribute to more than three times revenue growth and two times profit margins (BCG, 2012).

- Companies that hire managers based on their management capability saw a 48 per cent increase in profitability (Gallup, 2020).

- Research from Gallup (2020) also found that one in two employees left a job because of their manager.

- Thirty-six per cent of people switching jobs left because they were 'unsatisfied with the work environment/culture' of their previous employer (LinkedIn, 2014).

There is further research in the public domain that makes the case for the ROI of a wide range of people strategies and activities. For example, John Kotter's (Kotter and Heskett, 1992) research on culture found a link between a strong culture and commercial performance:

- Revenues increased in these companies four times faster.
- Job creation rates grew to seven times higher.
- Stock prices increased 12 times faster.

- Profits climbed 750 per cent higher.
- New revenue grew 700 per cent.
- Customer satisfaction doubled.

How to measure EX

Developing your umbrella EX measurement approach – to survey or not to survey?

We're already seeing a rise in survey providers offering tools and approaches to measure and benchmark your EX. Their approaches are based on research that results in a list of attributes, which the authors argue either measure EX itself or have a real and measurable impact on EX. The problem with this approach is that, first, there is no single universal definition of EX. Second, what constitutes a great EX is not universal or uniform. And third, what drives a great EX within the context of your organization will be unique to you. There are almost certainly some universal elements of what constitutes and drives a great EX, but at the same time there will always be organizational differences too. If we take an 'off the shelf' approach to measuring EX, we are making assumptions about what a great EX is and what drives it, and subsequently the findings we get could lead us to work on the wrong things.

For example, IBM (2017) conducted research to answer the following questions:

- What is the ideal employee experience in today's workplace?
- What impact could a positive employee experience have on key outcomes?
- How can organizations drive more positive and human employee experiences?

And following a literature review they defined EX as:

A set of perceptions that employees have about their experiences at work in response to their interactions with the organization.

Using this definition as a guiding framework, they then developed their EX Index, which measures:

- belonging – feeling part of a team, group or organization;
- purpose – understanding why one's work matters;
- achievement – a sense of accomplishment in the work that is done;
- happiness – the pleasant feeling arising in and around work;
- vigour – the presence of energy, enthusiasm and excitement at work.

While this all sounds very reasonable, the problem is that if we take IBM's definition, it is organization-specific. That is, EX is about the perceptions we have about our experiences in response to interactions with the organization we are working for. We believe that the elements of the IBM model outlined above will most likely feature in people's best experience stories. But critically, there will be more involved in a great EX, for example feeling valued, having autonomy and more. This is why it is so important for you to invest time to understand what good looks like for your people and use this insight as your foundation for any EX efforts.

To measure your umbrella EX you might be tempted to try and develop an EX index, but our advice is please don't! While it's tempting to combine a number of elements into an overall score, the problem is that this is pretty meaningless, and it won't give you a measure of the umbrella EX. In addition, an EX index score might give you a temperature check of how your people experience your organization, but it doesn't give direction on what to work on to improve your EX. You may find you get a top-quartile EX index score from an off-the-shelf survey, but this doesn't really demonstrate the value add, and positive impact, achieving a score like this actually has on a business.

We recommend that if you do wish to run a survey to measure your EX, whatever this means for you, you develop your own set of measures to do this. And it isn't as complex as it sounds. This process starts with running some best EX workshops across your organization. The insights from these workshops will shed light on what great experiences look and feel like for your people. You can then use this insight to develop a survey to understand how near or far you are from this ideal experience as defined by your people. Of course you can add in further questions relevant to your organizational context, but this is really the best way to approach measuring your umbrella EX.

EXERCISE
Measuring EX at ING

ING is a global bank with a strong European base. They have 55,000 employees who serve around 38.4 million customers, corporate clients and financial institutions in over 40 countries. Their purpose is to empower people to stay a step ahead in life and in business. And they are investing in EX, endeavouring to make sense of measuring EX. We wanted to share their approach to EX measurement to shine a light on how you can approach this. (EX Measurement at ING was developed in close co-operation with TI-People, inventors of the Employee Experience Index©.)

ING have recognized that, historically, measurement in HR has been focused on engagement rather than EX. In order to actively manage EX, they identified the need for a mechanism to capture immediate feedback from experiences at the important touchpoints in relevant journeys.

They identified that time is a crucial factor when evaluating EX. When reacting to negative experiences, the journey and touchpoint owners needed to learn about issues as soon as possible after they occur. They also wanted an approach to enable feedback at touchpoints. This then enabled negative experiences to be directly linked to touchpoints, therefore making it possible to assign responsibility to improve an experience.

ING recognized that existing indicators that are sometimes thought to provide insights on EX, such as pulse checks or exit interviews, are EX retrospectives. By definition they have a time lag and lack a clear link to touchpoints. Their approach therefore covers both individual touchpoints and entire journeys, ultimately aiming at gathering real-time data.

Their approach very deliberately looks at both journey-level EX data and touchpoint data to ensure the insight is actionable. For example, the overall journey EX may seem acceptable – even though one or more important touchpoints may show negative EX. This means missing out on the opportunity to enhance EX at these touchpoints. And if you only measure at the touchpoint level, EX across all touchpoints could be deemed acceptable. However, the journey EX could be negative due to average touchpoints that should be improved to drive engagement.

Their approach to measuring the EX at each employee touchpoint helps them to understand those that need to be redesigned. Here is an example of a case where a touchpoint needs to be redesigned:

1 EX at that touchpoint is currently very negative, causing a pain point.

2 The touchpoint is a Moment-of-Truth: an emotionally loaded touchpoint that has a disproportional impact on engagement.

3 Redesign might require the involvement of multiple stakeholders across ING. These stakeholders may own touchpoints or specific channels and sit across multiple teams and functions.

4 The change required to redesign the touchpoint is assessed from the employee's perspective. The solution may be a quick fix or involve a larger-scale change such as implementing a new technology solution, like an onboarding app.

They have also identified and measure EX via three KPIs: one at journey level and two at touchpoint level.

1 KPI for employee journeys: evaluation of EX at journey level uses net promoter score (NPS).

2 KPI for touchpoints: Moments-of-Truth that require a higher service level are evaluated by customer satisfaction (CSAT) – effortless touchpoints that are more likely to leverage technology may be assessed using a customer effort score (CES).

This example of a measurement plan covers both the overall EX as well as specific experiences, and is a great example to illustrate how you could approach it.

What EX metrics could you use?

Dr Wilmar Schaufeli, professor of work and organizational psychology at the University of Utrecht, has made the case for using the Utrecht Work Engagement Scale (UWES) to develop EX metrics. The UWES argues that there are three elements involved in engagement with work: vigour, absorption and dedication. Schaufeli argues that we can use these elements to understand how our people experience the company (Schaufeli and Bakker, 2004).

1. VIGOUR

Vigour is characterized by high levels of energy and mental resilience, the willingness to invest effort in one's work, and persistence even in the face of difficulties. Survey questions that measure vigour include:

- Do you look forward to coming to work most days?
- Do you feel energized and inspired by the work you do daily?
- Do you believe your work helps you achieve your personal career goals?

2. ABSORPTION

Absorption is characterized by being fully concentrated and happily engrossed in one's work, whereby time passes quickly and one has difficulties with detaching oneself from work. Survey questions that measure absorption include:

- True or false: When I'm performing my job responsibilities, time passes quickly.
- True or false: There are many parts of my job when I feel fully engrossed, invested, etc.

3. DEDICATION

Dedication refers to being strongly involved in one's work and experiencing a sense of significance, enthusiasm, inspiration, pride and challenge. Survey questions that measure dedication include:

- If you were offered a similar job with the same pay and benefits, how likely are you to take it?
- Do you think you'll be working here in six months?

Of course EX is about more than engagement in the work you do. There are a range of other factors we might choose to include when measuring the umbrella EX. These include:

- questions relating to the EX of hygiene factors, eg pay and conditions, tools to do your job, workplace environment, quality, rewards and more;
- questions relating to the EX of the employee 'lifecycle', eg the way my performance is managed, my experience of career development;
- questions relating to the everyday EX, eg culture, the way I'm managed, pride, employee net promoter questions;
- questions relating to employee EX mindset, eg belief in the contribution I can make, opportunity to make a difference, overcoming setbacks.

Consider the context, strategy and brand of your organization when designing your measurement approach. For example, a retail company focused on customers should include some measures relating to this. If you're a tech company, your employees' experience of your tech might be important. In addition to the themes, you also might want to explore attitudes, beliefs, behaviours, norms, preconditions of EX and outcomes of EX. To understand these themes, you may begin by asking some questions such as:

- What is the current experience?
- What makes it a good experience, or not?
- What is the ideal experience?
- How important is this experience to your employees?

Desired outcomes of EX

If you decide to run a survey to gather your data and measure your EX success, be mindful that often survey design can become unwieldy. We recommend getting really clear about the purpose of your survey: what is it you're trying to measure and why? Do you simply want to evaluate the current EX, or understand the drivers behind EX? Are you looking at the intended EX or the perceptions of the EX? Or are you looking at the desired EX?

EXERCISE

Running an EX survey – questions to consider

If you are thinking about running an EX survey, we recommend working through the questions below to help you get the most out of your research.

Be clear on why you want to run an EX survey

Make sure you are clear about why you are running a survey and how this insight can be used to inform your EX approach. What will you do with the results? How often will you run the survey? Are you looking to measure ongoing EX or specific experiences?

Understand what a successful survey programme looks like

Spend some time considering what success looks like and what insights will be useful. Do you want to look at outcomes, or the current experience? Think about how you want to use the data. Think about what demographic splits might be useful.

Think about where you might need some help

There is considerable technical skill involved in writing good survey questions and designing research, so ensure that a qualified member of your HR team, or other, is involved. You can run your survey yourself if you have the right tech internally or you can use a platform such as Survey Monkey or Qualtrics.

Alternatively, you might decide to bring in some external expertise to help you design and run your survey. Using an external supplier has many benefits, for example use of the latest technology, ease of reporting, confidentiality of responses and access to the behavioural research and approaches.

Consider the ideal survey experience

This is really important – if we are interested in developing EX, we need to design a decent survey experience. When running a survey you're asking employees to take the time to complete it, so it's a good idea to think about how you can make this a positive experience for them: from the way the survey is positioned, to how participation is encouraged, through to the way in which results are shared with employees and what will happen with data. These elements should all be considered to help make the survey experience a good one for your people.

These are some useful questions to consider if you're thinking about looking for a survey partner:

- Does their definition and model of EX work with your definition and model?
- Do their key driver questions align with your company context, strategy and focus?
- Is there an opportunity for their survey design to be bespoke for your organization or is it an off-the-shelf solution?
- Will their survey design include open-response questions to collect employee comments?
- How has their tool been validated and tested?
- Are they able to offer translation services if required?
- Can they offer multi-format surveys if required, eg online and paper?
- Can they provide different cuts of the data as required, eg by department, team, manager, etc?
- What reporting tools do they offer and how easy are they to use?
- What type of statistical analysis do they offer?
- Have they got any recommendations from other clients?
- What is the cost? Be sure to enquire about any extras such as requesting further data cuts or special reports.

It's not all about the survey

If you do decide to run an EX survey, it is helpful to run some qualitative research to delve deeper into areas of interest arising from the process. In fact, it's useful to run qualitative research even if you don't run an EX survey. Often quantitative research via a survey raises more questions than it answers, and you need to understand what sits behind the results and find out why you are seeing certain patterns and trends. There are a range of qualitative methodologies that can be used to further explore the data from the survey process:

1 focus groups;
2 follow-up interviews;
3 world café events;
4 online discussion groups;
5 facilitated team discussions.

It's also important to remember that qualitative research and insight are not only useful for measuring the success of your EX efforts, but you can also use it during the insight and empathy phase of the design thinking process. Depending on the topic for the qualitative research, it is sometimes preferable to use an external facilitator to ensure objectivity and confidentiality. Some questions that it will be useful to consider include:

- What do we want to further explore and why?
- Which qualitative technique will work best: a group technique or a one-to-one technique?
- Who do we want to speak to?
- How will we ensure confidentiality?
- What questions would we like answered?

How to run a focus group

What is a focus group?

Focus groups typically gather 6–10 people to share their opinions, suggestions and feedback on a topic. A small number of questions, developed in advance, are used to generate in-depth consideration of a narrowly defined topic. Focus groups examine perceptions, feelings, attitudes and ideas.

How to run a successful focus group

If appropriate, ask the participants to introduce themselves and/or wear name tags. Most importantly, all questions you ask should be open and neutral. It's also important for the moderator to be aware of participants' energy and concentration levels and provide short breaks if necessary. The moderator should encourage free-flowing discussion around the relevant issue(s).

Other tips for running focus groups include:

- Start with an issue people have strong feelings about and are familiar with.
- Phrase issues in terms people will be familiar with.
- Let participants know their contributions are valuable (both through what you say and also your body language).
- It's also important that the moderator realizes that:
  - It may be necessary for them to step in and keep the session on track.
  - Disagreements and debates are useful when they lead to new and interesting ideas, but have to be managed carefully.
  - Issues of power and privacy need to be managed sensitively.
  - Focus groups should end with the moderator winding up the session by stressing all that has been achieved during the session and casting it in a positive light.

Moderating your session

- Introduce yourself and any note-takers present.
- Set the scene – the bullets below may help to do this.

WHY ARE WE HERE? AN EXAMPLE

- We are here to quickly gain a deeper understanding of the recent EX survey results, specifically in relation to some feedback about our communication approach.
- We want to use this feedback and insight to inform planning and next steps on our communication approach, to help us design and create a positive experience.
- We want to demonstrate that we are serious about addressing this issue.

Explain

- Clarify the means of recording the session.

- Go through the rules and confidentiality:
  - It's a safe environment to express your opinion.
  - No one person will be named in the write-up.
  - Try and stick to the focus of the session.
  - Be constructive.
- Carefully word questions and allow the group time to think about it – make friends with the silence if there is any.
- Try to address participants by their name to encourage trust and also to bring in those participants who are not really contributing.
- Try to avoid one person dominating the session by addressing questions to other individuals.
- After questions, carefully reflect back a summary of what you have heard to ensure understanding.
- Closing the session – explain next steps and thank everyone for their contribution.
- Immediately after the session – feed back any observations to the note-taker.

In Table 10.1 we outline an example question set for a focus group exploring communication within the organization.

TABLE 10.1 Prompt questions about communication

Topic	Prompt questions
General communication	<ul><li>What is your overall communication experience like?</li><li>Do you think effective communication exists across the business?</li><li>Talk about the strengths and the development areas with respect to communication within Company X.</li><li>Do you understand the communication you receive?</li><li>What improvements would you make?</li><li>Do you receive information quickly enough?</li><li>What are the barriers to effective communication and how do you think they could be overcome?</li></ul>
Leadership communication	<ul><li>How would you rate communication with your line manager?</li><li>What is the experience like?</li><li>What about communication from the senior leadership team?</li></ul>

(continued)

TABLE 10.1 (Continued)

Topic	Prompt questions
Understanding our business	• Do you understand the priorities in Company X?
	• Where are we going?
	• Do you understand your contribution?
	• Do you feel well informed?
	• Do you know how you're performing? Or how your team is doing?
	• Are successes celebrated?
Channels	• How do you currently receive information?
	• Do you have ready access to the information needed to do your job?
	• What channels do/don't you use and why?
	• What is the best way to communicate with you?
Communication style	• How would you describe the communication style within Company X today?
	• In the future, for communication to improve, what should the style be like?
	• Are ideas and best practice shared across the business?
	• How open is the communication within Company X?
Audience	• How well do you think communications are targeted to you?
	• Do you feel like you are understood as an audience?
	• What do you do to make yourself better understood?
	• What needs to change?
Content/ messages	Thinking about some of the recent communication campaigns within Company X:
	• Did you understand the content and messages?
	• Were you able to relate the communication to your role?
	• How could messages/content be improved?
Feel-good factor	• Do you care about the future of Company X?
	• Are you proud to work here?
	• Would you recommend it to your friends?
	• What is your overall experience of working here like?
	• Is your work interesting?
	• How could we bring some fun back into the workplace?
Open floor	• Anything else you'd like to discuss?

Our recommended approach for measuring EX

In Chapter 3 we introduced you to our MAGIC-CA model of EX. The themes included in the model were the results of analysing hundreds of best EX stories across hundreds of companies. The model argues that when employees have a best experience, it gives them:

Meaning

Appreciation

Growth

Impact

Connection

Challenge

Autonomy

We recommend using the attributes within the MAGIC-CA model as part of your EX measurement plan. Our research shows that they are present when employees have a 'best experience'. Consider ways of gathering insight to help you understand how you are performing in each of these areas. This could be via questions in a survey, qualitative methods, or analysing data that already exists as part of your HR metrics approach.

Equally, though, the model also emphasizes the need to understand individual differences and deliberately places the individual at its centre. We strongly recommend running best EX workshops to gather your own insight first to build your bespoke measurement plan and add to the attributes outlined here. By combining the MAGIC-CA model elements and your own insights you will have a really clear understanding of what a best EX looks like for your people. You can then use this knowledge to build your measurement approach and plan. For example, with one company we worked with, while the MAGIC-CA themes were present when they conducted their best EX workshops, they also found that for great experiences their people needed fun, a big social element and an element of risk and adventure.

These themes were very relevant to the culture of this specific organization and the nature of the work they did, which often involved travel and long stays in different parts of the world, often at a moment's notice. They built in these aspects of the EX into their measurement approach to understand how they were performing against them.

Using HR analytics to measure your EX

HR analytics is now a key strategic enabler in many organizations. Using HR analytics enables organizations to improve the EX, via the application of company data, statistics and technology. Typically analytics expertise is applied to large sets of people data to make connections, spot trends and understand what impacts the EX and how to measure success. There are a range of tech solutions in the marketplace to help to do this and HR analytics teams are becoming more common as part of the HR department in companies today. For example, Google uses analytics to predict which employees are at risk of leaving. This is a growing area and can provide useful insight during the design phase for EX as well as when measuring progress.

Measuring the impact of your EX

When considering how to measure your EX efforts, a good place to start is by going back to your goals and outcomes. Understanding the change we wish to see as a result of EX activity helps to focus on what we should then measure. The goals and outcomes you have set should define how you will measure the work you are doing and demonstrate the value you are adding. We're going to share a simple approach to evaluation to help you to measure the impact of the EX within your organization.

Typically evaluation falls into the categories outlined in Figure 10.2.

FIGURE 10.2   Measuring your impact

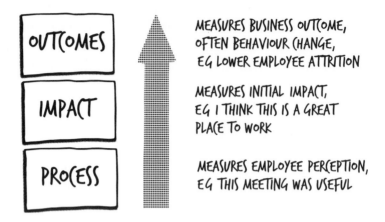

Process evaluation

This is an assessment of employee perceptions. It focuses on the perception of their experience – whether or not it was positive. Examples of process questions could include:

- The EX workshop was a good use of my time.
- My performance management conversation was a positive experience.
- My manager did a good job of answering any questions arising.

Impact evaluation

This measures the immediate effects of any EX activity. Impact evaluation tends to look at areas such as employee understanding, buy-in and commitment to activities or plans. Examples of impact questions include:

- I understand the contribution I make.
- I intend to be working here in 12 months' time.
- I believe in our company purpose.

Outcome evaluation

This measures the longer-term impact of EX activities on desired organizational outcomes. Outcome evaluation tends to look at behavioural outcomes, or business outcomes you are looking to impact via your EX focus. Examples of outcome measures include:

• reduction in employee attrition;

• increase in productivity;

• increases in employee referrals.

When thinking about how you will measure you EX efforts, you also need to consider the approach and methodology you will use. It is not always necessary to run a full-scale quantitative evaluation programme such as a survey; sometimes qualitative methods are the right answer. Table 10.2 summarizes the different approaches.

When selecting your chosen research and data collection methods, remember that you can use a mixture of both quantitative and qualitative methodologies: your decisions will depend on what is being measured and the most appropriate means of gathering that information.

TABLE 10.2 Approaches for measuring EX

	Quantitative	Qualitative
Objective	To quantify data and generalize results from a sample to the population of interest	To gain an understanding of underlying reasons and motivations
	To measure the incidence of various views and opinions in a chosen sample	To provide insights into the setting of a problem, generating ideas and/ or hypotheses for later quantitative research
	Sometimes followed by qualitative research, which is used to explore some findings further	To uncover prevalent trends in thought and opinion
Sample	Usually a large number of cases representing the population of interest	Usually a small number of non-representative cases
	Randomly selected respondents	Respondents selected to fulfil a given quota
Data collection	Questionnaires; online, telephone, face to face, experiments, secondary data, HR analytics	Interviews, focus groups, content analysis, conversation, observations

There is also a growing industry of tech solutions that offer innovative ways to gather data and measure your EX – for example, real-time pulse surveys, online crowdsourcing of feedback, using data from 'wearables', even an app that provides body language feedback using videos. Once again we recommend returning to your purpose to help you navigate the wide range of options out there.

EXERCISE
Measuring your impact

What this is: This activity will enable you to demonstrate the impact the work you do has on the business.

Why use it: It's important that key stakeholders understand the impact the work you do has on the business. This activity will give you a process and tools to do this.

You can use this activity alone to help you develop your own evaluation or impact plan, which you can then put into practice.

Background notes

As well as measuring the EX itself, it's also important to measure the impact of EX. The goals and outcomes you have set should define how you will measure the work you are doing and demonstrate the value you are adding:

- First, revisit your EX goals and outcomes.

- Now consider how you can demonstrate you have achieved these objectives. If you are struggling to define how you will measure your goals and outcomes, they are probably not tangible enough. With good goals and outcomes it is usually clear how you will measure them and demonstrate you have achieved them.

- Take a look at the example measurement plan below to give you some ideas on how you can evaluate your impact or the impact of work you are involved with.

Example measurement plan

You wish to improve the EX of your onboarding. Your measurement plan could look like this:

Objective: to ensure a positive onboarding EX that delivers reduction of employee turnover within the first six months of tenure.

Process measures:

- Onboarding activities were a good use of my time.
- I enjoyed my onboarding.
- My onboarding was a positive experience.

Impact measures:

- I intend to still be working here in 12 months' time.
- Based on my experience of my first six months, I would recommend this as a great place to work to others.

Outcome measures:

- Reduction of employee turnover during the first six months of tenure by 18 per cent.

Completing your measurement plan

Use the template shown in Table 10.3 to consider how you can measure the impact you will have. We have included some further examples to help bring this to life.

TABLE 10.3   Example measurement plan

EX objective	How	Measured by
Ensure employees have a positive communication experience	Help employees understand the vision, values, strategy and brand promise	Over 80% answer positively to: • I understand our vision/ purpose, etc.
Ensure employees have meaning at work to contribute towards their EX	Clarify individuals' role within the organization and the difference they make	Over 80% answer positively to: • I understand the role I play in achieving our vision. • I understand how I contribute to the success of this organization. • I believe I have a role to play in delivering our goals.
Insert your objectives here	*Insert the 'how' here*	*Insert your measures here*

Takeaways

In this chapter we have outlined the ways in which you measure the success of your EX efforts and made the case for why this is so important. By measuring the work we do, we can demonstrate the value we add to the organization with EX as well as ensure we are doing the right things and having an impact. In summary:

- Be clear about what you are measuring.
- Put a ROX case together if at all possible.
- Revisit your objectives to help you design your measurement plan.
- Use the MAGIC-CA model of EX plus best EX insight to uncover what matters to your people so you can ensure you measure the right things.
- Qualitative methods are just as useful as the survey.
- And consider how you will measure and demonstrate your impact.

References

BCG (2012) [accessed 10 August 2020] Realising the vales of people management [Online] https://www.bcg.com/publications/2012/people-management-human-resources-leadership-from-capability-to-profitability (archived at https://perma.cc/724Z-4H8E)

Bock, L (2016) *Work Rules*, John Murray, London

Gallup (2020) [accessed 10 August 2020] State of the American manager [Online] https://www.gallup.com/services/182138/state-american-manager.aspx (archived at https://perma.cc/F6K4-JCGA)

HR Wins and Culture Amp (2020) [accessed 10 August 2020] The value of employee experience and culture: Calculating the impact of employee experience in times of growth or crisis [Online] https://www.cultureamp.com/resources-a/whitepapers-ebooks/ (archived at https://perma.cc/RJ47-C7F5)

IBM (2017) [accessed 10 August 2020] The Employee Experience Index: A new global measure of a human workplace and its impact [Online] https://www.ibm.com/downloads/cas/JDMXPMBM (archived at https://perma.cc/J4EB-RN9W)

Kotter, J and Heskett, J (1992) *Corporate Culture and Performance*, The Free Press, New York

LinkedIn (2014) [accessed 10 August 2020] Why and how people change jobs [Online] https://business.linkedin.com/content/dam/business/talent-solutions/global/en_us/job-switchers/PDF/job-switchers-global-report-english.pdf (archived at https://perma.cc/X6CC-7MDD)

Maylett, T and Wride, M (2017) *The Employee Experience: How to attract talent, retain performers and deliver results*, Wiley, Hoboken, NJ

Morgan, J (2017) *The Employee Experience Advantage: How to win the war for talent by giving employees the workspaces they want, the tools they need, and a culture they can celebrate*, Wiley, Hoboken, NJ

Peterson, A (2020) [accessed 10 August 2020] The hidden cost of onboarding a new employee, Glassdoor [Online] https://www.glassdoor.com/employers/blog/hidden-costs-employee-onboarding-reduce/# (archived at https://perma.cc/BV7R-HWEY)

Schaufeli, WB and Bakker, AB (2004) Job demands, job resources, and their relationship with burnout and engagement: A multi-sample study, *Journal of Organizational Behavior*, **25**, pp 293–315

11

What next in EX?

In this chapter we'll cover:

- how the future of work will change EX;
- the impact of hybrid locations;
- the evolution of learning at work;
- leading and designing for employee energy and wellbeing (when it's more than just another people initiative);
- the opportunities (and risks) of using data to personalize EX;
- what it means when what we understand by 'experience' is transformed;
- is human connection the future of EX?

What next in EX?

When it comes to discussions about the 'future' of work, the truth is that, more often than not, what is framed as 'the future' is in fact already here – at least in part. And the same is true for employee experience. EX early adopters are pushing the boundaries of what it means to understand and design the human experience at work.

In our final chapter we look at the forces reframing work and how we think about employee experience. This is a vast subject that could easily fill the pages of multiple books. And it's complicated further by the ramifications of COVID-19, which has fast-forwarded many of these developments and added new dimensions to future of work discussions. Our aim isn't to paint a picture of what we think the future of work looks like. Rather, we want to ask what these possible future scenarios could mean for employee experience and how we approach it. We want to leave you with thought-provoking questions that fuel your curiosity and ongoing exploration.

To help us navigate, we kick off the chapter by looking at what's changing through our three lenses (Figure 1.1):

• the evolving nature of work;

• people's shifting expectations of their experiences with and at work;

• the resulting questions this asks of organizations: their strategy, purpose, culture and more.

We then invite people who are pioneers in their field to explore the standout elements that are and will continue to influence how organizations should and will think about EX, including:

• the impact of hybrid locations;

• the evolution of learning at work;

• leading and designing for employee energy and wellbeing (when it's more than just another people initiative);

• the opportunities (and risks) of using data to personalize EX;

• plus, what it means when even what we understand by the concept of 'experience' is transformed.

The future through three lenses

The work

It is impossible to underplay the impact of the tech revolution on the world of work. For a simple, accessible and actionable view, we like Heather McGowan and Chris Shipley's book *The Adaptation Advantage*

(2020). In it they highlight three key impacts on how work gets done: augmentation, automation and atomization.

AUGMENTATION AND AUTOMATION

Augmentation is about making tasks easier to do, quicker to complete or creating better outcomes. As with automation, where computers do the work for us, there are optimists and pessimists when it comes to what this means for people and their experience of work. What is less up for debate is that COVID-19 has accelerated the adoption of automation technologies – including robotics and AI-driven software that can process workflows at a social distance and without the risk of getting sick. For example, during the pandemic, fashion retailers deployed robots to sort clothes in warehouses to meet a surge of online orders. And robots are expected to pick up a lot of the additional cleaning and hygiene tasks in workplaces and other commercial and public premises in the months and years ahead.

When it comes to EX, we like to think augmentation and automation offer a significant opportunity for employers to create richer experiences at work. If routine and predictable work becomes easier and quicker to do (or done by computers), there may be more time for employees to spend on work that has greater meaning for them. Think back to the MAGIC-CA framework and the universal themes associated with a great EX (Chapter 3), specifically the elements of challenge and growth. If organizations handle this transformation well, if they support and equip their people to learn and take on new challenges, could the impact on people's experience of work be a positive one?

What is certain is that the impact of the three As on the world of work means it's never been more vital for people to upskill – and at speed. In 2019, IBM predicted that 120 million people in the 12 largest economies alone would need to retrain or reskill in the next three years to keep pace with rapidly changing technological capabilities impacting work. So the impact of technology on the nature of work is a challenge for EX, yes, but it is also an opportunity if organizations embrace this and help their people to grow their skills and adapt to take on new and unpredictable tasks. But we're not talking purely technical skills. Future skills highlighted by many organizations (from the World Economic Forum to the Institute for the Future) point at the fact that the skills most needed in the future of work are largely human skills – how we think, solve problems, collaborate with each other and technology, and how we flex and adapt. Honing and deploying such human skills touches on many of the elements of what creates a great EX – meaning, growth, impact, connection, challenge, and autonomy.

If, on the other hand, employers do not provide this support, people could find their experience suffers dramatically as technology changes the nature of work in rapid and unpredictable ways and, ultimately, threatens their job security. The lack of control over what is happening to them will impact not just how employees feel, but potentially how they connect with each other in the workplace – so the negative impact on experience could be further compounded by a breakdown in social connections.

ATOMIZATION

Atomization, the third of the three As, is about breaking tasks into separate, discrete pieces that can be solved by the best and lowest-cost provider anywhere in the world. Atomization is already having an impact on people's experience of work. Enabled by crowd-work platforms such as Fiverr, Upwork, and TaskRabbit, more and more companies now split virtual jobs into small tasks, then offer them to homeworkers to compete for and perform anywhere in the world. The numbers of people signing up to such platforms surged during COVID-19 with more people looking for ways to supplement their income, perhaps while juggling the demands of caring responsibilities, or because they were unable to access other forms of work.

Like Uber drivers and other gig economy participants, crowd-workers are classed as independent contractors and paid by the task. According to the *Financial Times* (O'Connor, 2020), these workers are virtually invisible, and no one knows how many there are. That's problematic because the conditions and life experience of people working in this way can be bleak, with increasingly long hours and very low pay as more and more people compete to do the work.

What does this mean for employee experience? Do we need to rethink what we mean by 'employee'? Or is it right that we should only consider the experience we create for someone who is in this contract with us? In a world of transparency and increased scrutiny of the social impact of organizations, we suggest organizations need to think about and take care of the experience of everyone carrying out work for them. It is, of course, the right and responsible thing to do. On top of that, failing to do so will not only risk reputational damage, but will impact your 'employee's' experience because your people want to be proud of who they work for, what they do and how they do it.

People

Increasing diversity in the workplace is a huge trend impacting employee experience. As we live longer, age diversity is on the rise at companies around the world. Talent professionals overwhelmingly see this as a good thing and a path to success, helping to attract and retain talent, as well as driving innovation, productivity and brand relevance and reputation. But it's not just age that is more diverse. A shortage of knowledge workers around the world and a predicted squeeze on blue-collar workers in some countries mean organizations are casting the net wider to find the people they need. This means workforces are more diverse across multiple dimensions – nationality, employment background, education and location. Teams are more far-flung, have different backgrounds and a variety of communication preferences.

When it comes to the impact on EX, much will depend on how well organizations create inclusive environments where everyone can feel equally in control of their experience, connected to the people they work with, able to grow and have an impact, and appreciated for what they do. There are many elements to creating such a culture and it is vital that organizations show leadership and invest time and energy to achieve it. If they don't, EX won't swim in the cultural soup; it will sink.

Organizational context

Technological, societal and economic forces have always influenced employers – who they are, what they do and how they do it. Today is no different. However, COVID-19 unleashed new forces of change on such a variety of fronts, while super-charging many forces already in play, that few organizations have been left unscathed. How organizations choose or are forced to respond will significantly impact the employee experience.

Below we invite six experts to share their views on what organizations need to do to thrive and how that will impact EX.

Where work happens and what it means for EX

For anyone who has been able to work from home during the pandemic, it's easy to assume this option is commonly available. Rather, it is a privilege available largely to the well off. According to the *Financial Times* (O'Connor, 2020), European data suggests three-quarters of jobs in the highest-paying quintile can be done remotely, compared with just 3 per cent of those in the lowest quintile. In looking at the impact of remote working on EX, we are aware we're only talking about the experience of a portion of the working population. However, it is a significant portion.

According to Stanford University Professor of Economics Nicholas Bloom, by sheer numbers, the US is now a working-from-home economy, with almost twice as many employees working from home as at work (Wong, 2020). Similarly, in the UK, Office for National Statistics figures suggest that in September 2020 nearly a quarter of people worked exclusively from home (Webber, 2020). And this new working-from-home economy is likely to persist long after the pandemic. So, what does it mean for employee experience?

Sacha Connor, founder and CEO of Virtual Work Insider, trains hybrid, geographically distributed and remote teams in the skills to lead, collaborate and communicate across distance. Here she explores the impact on employee experience of location inclusion (and exclusion) – and how to achieve it in a hybrid world.

Sacha Connor

Unprecedented location inclusion is one of COVID's positive unintended consequences. The office shutdowns forced so many of us into FROGs – fully remote organizations. For the first time in many companies, all team members were forced to be on an equal, location-agnostic, playing field.

For many, the frequent faux pas of only inviting people that live or work nearby to participate in a meeting, a brainstorm, or social gathering has vanished. Those invisible fences have fallen in favour of location inclusion – people are being included based on merit, not proximity.

Before COVID, so many of us were being called upon to lead teams that were geographically distributed across the country and the globe. The COVID office shutdowns took that one step further, jumping us all the way into fully remote teams. It sped up the acceptance of workplace flexibility by many years and it became a great empathy exercise in that it gave everyone a taste of the challenges of remote work and a realization that it's *not* what the media used to depict it as – eating bonbons on the couch all day in pyjamas.

THE FUTURE IS HYBRID

While I believe that many more companies will include remote work as part of their workforce strategy moving forward after COVID, I believe that the future is not remote; the future is hybrid. And hybrid is harder than fully remote – and the consequences on employee experience of not getting this right are extreme.

Future team anatomy will be made up of people more equally spread across a company's headquarters, satellite offices and work-from-anywhere locations (home, co-working spaces, on the road).

Even the people that work from HQ or a satellite office will likely have the flexibility to work from a remote location a few days per week.

Leaders, teams and employees need to be aware that transitioning into these new hybrid teams is going to be a bumpy road, one that will take upskilling and intention.

In hybrid teams the power, flow of communication, and inclusion usually sit with the co-located majority, and those in the location minority have to fight like crazy to get that information and be included. What is at play is what the NeuroLeadership Institute (https://neuroleadership.com/the-seeds-model/) calls distance bias – our brain's natural tendency to put more value on the people and things that are closer to us than those that are further away. So, if you are not in close proximity with others, you might literally be out of sight and out of mind, and beyond that the value of your ideas and contributions may actually be discounted compared with those of someone more closely located to a decision-maker.

MODERN, VIRTUAL LEADERSHIP SKILLS ARE REQUIRED TO WIN

Old-school in-person management, communication and leadership techniques are no longer enough to succeed while working in fully remote and hybrid teams. Nothing has proven this more than the pandemic. To be effective, it's imperative that today's leaders know how to lead across distance and not rely on being within eyeshot and earshot of their teams.

What is virtual leadership? I define it as demonstrating your thought and people leadership skills by adjusting behaviours to account for the distance – such as how you lead effective, inclusive and engaging virtual meetings, how you influence others across distance, how you approach asynchronous collaboration and how you foster a positive and inclusive culture across locations.

WHERE TO GO FROM HERE

It's vital we don't slip back into old ways of proximity as paramount. If we do, the consequences for employee experience (and more) will be profound. The secret to getting this right lies in four areas.

1. New virtual leadership principles and communication norms
Organizations should not try to replicate how they worked when they were co-located. They should be learning from the leading-edge FROGs and virtual work experts on what it takes to transition to successful virtual and hybrid teams. That includes being very intentional and deliberate with setting expectations and new norms. For example, teams need to decide on the best balance of synchronous versus asynchronous communication to meet their objectives. They should agree to core meeting hours and set expectations for responsiveness and how to communicate across time zones. It also requires empathy and flexibility, understanding what works for different people and being as responsive as possible in terms of creating different options about how and where people work.

2. Career development and hiring   Organizations must embrace location inclusion and location diversity when it comes to development and recruitment. Old-school attitudes need to change. The best project assignments, the best role rotations and the fastest speed to promotion should no longer be based on proximity to HQ or the decision-makers; it should be merit based. Dropping the constraints of hiring within a certain distance of HQ or an office site will also open up incredible talent pools that were not accessible before because of self-imposed geographic restrictions.

3. Upskilling   Employees at all levels need to learn virtual leadership, communication and collaboration skills. This can be done through hiring an external virtual leadership skills training company or by finding the pockets of people within your organization who are experts in these skills and ask them to take on a role of teacher and mentor.

4. Create accountability   Some companies as of late have created a head of remote role, but I want to push it further to head of hybrid, because that person's responsibility is not just to help those who are remote, but to help the full ecosystem across all locations. Companies will need someone who is responsible and accountable for ensuring that the organization is mitigating distance bias, that its culture is location-inclusive in all aspects, that it is getting the training that it needs and that it is putting the right processes, policies and tools in place to support the hybrid workforce.

Let's face it – the focus shouldn't be on where you work; it should be about getting the work done well, on time and collaborating fully with your co-workers, senior leaders, external partners and clients. You can be on track to do this successfully if you put the right principles, policies, processes, training and tools in place to drive business results, create a culture of inclusion and keep employees feeling engaged regardless of location.

How learning happens and the impact on EX

As Heather McGowan and Chris Shipley write in *The Adaptation Advantage* (2020):

> Our relationship to work is no longer a monolithic career based on a single dose of early learning and compiled experiences. Instead, our careers will be defined by a state of constant learning and adaptation as new technologies, applications, and data alter the current state.

So can constant learning and adaptation provide the growth and challenge that impact a positive employee experience?

Dr Bonnie Cheuk is a digital and business transformation leader who has led multiple enterprise-wide digital transformations, building digital capability, knowledge-sharing, and learning culture for global workforces. Here Bonnie looks at the need for continuous learning and unlearning to underpin agile organizations and the impact on the employee experience.

Dr Bonnie Cheuk

The world is changing and so is the future of work. In order to be responsive to internal and external change, corporations need to be both stable and able to flex. This requires a connected workforce that can thrive in ambiguity and be able to innovate, while at the same time be capable of achieving stability and driving efficiency by stream-lining and standardizing processes.

The assumption that work is stable – ie that the output of work can be clearly defined, and that employees can be managed through set management processes – is today only partially true. When change is the new constant, we need to assume that work is both 'stable' and 'gappy', that work is both 'stable' and 'unstable'. Increasingly, employees face new challenges that do not have known answers. Organizations need to learn to handle the 'gaps' because they are not outliers – or risks to be mitigated or eliminated – they are part of the future of work.

UNDERSTANDING GAPS

Take a look at an employee working in a role who faces different situations. In some cases, the tasks can be clearly defined and the output of work is predictable. Other times, the employee has to navigate uncertainty and the work output cannot be predefined. In such situations, the employee needs to be able to flex. Increasingly, AI-assisted robots handle all the predictable work. As human beings we need to use our inductive capability to explore, learn, create, adapt and adjust, read between the lines and connect emotionally with others. These are critical capabilities for the future workplace (Cheuk, 2020). When 'gaps' are a part of day-to-day work, leaders and managers have to become coaches to support their team to navigate ambiguity. In doing so, leaders and managers are learning themselves as they collaborate with the teams trying to figure things out. And the future of work is all about the future of learning, which goes beyond attending formal training or adding social interaction to the training programmes.

WORK IS LEARNING AND LEARNING IS WORK

Executives want their corporations to become responsive organizations. This focus on improving business agility and learning agility touches organizations at all levels – company, leaders, teams and individuals. Leaders need the capability to sense, adapt, innovate and continuously improve the business. Teams need to assemble in fluid ways, bringing out diverse viewpoints to challenge the status quo, to innovate and to solve challenges. Every employee needs to embrace a growth mindset, to learn, unlearn and relearn, so that they can quickly apply new ideas and gain new experience when facing different situations. To meet this need, corporate learning needs to be reimagined. The focus needs to be on enabling informal learning in the flow of work.

This is a big ask. It's about reimagining the future of work.

LOOKING FORWARD – CONTINUOUSLY LEARNING, UNLEARNING AND RELEARNING IN THE FLOW OF WORK

As the global capability lead for learning agility and learning culture of a large multinational pharmaceutical company, I have recently created our definition of learning agility. Based on the assumption that work is both certain and uncertain, I have developed principles to design the future of work, where learning is seamlessly embedded into the way we work. Informed by Dervin's sense-making methodology (Cheuk and Dervin, 2011), these principles can guide the redesign of learning in any organization:

1 Learning cannot be limited to formal education. Enabled by digital tools, learners should be empowered to learn, anytime, anywhere, in the flow of work/life. Individuals and teams continuously learn, unlearn and relearn on the job, in both certain and uncertain situations.

2 The workforce has to become more human, especially when we delegate repetitive physical and cognitive tasks to machines. Human beings are unique and we should leverage our strengths, ie our inductive capability to navigate ambiguity, to create connections, to handle serendipity and to imagine.

3 Focus on creating and sustaining micro-moment work habits that can be applied just-in-time in any work context. These work habits are grouped into five areas: (1) self/team reflection moment; (2) innovation and growth mindset to create rituals to break habits and build habits; (3) follow good conversation and meeting protocols;

(4) creating space for psychological safety and allowing diverse and dissenting voices to be heard; and (5) working out loud and tapping into the global network to collaborate/work/learn together. They can be re-mixed to suit any work context. By applying these work habits, learning continuously becomes an output of work, which becomes input to new work and an agent for further work improvement or to drive innovation.

This represents a significant shift. We need to resist the urge to provide the workforce with more training in learning agility and innovation. Instead, we need to design micro-moment work habits to allow employees to interact, to agree and disagree, to follow and to challenge, to stabilize and to disrupt in the natural flow of work.

This has the potential to impact experience in multiple ways, not least in how we empower individuals and teams to adopt new continuous learning practices in their day-to-day work. Such practices will require not just new behaviours, but cultural adjustments to support employees to:

- Slow down to pause, reflect, learn and unlearn.
- Be more self-aware and set goals based on dreams, purpose and passion – a purposeful discovery journey.
- Enjoy 'gaps' at work, accepting you don't always have all the answers and using the opportunity to seek help and show vulnerability.
- Be curious, ask questions, build in serendipity and connect with unfamiliar people and situations.
- Develop good collaboration, communication and meeting habits. Look for agreement and disagreement and cherish diverse viewpoints.
- Talk less and listen more – not just to validate your own viewpoints. Be conscious of power issues and ensuring that voices are not suppressed or hidden. Give permission for others to challenge, raise concerns and disagree with psychological safety.
- Create and build networks by working out loud, sharing ideas and giving value to others first to grow followership. Think beyond collaborating with the immediate team. Don't be afraid to reach out to strangers and communities.

- Be a critical thinker and alert to biases, including in the algorithms of AI-driven robots.

- Challenge the assumption that what was appropriate last month will continue to work next year.

THE FUTURE OF WORK IS ABOUT BEING HUMAN AT WORK

Work is filled with moments of certainty and uncertainty. We cannot tell our workforce 'you need to be adaptive, learn and unlearn', when all the systems/services/processes are set up to be inflexible. Conventional learning solutions focus on transferring best practices at the right time to the right learners, so that they can adopt the right mindset and behaviours. This convention sets incoherent expectations that our people need to be passive recipients of information – or followers of procedures – while paradoxically continuously learning, unlearning and adapting. Looking after people's experience will mean consciously moving beyond this paradox by paying attention to how we design processes, systems, services, learning solutions and roles that account for all types of human experiences.

The future of work is about bringing our humanness to work (Dervin, 2020; Hamel, 2020). If we only design for certainty, we will never develop human-centric learning solutions and the experience our employees have will be incoherent and disjointed.

How to design work for energy and what it means for EX

As the world made sense of the creeping new reality of living in a pandemic, human energy – how we use, conserve and focus it – became an increasing subject of discussion. And we predict it will continue to be a focus as more individuals, leaders and whole organizations come to realize the value of this precious commodity – and how easily it can be squandered. As leading mental health campaigner and former Unilever VP of HR Geoff McDonald asks: 'If we accept that the most important driver of individual, team and organizational performance is people's "energy", then why aren't organizations actively making it a strategic priority and investing in the health of their workforce?'

Perry Timms, MCIPD and FRSA, founder and chief energy officer at PTHR, says there is an opportunity to create new models of work that inspire and enable more energy and that don't just create a better EX, but recast it all together.

Perry Timms

What if our entire approach to employee experience – with clarity of role, cohesion with our mission, team charter and own objectives and key results (OKRs) – was *still* misfiring? What might be behind that?

In my experience, that could be down to energy. Human energy and the impact of the design of work are more explicitly linked than many of us might give it credit for.

The famous stairway to competence (four levels of unconscious incompetence right through to unconscious competence) shows us that we are applying our energies and our intellect in different ways. When we're new to a role, we suddenly become aware of our incompetence and our energies are all attuned to learning: not making mistakes, mastery and focus. As we become more competent, there is a degree of comfort in our capability and, with that, new energies: experimentation, improvement, teaching others, making it your own. Enterprise management becomes a thing as this 'corner' of the organization becomes our own lean start-up. And then, when totally on our game, a different set of energies are at play: boredom, over-tinkering, distraction. It's at this point that we realize what human energy at work needs more than anything – like the spark in a piston chamber – a catalytic stimulus.

So, if our employee experience is not littered with stimuli, our experience can suffer from seemingly inescapable monotony.

ENERGY AND WORK DESIGN – CRAFTING A BETTER EX
In my research into human energy and work design (Timms, 2020), I've come across a number of factors that create that stimulus – some obvious, some small, others less obvious and some huge.

What, then, are my key elements for a stimulated EX that sparks human energy and creates fulfilling work and flourishing people?

1. LEARNING

The most obvious. If you're under-stimulated or over-pressured in work that is impairing the EX 'ratings', learning something new is a stimulator. This could be any number of things, from a productivity hack, to a new psychological discipline in influencing others, insight into avoiding procrastination, or taking to a new app that manages your workflow.

2. EXPERIMENTING

Distinct from, but still part of, the overall opus of learning, here we see you creating a spinout from your core work to develop and test new solutions, ways of working, create a new software platform, or depart from overly bureaucratic processes you feel are choking your EX. I've seen IT, finance and HR professionals create revenue-generating offshoots that have become new parts of the overall business model.

3. INTERPLAY

Knowing your part in the system you're in can help you map, utilize and understand your energy even more. If you're in a tiring meeting-culture-based organization, you may feel frustrated (like I did in my previous corporate life) to be shuffling from meeting to meeting and not getting any 'work' done. Or you may be in a chaotic start-up with no processes and with duplication, waste and forgotten deadlines all over the place. Naming, defining and then managing the systems you're part of may seem beyond your control, but it's an important element in finding the 'you are here' place on the map of workflow and decisions, power dynamics and influence. You can then start to craft your responses and actions within that system and help others do the same to improve the way things get done and regain some control. EX is only as good as the system you operate in. Well-intended shifts to EX often stutter and fail because of poor organization design.

4. FLOW

Mihaly Csikszentmihalyi (1998), the American-Hungarian professor of psychology, is perhaps most famous for his concept of flow: the 'right' degree of confident competence and the right degree of pressure and stimulation. When you're in flow, you don't notice time (or the pressure of time), you feel the sense of accomplishment, and overall your energy is like a purring F1 engine. Some of this can come in two simple calibrating mechanisms for your work: high cognition and low cognition. High cognition is the deep stuff, the complex, the creative. You need space, focus, concentration, creative tools and avoidance of distractions. Low cognition is the admin, the emails, the short check-ins with colleagues. Knowing when you need to be high- or low-cog is key to achieving flow and optimizing energy. In writing this piece, I chose deliberately to do it before 8 am – when I know my brainpower is cleanest, clearest and clutter-free.

5. RELATIONSHIPS

Honestly, forget the Gallup question, 'Do you have a best friend at work?' I really don't hold any stock in that. Do you relish and respect the people you work with for their attention to things you don't have as part of your modus operandi? That's more like it. We, of course, gravitate towards people who appear to be ignited by things in ways similar to ourselves. And we're beginning to understand and regard more difference too – cultural, intellectual and attitudinal differences. Yet, however we define our 'bench', we need good relationships to foster good energy in our work and therefore an enhanced EX.

IN SUMMARY

Learning, experimenting, designed systems, flow and relationships are some of the core tenets of being energized in your work and form components of a good work situation where the EX is considered in full effect.

Clearly the 'deal' you have with your employer will also factor heavily in this – the culture, the leadership on display, the growth and diversification of the business also feature. These are the conditions that stimulate a positive and fulfilling EX.

What is most stark in all aspects of a thriving EX is that it has to be founded on two key principles: safety and agency. By that, I mean the now-classic work of Professor Amy Edmonson on psychological safety (Edmonson, 2018). But also the safety found in a well-run business that pays attention to its capital and capabilities and also in speaking up and sharing issues, errors and creative suggestions. Then agency in having the intent and the actualized aspects of self-direction, support and choice. These are two factors that perhaps have been underestimated in organization design, culture and ways of working more generally.

At the time of writing, these elements are proving even more relevant in a mid- and post-pandemic world, and more than ever we need that safe-house feel (see the Edelman Trust Barometer's work year on year for the last three) and the increase in trust and choice through dispersed working conditions for many office-based employees.

I would say that now, more than ever, a book like this is needed as we head into employee experience (at least) version 2.0 and a new social contract in work. As Frederic Laloux (2014) said in his landmark book *Reinventing Organizations*, 'there's something in the air'. And that 'something' is potentially a recast EX set against the new models for good work.

Data, personalization and the impact on EX

In an increasingly data-driven world where algorithms know and provide exactly what we need and when, people increasingly expect the same personalization from their experience at work. It's not about perks, but about work projects that challenge their abilities; personalized and insightful advice to help them grow; rotational assignments where they can apply fresh skills in new roles to have an impact; agile work across teams and functions where people can connect in new ways to colleagues and organizations and more besides.

Personalization can be applied across the spectrum of employee experience. Artificial intelligence alongside such tools as sentiment analysis in employee engagement platforms is already being used to understand people's experience beyond what they say in surveys – even to make predictions about who is at risk of leaving. With this knowledge, EX interventions can be made to turn experience around. At least that's the theory. And there is significant potential for more advanced technologies to help organizations find deeper, and more human, insights into the feelings and opinions of employees for a more accurate and real-time understanding of employee experience. However, this potential doesn't come without risks.

Damon Deaner, IBM's director of employee experience design, explains why it's vital that data technologies are used with care to create even more personalized, consumer-grade employee experiences.

Damon Deaner

Outside of work, we've all become accustomed to thoughtfully designed in-person and digital experiences from services organizations, retailers, social media applications and others. In response to growing business and employee demands, organizations are bringing together cross-functional and multi-disciplinary teams to collaborate in new ways and leverage their strengths to design and deliver consumer-grade employee experiences – experiences that are more in line with the simple, intuitive, accessible and deeply personalized experiences we have from service organizations, social media applications, retailers and more – nearly all of which are powered by advanced data and AI technologies. These teams often face significant pressure to quickly apply modern technologies and use increasing amounts of employee data, analytics and inference – typically augmented by AI to surface insights, recommendations, personalized content and decision support. Teams wielding these powerful new data technologies can indeed achieve exceptional employee experience outcomes that often include individual employee-level personalization and support. However, without intentional and thoughtful consideration of their use, these new data technologies can also unintentionally cause great harm by breaching legal or ethical boundaries or by simply creating a big brother feeling of being watched.

So how will organizations avoid these pitfalls? I suggest by focusing on five areas it will be possible to ethically use AI-powered data to underpin the employee experiences we create.

1. ACCOUNTABILITY

No matter our role in helping to craft an employee experience, whether an HR professional, developer, designer, leader or any other, we are all accountable for carefully considering the impact that using any AI-powered data and analytics can have on an individual employee or the organization at large. We should ensure that our data and AI policies are accessible and that everyone is clear on their responsibility and accountability. Detailed documentation on the use of data and AI is vital for tracking changes at every iteration. This documentation can often become an essential collaboration tool to keep the team aligned and focused on the importance of the ethical use of data and AI. This is in addition to the organization's business conduct guidelines, national and international laws, regulations and guidelines.

2. VALUE ALIGNMENT

Data usage and AI need to align with the values, norms and expectations of our employees and our organization. Every organization has a bespoke culture that can change over time. Collaborating closely with both employees and leaders is critical to understanding how the use of data and AI could be perceived positively or negatively by those we're trying to support. Using the methods of design thinking and agile to co-create solutions with employee sponsor users can be a crucial source of alignment.

3. EXPLAINABILITY

With every increase in the use of and reliance on data and AI needs to come a corresponding focus on maintaining the ease with which every employee can understand those inputs. Employees should always be aware of when and how they interact with AI-powered data, analytics, inference and recommendations. Organizations must provide methods and obvious cues for employees to easily perceive, detect and understand the use of personalized data, analytics and inference. Transparency should be maintained by plainly explaining when and where personalized data is used and from where it was sourced. Openness and transparency build trust. We should not sacrifice transparency in creating simple, seamless experiences. Imperceptible AI is not ethical AI.

4. FAIRNESS

Ensuring fairness and equity for employees is something that must be intentionally designed, monitored and managed. Minimizing bias and promoting inclusion and equity can be vastly improved by employee data. However, they can also be severely hampered without careful, thoughtful consideration of the quality, completeness and accuracy of employee data, and most importantly, how it's applied. Humans are inherently vulnerable to biases and are responsible for building AI, which means biases can easily find their way into the data we capture, the insights and inference we develop and the systems we create.

We must always carefully consider each piece of data, its source, and its use by exploring, as a team, any potential biases it could include. When bias is suspected or found, we must investigate it, as a team, to understand where it originated and how it can be mitigated. Teams should schedule regular reviews to help avoid and identify unintentional biases within the experience.

5. USER DATA RIGHTS

Within the employee experiences we create, there are often opportunities to allow employees to provide input on data related to them and allow for greater control of its use. For example, providing the ability for them to update or add data directly or to control the visibility or sharing settings of certain data with colleagues, managers and leaders. We must always adhere to applicable national and international laws on employee data rights. We should explore opportunities to provide employees the ability to control what data is used and how. We should provide opportunities for employees to update or augment data to improve AI-powered insights and inference.

We should clearly articulate when and how employee input data is being used and shared.

As creators of employee experience, the future will have us becoming even more empowered by increasing sources and volume of employee data. We can now also wield this data with quickly advancing AI capabilities, allowing us to use it in exciting and interesting new ways. However, with great power comes great responsibility. As these technologies continue to mature and evolve at an exciting pace, we must all do our part to ensure the experiences our employees have aren't harmed by these new capabilities, but instead, benefit from our ethical use of our employee data.

When tech reframes what we mean by experience

There is growing interest in how virtual reality (VR) will impact the employee experience. From recruitment to onboarding, workshops, and leadership development, the applications are increasingly wide ranging. However, as yet they are somewhat limited in scope. VR isn't just another 'tech' – although, in truth, it is often treated like that, as if 'doing VR' is an item on a to-do list. VR is different and interesting when it comes to EX because it creates entirely new experiences – immersive experiences that don't fit on our current radar of what constitutes an employee experience.

Tim Fleming, founder of VR training solutions company Future Visual, brings VR to life and looks at what it could tell us about where VR may impact EX.

Tim Fleming

Virtual reality enables us to experience ourselves, our environment and our interactions with others in a way that challenges the basic building blocks of our learned experiences to date. The ramifications and possibilities this can deliver are huge. To illustrate this, let's compare a real-life event and the VR version.

There is a little festival in the UK called Glastonbury (250,000 people small) and within it an area with a reputation. Shangri-La is the furthest corner of the festival, but it is more than just a party in a field. It is an outdoor gallery and interdisciplinary space that connects, inspires and educates festival-goers on a wide variety of causes, knowledge and movements. Shangri-La opens when everything else closes. It's where you find yourself on the dance floor at 3 am.

In 2020, COVID-19 cancelled Glastonbury. However, the Shangri-La crew rebuilt it with virtual reality. I frequently explain that VR can deliver experiences that are physically impossible or prohibitively expensive in real life. Could Shangri-La be captured, or more pertinently, could it be improved using VR?

HOW IT DELIVERED

The day approached with palpable excitement – but no four-hour road trip, two-hour queue, or £250 spent on a ticket. My wife and I got ready with our headsets at home – who doesn't want to go raving without a partner in crime (even though the point of networked applications is that you can meet friends who aren't in the same physical space)?

We launched the app and moments later we were in a lobby approaching the virtual doorway. Throughout the evening as we re-entered the experience, we spent a few moments here, where we had the random conversations you get in a queue for a club. This was our first sense that VR could replicate something close to reality.

From here we 'arrived' at a staging environment with other party-goers and were admitted to the 'virtual' festival space. We had arranged to meet friends, but I couldn't find them. This is familiar for a festival. However, in this VR world, the handy menu on my wrist allowed me to 'teleport to friend': 1–0 to VR.

With the help of a guide, I chose to adopt the persona of a comedy shark with a huge tongue. This served two purposes. First, it looked like I wasn't trying too hard to be a club kid. Second, the avatar inspired lots of conversations I probably wouldn't otherwise have had. My wife was similarly delightfully entertained by some youthful drum and bass MCs. Perhaps fantastical avatars break down normal social barriers of age and culture and challenge learned social behaviours: 2–0 to VR.

What was truly astounding was the convenience of 'jumping' in and out of an environment delivering a peak experience. Getting to an event and moment like this usually takes days, travel and expense. The ease of access to this peak experience added to the intensity of the moment.

In summary, VR allowed us to:

- meet people who were distributed around the world, at an event we were not physically close to;
- enjoy an identity that we would not have used in real life;
- reduce judgement-loaded interactions – being a shark (or whatever else) removes initial judgements around age, gender and race;
- explore an environment where in real life I might have felt unsafe;
- access peak experience environments easily and without fuss.

WHAT DID SHANGRI-LA SUGGEST IS POSSIBLE FOR EX?

VR can deliver experiences that are physically impossible or prohibitively expensive in real life. Organizations are and will continue to experiment with building this in to key moments of the employee experience. For example, by building content relevant to the role, organizations will be able to not only spot talent and personality types, but build training programmes that can deliver close to real-world experiences. Such experiences could offer faster routes to competency and excellence, both in practical high-risk training, but also in the delivery of people skills, such as inclusive communication or leadership skills, and emotional intelligence. For example, it could be valuable to experience life from both colleagues' and customers' perspectives. And the ability to quickly access emotionally charged environments could add a real dynamism to such experiential learning.

I'm not suggesting immersive experiences will be a panacea for tackling traditionally tough development topics, but they can be a catalyst to conversations about how we might work with these areas of emotion and performance that have traditionally been difficult to access in the workplace.

Beyond this we can see that immersive spaces can provide a new virtual layer to the hierarchical modalities of behaviour that exist in the traditional workplace. As we now live in a world of more remote work, this is a strong opportunity to embrace new layers of digital transformation and interaction. At the moment we have MS Teams and Zoom. Immersive tech enables the development of a third space with a much wider range of possibilities to bring people together in ways that are both playful and powerful.

This is only touching the tip of the iceberg of what is possible. The real opportunity lies for those organizations who are willing to explore the wider potential of the immersive experience to extend the template of what work-based environments look and feel like, and enable people to allow their best qualities to shine.

Back to us: is human connection the future of EX?

We have a genuine desire to make the world of work better for everyone. We spend our days working to make this a reality. Work shouldn't be a miserable experience, and the irony is that everyone benefits when the EX is good. And yet the current truth is that many of us have had pretty poor experiences at work. Our over-riding desire for the future of EX is to change this. And we believe the COVID-19 pandemic has provided a unique opportunity to accelerate this and ensure more people have a great experience at work.

At the outset of this chapter we explained our aim to understand what possible future scenarios could mean for EX, rather than paint a picture of what the future of work will look like. The pandemic fast-tracked many of the positive changes we were already observing, from where we work to how we work, when we work and more. When we reflected on these changes, what became clear is that human connection is a theme that is central to a good EX. As human beings we have an innate need to connect, and there is a real opportunity to transform EX when we focus on meeting this need. Fundamentally this is about connecting with each other, with colleagues, with our boss, with our team, with friends at work, with the organization itself, with customers and suppliers and more. But there is also an opportunity to consider how the EX can support connection with our local community, with family, with friends and even with ourselves.

At its heart EX design is a human-centred approach. We know this works for all of the reasons laid out in the chapters of this book. Human connection is a key feature of the best EX stories we have gathered over the years. And those companies getting their EX right today ensure that human connection is fundamental to their approach. And when we look at the views on the future of EX expressed in this chapter, human is a central theme.

For example, in *The Adaptation Advantage*, Heather McGowan and Chris Shipley (2020) argue that while technology is driving exponential change, humans remain in the driver's seat. They argue that collaboration will be key to build meaningful experiences and collaboration can only happen when we make meaningful connections. Collaboration is not about shiny apps or tech; it is about enabling connections to happen that benefit people.

One of the unintended consequences of the increase in remote working as a result of the pandemic has actually been greater inclusion and connection for many employees. While this is not universal, and of course needs care and attention to sustain, it has been interesting to observe that working more remotely can result in greater connection. And this has had a positive impact on EX. We have worked with teams during lockdown who now have a deeper connection to their colleagues as a result of working in this new way.

When considering the future of learning at work we heard that teams need to assemble in fluid ways, sharing diverse viewpoints to solve challenges. Learning in the future will likely move further away from formal, classroom-based training programmes. And we know that growth and mastery are fundamental to a good EX. This emerging focus for learning again requires greater emphasis on human connection.

When considering how we use energy at work to facilitate a great EX, the link to human connection is obvious. Understanding our connections and who gives us positive energy, and who zaps our energy, can help to improve our experience at work. And advancing technology can help to foster more human connection, not less. Using VR to meet and work with colleagues in a virtual space has far-reaching implications, not least in a world where social distancing applies.

We want to use these changes as a force for good, to improve EX and make the world of work better for everyone. We believe we can take advantage of the changes brought about by the pandemic to reset our approach to EX. And human connection should be at the heart of everything we do.

References

Cheuk, B (2020) [accessed 15 October 2020] Dr Bonnie Cheuk: IDC Future of Work Keynote: Workforce transformation human machine collaboration, 3 March [Online] https://www.slideshare.net/BonnieCheuk/bonnie-cheuk-idc-future-of-work-keynote-workforce-transformation-human-machine-collaboration (archived at https://perma.cc/S7HU-2KJ4)

Cheuk, B and Dervin, B (2011) [accessed 15 October 2020] Leadership 2.0 in action: A journey from knowledge management to knowledging [Online] https://sense-making.org/my-journey-from-knowledge-management-to-knowledging-and-learning/ (archived at https://perma.cc/5YAF-663P)

Csikszentmihalyi, M (1998) *Finding Flow: The psychology of engagement with everyday life*, Basic Books, New York

Dervin, B (2020) [accessed 15 October 2020] A range of Dervin and her students' papers are made available on the Sense-Making Methodology Institute website [Online] http://sense-making.org/ (archived at https://perma.cc/TR6K-8AQ9)

Edmonson, A (2018) *The Fearless Organization: Creating psychological safety in the workplace for learning, innovation, and growth*, John Wiley & Sons, Upper Saddle River, NJ

Hamel, G (2020) *Humanocracy: Creating organizations as amazing as the people inside them*, Harvard Business Review Press, Boston

IBM (2019) [accessed 15 October 2020] The enterprise guide to closing the skills gap [Online] https://www.ibm.com/thought-leadership/institute-business-value/report/closing-skills-gap (archived at https://perma.cc/8NZH-54RA)

Laloux, F (2014) *Reinventing Organizations: A guide to creating organizations inspired by the next stage in human consciousness*, Nelson Parker, Brussels

McGowan, HE and Shipley, C (2020) *The Adaptation Advantage*, Wiley, Hoboken, NJ

O'Connor, S (2020) [accessed 15 October 2020] Do not let homeworking become digital piecework for the poor, *Financial Times*, 15 September [Online] https://www.ft.com/content/ab83270c-253a-4d7a-9ef8-a360d2e04aab (archived at https://perma.cc/N4DY-HN3J)

Timms, P (2020) *The Energized Workplace: Designing organizations where people flourish*, Kogan Page, London

Webber, A (2020) [accessed 15 October 2020] Working from home increased after guidance U-turn, *Personnel Today* [Online] https://www.personneltoday.com/hr/working-from-home-increased-after-guidance-u-turn/ (archived at https://perma.cc/42BD-FBY6)

Wong, M (2020) [accessed 15 October 2020] Stanford research provides a snapshot of a new working-from-home economy, *Stanford News* [Online] https://news.stanford.edu/2020/06/29/snapshot-new-working-home-economy/ (archived at https://perma.cc/S6H6-XWUT)

INDEX

<cite></cite>